THEOLOGY AFTER THE STORM

Theology after the Storm

John McIntyre

The Humanity of Christ,
Theology of Prayer,
The Cliché as a Theological Medium

Edited, with a Critical Introduction by

Gary D. Badcock

William B. Eerdmans Publishing Company
Grand Rapids, Michigan / Cambridge, U.K.

255 Jefferson Ave. S.E., Grand Rapids, Michigan 49503 /
P.O. Box 163, Cambridge CB3 9PU U.K.

Printed in the United States of America

02 01 00 99 98 97 7 6 5 4 3 2 1

Library of Congress Cataloging-in-Publication Data

McIntyre, John, 1916-
[Selections. 1997]
Theology after the storm / John McIntyre; edited, with a critical introduction by Gary D. Badcock.
p. cm.
Includes bibliographical references.
Contents: The humanity of Christ — Theology of prayer — The cliché as a theological medium.
ISBN 0-8028-4110-4 (pbk.: alk. paper)
1. Jesus Christ — Humanity. 2. Prayer — Christianity.
3. McIntyre, John, 1916- . I. Badcock, Gary D. II. Title.
BT218.M35 1997
232′.8 — dc20 96-35273
CIP

Contents

Acknowledgments

A number of people have assisted in the production of *Theology After the Storm.* Dr. Neil MacDonald helped in the early stages with scanning typescript and editing the resulting, rather convoluted, electronic text. Dr. Andrew Ross of the University of Edinburgh has helped to fill in some of John McIntyre's biographical details. Professor McIntyre himself consented to my work on his papers and has re-read and occasionally re-written material from them. He has also commented judiciously on my editorial introduction. My wife Susan tirelessly typed some of the manuscript. Finally, the support of the publishers is gratefully acknowledged.

GARY D. BADCOCK

I should like to express my appreciation of the kindness of Dr. Badcock in selecting these essays for publication and of the care and diligence with which he applied himself to their preparation for the publisher.

JOHN MCINTYRE

The Theology of John McIntyre: A Critical Introduction

Life and Work

John McIntyre, CVO, DD, DLitt, DHL, FRSE, Professor Emeritus of Divinity in the University of Edinburgh, former Chaplain to Her Majesty the Queen in Scotland, and former Moderator of the General Assembly of the Church of Scotland, to name only some of his distinctions, was born in Glasgow in 1916, the son of a joiner. The family left Glasgow to live near Bathgate along the Forth estuary from Edinburgh in West Lothian when he was a boy, and remained in this coal mining and industrial area during his formative years from 1924 to 1935. Though he was to become one of the great Scottish scholars of his generation, family background and childhood experience of working class life during the years of the Great Depression seem to have left a mark upon him, for McIntyre has been known to generations of students and friends as an approachable, down-to-earth and humble man.

McIntyre's schooling at Bathgate Academy was significant for what would become one of his abiding theological interests. There had been in the University of Edinburgh for generations a great succession of Professors of History, who, in the Scottish tradition, had in their turn educated significant numbers of history teachers for the schools. Even Bathgate had its share of excellent teachers of history, and McIntyre as a budding scholar fell under their spell. When, in his final year at school, he decided to train for the Ministry of the Church of Scotland, it seemed that the most obvious route to follow would be by way of an Edinburgh MA in history, through to a subsequent Divinity Degree. In the event, in his first year at University in 1933, the then Professor of History proved an exception to the rule and a disappointment, and McIntyre turned from his second year on to the study of Philosophy under A. E. Taylor, Professor of Moral Philosophy, and Norman Kemp Smith, Professor of Logic and Metaphysics. He graduated MA in 1938 with First Class Honors in Mental Philosophy.

Both Taylor and Kemp Smith had an important influence on McIntyre's intellectual development. Taylor was an English Anglo-Catholic, who took the classical philosophical tradition to have genuinely religious significance, and the religious development of the philosophical tradition to be of genuine philosophical interest. Taylor had given a notable series of the Gifford Lectures on Natural Theology in 1926-28, later published under the title, *The Faith of a Moralist,*[1] which even today, and perhaps especially today, repays careful reading. Kemp Smith, who also had a lively interest in religious questions, but who is best known as a commentator on the modern philosophers Descartes, Hume, and Kant, taught McIntyre the value of a realist slant on the problems of epistemology, even in the context of modern philosophy; this epistemological realism, though developed with eyes open to the critical turn in modern philosophy, would become an important factor in later years in McIntyre's theological work.

When, in 1938, McIntyre went to New College in the University of Edinburgh to study for the BD and the Ministry, his teachers were some of the greatest scholars in the English-speaking Protestant theological world at that time: John Baillie in Theology, William Manson in New Testament, Norman Porteous in Old Testament, and J. H. S. Burleigh in Church History, to name only a few. Curiously, in Theology it was G. T. Thomson, the early Barthian, who had the greatest influence upon McIntyre at the time; though Baillie certainly had the finer theological mind, he was somewhat out of step with the prevailing Barthian certainties of the times. According to the Barthian tradition, the best apologetic, and in the final analysis the only apologetic for Christian faith, is dogmatics and preaching, since one comes to believe

1. A. E. Taylor, *The Faith of a Moralist,* 2 vols. (London, 1930).

only by a pure miracle, as the gift of the Spirit makes us hearers and doers of the Word. It was not until later years, when working on the theology of Anselm, that McIntyre would return to a more realistic appraisal of the importance of philosophy for the theologian, and to a sense of the interdependence of faith and reason in theology. More will be said of the significance of Anselm below.

During the whole of his studies in Arts and Divinity from 1933-41, McIntyre's "parish" work was done with the YMCA in North Merchiston, a working class area of Edinburgh. This gave him experience in working with young people and reveals an interest in their problems during very difficult years; it was an experience which marks much of his theology, most notably in his early interest in the Christian community as a theological ideal, in his openness in what can only be described as his own "pure" theology to the problems of "applied" theology, i.e., the practical religious questions which emerge in the "cure of souls," and to ordinary religious experience and faith. It is also consistent with his long association with the Iona Community in Scotland.

McIntyre completed his Divinity training in 1941, but as a Minister, was exempt from military service. He intended and was due to go to India to teach philosophy in the Scottish Churches College in Calcutta in 1941, but his pre-departure injections turned septic two days before the date of departure, and he was unable to leave as expected. There followed months of illness, as his injections proved to be no good thing medically, but he went on to serve as a Minister of the Church of Scotland from 1941-45, first as *Locum Tenens* in the parish of Glenorchy and Inishail, being called in 1943 to the parish of Fenwick, Kilmarnock, famous for its covenanting associations some three centuries earlier. In 1945, McIntyre was appointed to the Hunter Baillie Chair of Theology at St. Andrew's College, in the University of Sydney, Australia. His primary responsibility there involved teaching dogmatics to students for the Ministry of the Presbyterian, Methodist and Congregational Churches, and to candidates for the BD of the University of Sydney. In 1950, he became the Principal of St. Andrew's College, which, in addition to its theological function, provided a residence for students of all Faculties of the University; he held these joint positions until 1956, when he succeeded John Baillie in the Chair of Divinity in Edinburgh. It was in St. Andrew's College that he gained firsthand experience of the administration of a University College, with its social and sporting interests, in addition to his tutorial and other academic responsibilities — experience which proved to be invaluable in the project of the Pollock Halls of Residence in later years in Edinburgh.

The Australian years were some of the happiest of McIntyre's career, and were profoundly influential. He had married Jan Buick in 1945, and three children were born to them in Sydney. Many lifelong friends were made by the McIntyres, and an affection for Australia and Australians developed which is still evident in conversation with them. Professionally, John McIntyre was a successful theologian; he lectured and published extensively, especially in the *Reformed Theological Review.* One of the highlights of the Australian years was his public defense of Christian faith against the then Professor of Philosophy in Sydney, the fellow Scotsman John Anderson, a virulent atheist. The debate was wide-ranging, and attracted the interest of Christian students in Sydney and beyond. In Melbourne, John O'Neill,[2] a young student at the time, took refuge from the philosophical storm of the post-War years in the little booklet of McIntyre's which resulted, *Freethought and Christianity,* published in 1948 by SCM Press. It was in this context that McIntyre began to reassess the quality of the training he had received from John Baillie, and to understand and admire the intellectual and devotional depth of his writings.

Two of McIntyre's most important works have their origins in the Sydney years. First of all, although the interest in the Christian understanding of history predates his arrival in his new post — indeed, McIntyre had intended to take time out from his Divinity Degree in 1939 to do a Doctorate at Oxford on the concept of history under Collingwood when the War intervened — his inaugural lecture in Sydney set the scene for his abiding theological interest; it was entitled, "In the Fullness of Time."[3] His argument there anticipated much that was to come later in the book published in 1957 at the beginning of his years in Edinburgh, *The Christian Doctrine of History.*[4] The book actually followed on a series

2. John O'Neill was Professor of New Testament in the University of Edinburgh from 1985 to 1996.

3. John McIntyre, published in two parts: "In the Fullness of Life" [*sic*], *Australian Christian World,* July 18, 1847 [*sic*], pp. 5-6, and "In the Fullness of Time," *Australian Christian World,* July 25, 1947, pp. 3-4.

4. John McIntyre, *The Christian Doctrine of History* (Edinburgh and Grand Rapids, 1957).

of earlier publications on the question.[5] McIntyre's work on Anselm's soteriology belongs also to the Sydney period. He had begun to work on it in earnest by 1950, and published it in 1954 under the title, *St. Anselm and His Critics*.[6] It was to be in many ways the definitive study of Anselm's soteriology and one of the best general theological commentaries on Anselm written in the twentieth century. Reviewing the volume in the *Journal of Theological Studies*, his old teacher John Baillie praised it as a work of "real distinction," and wrote, "No more penetrating examination of St. Anselm's presuppositions, and of the relation of each of his works to the others, has ever been made."[7]

The move back to Scotland in 1956 was motivated both by a desire on the part of the McIntyres to be near their aging parents, and by the status of New College as one of the great centers of learning in the world of Reformed theology. They sailed on a ship which had to be rerouted via Capetown, South Africa, because the Suez crisis had closed the Red Sea to commercial vessels. As a result, McIntyre missed the beginning of the winter term, but took up teaching shortly afterwards. While his subject in Australia had been dogmatics, his new responsibility in Edinburgh as Professor of Divinity was philosophical theology and the philosophy of religion. But it was a difference which was sometimes honored in the breach, for while his colleague, Thomas F. Torrance, the Professor of Christian Dogmatics, was deeply interested in the logic and method of dogmatic science, McIntyre for several sessions taught a course on the Trinity, and in later years taught dogmatics alongside philosophical theology. Though there were the inevitable tensions endemic to scholarly life, the result was that the two men complemented one another in their teaching in Edinburgh — which was, of course, what those who had appointed McIntyre to the Chair in Divinity had intended. In addition to *The Christian Doctrine of History*, to which reference has already been made, he published two further studies during his first ten years in Edinburgh which demonstrate his continuing dog-

5. John McIntyre, "History and Meaning," *Reformed Theological Review* 6 (1947): 7-23; "Christ and History," *Reformed Theological Review* 8 (1949): 9-42; *Christ and History* (Melbourne, 1949).

6. John McIntyre, *St. Anselm and His Critics: A Re-Interpretation of the Cur Deus Homo* (Edinburgh, 1954).

7. John Baillie, review of *St. Anselm and His Critics* in the *Journal of Theological Studies* 7 (1956): 144-46.

matic interest: *On the Love of God* (1962) and *The Shape of Christology* (1966).

In 1968, however, McIntyre's academic career again took a change of direction, when he was elected Dean of the Faculty of Divinity and Principal of New College. In addition, he had in 1960 been appointed Principal Warden of the Pollock Halls of Residence, the major complex of student accommodation in Edinburgh. Though he resigned from the latter position in 1971, and from the Deanship in 1974, he was twice appointed Acting Principal and Vice-Chancellor of the University of Edinburgh — in 1973-74 and in 1979. The result was that, whereas from 1956-66 McIntyre had published the three major books mentioned above, relatively little even in the way of articles appeared in print in the whole period between 1967 and his retirement in 1986, although during this period, his involvement with SCM Press from 1958-73 as joint editor of the Library of Philosophy and Theology, forming a series of some thirty volumes, is also a factor to be remembered. Whatever the effect on his publications, McIntyre served the University selflessly. Among his administrative contributions was something that reveals a pastoral touch: during his time as Acting Principal of the University, he initiated the democratization of nonacademic University committees dealing with student affairs, the result of which was that Edinburgh experienced relatively few of the student upheavals which were then commonplace elsewhere in the Universities of Europe.

Despite his administrative workload, however, McIntyre still managed to lecture extensively during these years, meeting invitations to give lecture series in a variety of institutions in various countries: in Union Theological Seminary, Richmond, Virginia; in St. Andrews University and Edinburgh University; and in the universities of Melbourne and Sydney. In addition, he taught courses in Princeton Theological Seminary (on the Holy Spirit), in the College of Wooster (on religious language), and in the University of New England, Armidale, New South Wales (on the place of imagination in the history of philosophy from Plato to Mary Warnock). Most of these lectures were presented in prepublication form, and after his retirement, provided the basis of several publications. The bulk of the present volume is likewise based on such material.

The present writer was taught by McIntyre during his last two years at the University of Edinburgh, by which time the burden of administration had fallen to others. While not the most flamboyant of teachers, he was one of the clearest and most thorough that one could hope to encounter. McIntyre frequently lectured from full notes, which were also often distributed freely in advance to the class. His standard joke was that he not only sent students to sleep, but also gave them the sheets to sleep on. I for my part did not sleep. One of the advantages of his practice appears in the present introduction, since use has been made of such notes in what follows, along with the substantial quantity of manuscript material of McIntyre's which is lodged in the Library of New College.

Faith and Reason

Although it would be inaccurate to present McIntyre primarily as a philosophical theologian, his training in philosophy and his appointment to the Chair of Divinity in particular in Edinburgh in 1956 channeled his theology in the direction of philosophical theology. What was perhaps McIntyre's most fruitful period from the late 1940s through to the early 1960s coincided with the protracted debate in the English-speaking Protestant theological world between Barthian theology on the one side and the disciples of Tillich, Bultmann, and even Brunner on the other. In this context, and particularly in the Edinburgh context where this debate had a personal as well as a theological edge, McIntyre made it his business to defend the place of philosophical theology in the University and the Church, arguing that without an adequately defined philosophical conceptuality, and more importantly, an adequate conception of the proper relation between philosophical and dogmatic theology, the work of the Christian theologian is seriously undermined. In McIntyre's view, the polarization of philosophical and dogmatic theology which characterized this debate rested on a misunderstanding of the proper function and role of the two disciplines. In his philosophical theology, therefore, McIntyre did not simply side with the philosophical theologians against Barth. Indeed, it would be as fair to see him as a critic of Bultmann and the Bultmannian school, or of Tillich and his disciples, as it would be to see him as an opponent of the radical Barthian tendency in some recent theology. Whereas the great majority of theologians think in terms of a school in which they are located, McIntyre's theology is quite independent, drawing on a wide variety of sources for its inspiration. In this respect, McIntyre's theology is representative of a more general tendency in the best traditions of Scottish theology, which has tended frequently to be similarly open to a variety of influences, rather than to be narrowly conceived in terms of a single school of theological interpretation or method.

The question of whether a Christian theology can legitimately employ methods and arguments appropriate to philosophical enquiry without by that very fact turning its back on the revelation of God in Jesus Christ, and without jeopardizing the *uniqueness* of that revelation, is one of the key concerns of Barthian theology, as also of much Reformation theology. On this view, philosophical theology represents the attempt by human beings to gain a knowledge of God on the strength of rational argument, rather than by hearing the Word of God which is addressed to them. As such, philosophical theology can be construed pejoratively as an attempt to reach God without grace, and without revelation; in particular, it bypasses the central fact of revelation with which a legitimate Christian theology must begin and end, the revelation of God in Jesus Christ. A variety of elaborations on this basic theme are possible. For example, it might be argued that as a result of the Fall, human beings are incapable of discerning theological truth of themselves in any case, since the intellect is darkened and our creaturely capacity to know and to love God so impaired that we are, as Calvin put it, "blinder than moles" of ourselves in the area of religious belief. Grace, revelation, faith as the transcendent gift of the Holy Spirit, are therefore not merely *advisable* for those who set out on the religious quest in some general sense, but absolutely necessary and unavoidable as prerequisites in the whole enterprise. Alternatively, one might wish to point to the confusions which result from the introduction of philosophical methods and concepts into the Christian Church — a tactic frequently employed in the Reformation with reference to the theological decadence of the late medieval era, and resurrected in the twentieth century by Karl Barth with reference to the blasphemies of the "German Christians" under Hitler. Barth pointed to Nazi religious philosophy as the example *par excellence* of where philosophical, or "natural" theology, as he preferred to call it, leads, though one is driven to remark in response that the case is hardly proven; one might just as well conclude that parents should abandon the attempt to set a moral example to children, since in some cases it has been known to lead to psychological repressions and neuroses in later life. One further view which might be mentioned in this context takes the line of reasoning in favor of dogmatic rather than philosophical theology a stage further, and this one too can be found in Barth. It is that since God is literally defined by who he is in the Christ-event, there being no case for any distinction of content between God as he is in himself and as he is in his revelation, it is necessary for us to look to revelation rather than to reason to find out who God is, or even if he exists, since he is who he is nowhere else than in his revelation. One points to the crucified one, like the famous image of John the Baptist in Barth's own study from the Isenheim Altarpiece, with dramatically elongated finger, for it is there that God defines *himself*, and that, quite simply, is a result which is and always has been and will be opaque to the philosopher. The Pauline warrant for such an approach would appear to be clear: "But we proclaim Christ crucified, a stumbling block to Jews and foolishness to Gentiles" (1 Corinthians 1:23).

Such a view of the relation — or lack of relation — between philosophy and theology prevailed in much Christian theology for much of the interval between the First and Second World Wars, and continued on into the post-War era. It was a view which was often congenial to both sides in the debate, the view that an amalgam of Christian faith and the philosophy of religion involves a compromise on the question of truth being accepted almost *a priori* by both philosophers of religion and by theologians alike. On the one side, philosophy generally has, in the twentieth century, as in much of the modern era, sought to be unencumbered by religious claims and commitments, and to be a purely secular discipline. Any real *religious* interest in religion can almost be taken to be indicative of philosophical weakness, so inimical is the spirit of most modern philosophy to religious faith. On the other hand, where the ultimate criterion of truth is taken solely to be the self-revelation of God, whether in Jesus Christ, or in the pages of the Bible, or in Bible and tradition taken in tandem, it is clear that there can be little room left for the rational methods and ideals of philosophy.

In his theology, McIntyre rejects this dichotomy as a false one, or as "postulational" rather than real, to use a favorite expression. In short, it is possible to have a philosophy which is detached from religious belief, and a theology which is conceived purely as the elaboration of the content of the Christian *kerygma,* without reference to the world of human thought beyond, but this polarization is by no means necessary. McIntyre insists that there is such a thing as a Christian philosophy of religion, i.e., a philosophy of religion practiced in the context of faith, and which is therefore not presuppositionless — a philosophy of religion which is as opposed to the secularized versions of philosophy of religion which are current as it is to a dogmatics detached from the responsibility to explain itself and to interpret the faith for one's own generation. Furthermore, such philosophy of religion can be genuinely at the service of, and integral with, faith. In an unpublished lecture, McIntyre wrote of what the philosophy of religion detached from faith becomes: "the theology of Christian gentlemen who have only a flimsy acquaintance with the regular ordinances of the Church," or an "abstraction" which fails to reflect "the tensions in the Church's existence"; "even the Apologetics . . . [are] aimed more at the tutors and fellows of Balliol than at the riveters in Clydebank."[8] Over against this, McIntyre attempts to develop a philosophy of religion, a philosophical theology and apologetic, which is at the service of faith, and which is conceived in and of itself as an elaboration of the content of faith. If the dichotomy is a false one, then such an integration of the two is not only possible, but necessary.

In short, a complete Christian theology requires an integration of philosophical and dogmatic thought, in order to be both controlled by the content of faith and responsible to the generation in which we live. Anselm's *fides quaerens intellectum,* faith seeking understanding, is regulative in all of this, for it is only as such that faith becomes something understood and understandable. McIntyre sees this as something belonging not just to theological work in the university or in the study, but something which has to be undertaken in the work of the preacher and teacher in the ordinary congregation, among "the riveters of Clydebank" or, for that matter, among their modern equivalents, whether their descendants among Clydebank's long-term unemployed or those at work in the "Silicon Glens" of the new Scottish manufacturing industries. Rather than seeing the content of Christian revelation as eternal truth given once for all in history, therefore, McIntyre argues

8. John McIntyre, "Philosophy of Religion and Apologetics," pp. 3-4, in the McIntyre Papers, New College Library, the University of Edinburgh.

that the revelation of God in the pages of the Bible, precisely because it occurred in time, is something which is expressed in time-conditioned categories; the work of the philosopher as well as of the exegete and theologian is required both to understand what the original meaning of the revelation was and to express the same thing in the categories of the present day. The question is not one of having some timeless message in our minds which is readily understandable, and which we then attempt to translate into terms which our contemporaries can follow, but one of translating one time-conditioned message into another time-conditioned form without loss of content.[9]

One of the major consequences of this approach to his subject is an insistence by McIntyre that theology must always be willing to listen to and learn from the great trends and themes of contemporary culture, even if, at the end of the day, it stands in critical relation to them. Thus an important underlying theme in John McIntyre's theology is that of *openness*, an openness which stands in sharp contrast to the widespread attempt in much twentieth century theology to attempt to demonstrate its *exclusiveness*.[10] It is for this reason that McIntyre is unconvinced of the merits of the great theological dictionaries produced by the biblical theology movement in the middle years of this century. Although comprehension of the original world of thought in which the Biblical narratives and literature was cast is an important step in the process of theological argument, no real theology, he is convinced, can be developed on this basis alone; without taking the additional step of retranslation, in other words, the most important stage in the whole process of theological development is missed. For this, an adequate philosophical conceptuality is an absolute prerequisite.

Anselm's principle of faith seeking understanding is regulative throughout, but that principle, it should be said, as McIntyre conceives it and elaborates it in *St. Anselm and His Critics*. What is distinctive in McIntyre's understanding of Anselm can be seen in the position outlined above. He argues that Anselm's *credo ut intelligam* cannot be understood to assert a form of fideism, to the effect that there is literally no understanding without faith, on the grounds that the very method

9. McIntyre, "Philosophy of Religion and Apologetics," p. 8.

10. John McIntyre, "The Open-ness of Theology," *New College Bulletin* 4 (1968): 6-22.

Anselm uses in the *Cur Deus-homo,* the method of *remoto Christo,* of the *removal* of the content of faith, is the very mechanism by which the principle enunciated is carried into effect. This implies that, for Anselm, the respective roles of believing and knowing cannot be so easily regulated as this overly simplistic view asserts. The problem of how it is that the *remoto Christo* methodology is consistent with the basic Anselmian principle of *credo ut intelligam* preoccupies McIntyre throughout his analysis of Anselm's theology. The conclusion reached is that Anselm intends by this procedure to emphasize the necessity for an intellectual apprehension and appropriation of the facts of the faith by the believer, in the sense that it is necessary for us to see the faith to be comprehensible and true, in order for us fully to believe. Rejecting a whole series of misinterpretations of Anselm, deriving from those who wish to present him alternatively as an apologist, or a dogmatician, or a philosopher of religion, or a crypto-Barthian, McIntyre argues that Anselm's greatness lies in the honesty with which he pursues the theological task, employing a variety of methods. McIntyre's summation of Anselm's achievement could be read as a guide to his own theology, or at least to what he valued in theology, and it is an ideal to which more theologians could well afford to aspire:

> St. Anselm's greatness as a theologian, then, lies in the facility with which he checks one method by the other, and demonstrates clearly that all are necessary to a successful prosecution of theological enquiry. Above all, it is the spirit in which St. Anselm writes — a spirit of reverent devotion towards the God Whose nature and mighty acts he seeks to describe, of profound humility which recognizes that theological reflection is itself a gift of God Who is both *Deus absconditus* and *Deus revelatus,* and of sympathetic patience with those who have not been given to see what he has seen — which secures for him a place in the forefront of Christian theologians.[11]

The study of Anselm marked an important development in McIntyre's thinking about the nature of theology, a development which can be seen by a comparison of his work on the doctrine of history, published in 1957, and his later works from *On the Love of God,* published in 1962,

11. McIntyre, *St. Anselm and His Critics,* p. 51.

onwards. For though *St. Anselm and His Critics* dates from 1954, and is therefore his earliest book, the main lines of the arguments represented in *The Christian Doctrine of History* predate the study of Anselm, being discernible in a series of articles which belong to the Sydney period, beginning with his inaugural lecture in Sydney in 1946, and which have been noted above. To this extent, *The Christian Doctrine of History* is the most anomalous of McIntyre's works, for one might say that in it, more than in any of his other major writings, he is concerned to press the case for the regulative role of revelation in the Christian concept of history, so that such categories as fulfillment and incarnation come to have decisive significance for his exposition. The work is not closed to philosophical analysis, or to a real engagement with the claims of secular historiography, but it would be too much to say that it is entirely open to them. One might, in fact, describe it as the most Barthian of all McIntyre's books. Indeed, in it, he sets out on the first page his intention to remain "in organic union with 'the given' of Revelation and the record of Revelation."[12] One can justly imagine his old teacher, G. T. Thomson, making an approving noise at that point, at least, of his reading of the work. Although the regulative role of revelation never disappears from McIntyre's thinking in the years following, it becomes increasingly common in subsequent works to adopt the standpoint of the contemporary skeptic, or of contemporary secular culture or thought, in order thereby to come to a clearer understanding of the content of revelation itself. In McIntyre's later theology, it is only by doing so that the contemporary theologian, like Anselm before, with his *remoto Christo* methodology, can come to understand afresh what revelation means and what it implies, what is says to the contemporary world and what also, significantly, the contemporary world says to it.

Theological Models and the Theological Imagination

McIntyre's theology is often characterized by a particular theological method which also needs to be explored as a function of his philosophical theology. At times, to read him is to gain the impression of a heaping up of theological images, all conceived or designed to shed light on different

12. John McIntyre, *The Christian Doctrine of History* (Edinburgh, 1957), p. 1.

aspects of a given question. It is not always the case that one can follow a linear argument from start to finish in his theology. Perhaps the best example of this is his recent work, *The Shape of Soteriology,*[13] but the same thing can be seen in earlier works, and most especially, perhaps, in his extensive, unpublished lecture manuscripts. Without an adequate understanding of this method, or of what he understands by the term "model" and how he employs theological models in his work, it is not possible properly to understand McIntyre's theology. As we shall see, the question of the status of models as an epistemic device will also help to clarify other areas of potential confusion in the interpretation of his theology.

The use of the term "model" itself dates from *The Shape of Christology,* which was based on lectures delivered at Princeton Theological Seminary early in 1965. The concept of theological models is there presented as derived from Ian Ramsey's, *Models and Mystery,*[14] but McIntyre develops his own distinctive view of the nature and function of a model, based both on Ramsey's work and on his own, earlier studies of the concept of analogy. In fact, since McIntyre had made implicit use of the notion of theological models years before he encountered it in Ramsey, one might speak more of a confirmation of an earlier insight at this point than of any simple dependence. In *On the Love of God,* for example, one finds the following explanation of method, some years before explicit reference would be made to the concept of a model:

> In what follows, six terms will be offered as successive determinations of the nature of the love of God. No one of these by itself will be adequate as a definition of this love. They are not equivalent to one another, so that one says what another says, but does so in slightly different terms. Each has a quite separate contribution to make, and as we advance from one to the other we are taken more and more deeply into the wonder and the mystery of this thing of which we dare even now to speak. . . . So we say, in this order, that Love is Concern, Commitment, Communication, Community, Involvement, Identification, Response and Responsibility.[15]

13. John McIntyre, *The Shape of Soteriology* (Edinburgh, 1992).

14. John McIntyre, *The Shape of Christology* (London, 1966), pp. 56ff., with reference to Ian T. Ramsey, *Models and Mystery* (London, 1964).

15. John McIntyre, *On the Love of God* (London, 1962), p. 37.

In Ramsey's work, however, McIntyre found an elaborate, and for him a convincing, treatment of the relation between the use of models in theology, to which, as we have seen, he was already committed methodologically, and the use of models in the natural and social sciences. Ramsey himself was openly dependent on the earlier scientific and philosophical work of Max Black and even James Clerk Maxwell on the role of models in the sciences, and used the concept in his own theology to build a bridge between science and religious thought as analogous branches of human knowledge. Ramsey distinguished between scale, or "picture" models, which as a concept is more or less self-explanatory, and "analogue" or "disclosure" models, which attempt to provide an echo of the deeper structures of what is modeled rather than simply a depiction of it in miniature.[16] This latter type of model "chimes in" with the structures of the physical universe in science or with the theological reality in question in theology, and so discloses to us something which would otherwise be an inarticulate mystery.

McIntyre's position on the use of theological models follows from this. According to McIntyre, models are images basically related to reality, and as such are the means of apprehension, without which human knowledge would be a very poor thing indeed. Model language, however, is analogical language. Rather than taking the view, therefore, that in using such language, we are engaged in a kind of low-level enterprise which ought to be, or which ought to be able to be, transcended in some sort of speculative metaphysics, he argues that the models, or analogies, which we use in theological discourse are the only means of knowing available to us. We are, in other words, unable to translate such an analogy as that of Christ as the Good Shepherd into more abstract discourse without a loss of something along the way which cannot be easily regained, and in fact, we are not able to translate this analogy into anything other than another analogy, for all talk of God is analogical. This has a further consequence, in that the inherent difficulties involved in the attempt to transcend particular models or analogies in theology entails that the realities with which we are concerned cannot be comprehensively described. Thus, according to McIntyre, we cannot assume at any point in our Christology, for example, that we

16. McIntyre, *The Shape of Christology*, pp. 1-11, with reference to Ian T. Ramsey, *Models and Mystery*.

have "exhaustively described or defined the mystery of the Word made flesh," for we simply "never grasp it in the immediacy of nonanalogical language."[17] The model, in short, or the analogy, to use the more traditional term, is the medium of knowledge, and though its limitations must be admitted (for Christ is both a Good Shepherd and yet obviously not a shepherd), its epistemic role is indispensable.

To the question, "Whence do models derive?" McIntyre provides an interesting and important answer. In a programmatic publication in the early 1960s, he had signaled an interest in what was to become an abiding concern over the next twenty-five years of active academic study and teaching, the theology of imagination,[18] and in *The Shape of Christology,* he returned to this theme: "the creation of models is part of the function which imagination fulfills in theological activity."[19] Rather than being mere fantasy, the imagination for McIntyre serves an indispensable function in the knowing situation as a medium of truth. This view of the nature of imagination was to be developed over the years in a variety of ways, for example, through an unpublished study of the concept of imagination in the history of philosophy which is now among the McIntyre Papers in New College Library, but most obviously in his book on the concept of imagination and on its place in theology, *Faith Theology and Imagination.*[20] Here, McIntyre begins with the insights of the seminal nineteenth century Scottish writer George MacDonald, who had such an important influence on J. R. R. Tolkien and C. S. Lewis, and ends with what can only be, on McIntyre's terms, an "imaginative" enumeration of the varied roles which images play in the work of the theologian and, more importantly, in the life of the worshipping Church.

It is thus appropriate that it is in *Faith Theology and Imagination* that McIntyre's most sustained discussion of the concept of models, and of their role in theological methodology and epistemology, in fact appears.[21] Once again, reference is made to the work of Ramsey and Black, though McIntyre moves on from these writers to more recent contribu-

17. McIntyre, *The Shape of Christology,* p. 67.

18. John McIntyre, "The Place of Imagination in Faith and Theology: I & II," *Expository Times* 74 (1962-63): 16-21, 36-39.

19. McIntyre, *The Shape of Christology,* p. 173.

20. John McIntyre, *Faith Theology and Imagination* (Edinburgh, 1987).

21. McIntyre, *Faith Theology and Imagination,* pp. 127ff.

tions, and in particular, to that of Ian Barbour in his *Myths, Models and Paradigms.*[22] After an extended treatment of the variety of possible types of model, mainly drawn from these authors' treatments of recent philosophies of science, McIntyre draws particular attention to the conclusion reached separately by Black and Barbour, that the human imagination plays a significant role in the construction and application of the scientific model to reality. Furthermore, "The selection and construction of the model, in whichever of its forms, *precedes* the processes of detailed rational deductions and precise mathematical verifications, and is not derived from them *a posteriori*."[23] In other words, it is basic to the work of the modern scientist to engage in an act of perceptive imagination before detailed measurement or experimentation can take place, since it is only on the grounds of some imaginative insight, or of some theoretical model, in other words, that the precise kind of experiments to be undertaken or range of measurements to be made can be designed and executed. Imagination thus serves a crucial role in the process of scientific discovery, and so important is this role that science and scientific discovery could not exist without it.

What this discussion reveals is that the term "imagination" in McIntyre's thought refers to far more than simply my capacity to daydream, to imagine, for example, that I am on a tiny tropical island in some ocean paradise rather than sitting at my desk at work in wintry Scotland. Rather, the term "imagination" serves as a synonym in McIntyre's thought for human creativity, or for what might be called the freedom of human thought and will, our capacity to transcend the boundaries of convention or habit or fixed circumstance, and to know or act in freedom. From this point of view, the human imagination is that which makes our thought and action distinctively *human,* for it is as beings capable of such creative, imaginative thought and imaginative action that we are free. It is as such that the category of imagination does service in McIntyre's theology as the essential feature of the *imago Dei* in humankind, and thus, by implication, that it does service also as a divine perfection — and perhaps even as the divine perfection *par excellence.*[24]

22. Ian Barbour, *Myths, Models and Paradigms* (London, 1974).
23. McIntyre, *Faith Theology and Imagination,* p. 129.
24. McIntyre, *Faith Theology and Imagination,* pp. 13ff., 41ff.

Several points remain to be made before we leave this discussion of the concept of imagination and its role in the construction of models. First of all, McIntyre draws particular attention to what might be called the fecundity of theological models, to their own inner capacity to create further insights which were not originally in view when the model was first conceived. He provides a number of examples of this capacity of the model from recent theological literature.[25] For example, Walther Eichrodt's concept of the covenant as the regulative idea in Old Testament theology in his two-volume study, *Theology of the Old Testament*,[26] issued from an act of creative perception, in which it was recognized that most of the essential themes of Old Testament literature could be gathered around this concept and illuminated through it. The fact has to be recognized, however, that in order to sustain his thesis, Eichrodt had to apply the concept of covenant to biblical texts which do not mention it. While this has brought criticism from Old Testament scholars, Eichrodt's insight is perfectly compatible with the role of models in science and in theology, for any model's explanatory power potentially reaches beyond its original field of reference. Eichrodt's theology of the covenant implicitly depends upon this basic feature of the model in its employment in human knowing. The fact that the model in this case does illuminate texts which make no mention of covenant, on the one hand, and yet, on the other, that the limitations of the concept of the covenant, or the model of the covenant, have therefore to be recognized as well, is catered for in McIntyre's theology. The truth is that any model, like any analogy, has a positive and a negative content: a positive content in what it legitimately says, and a negative content in what it is unable to say. For McIntyre, all theological language is like this, so that there is no real mystery or dilemma to contend with in the case of Eichrodt's conception of the covenant, so hotly debated by the Old Testament theologians. Like everything else in theology, it has its applications and its limitations, but both have their origins in the creative human capacity to construct imaginative models as the medium of knowledge.

Secondly, one might say that one of the tests of any particular

25. McIntyre, *Faith Theology and Imagination*, pp. 136ff.

26. Walther Eichrodt, *Theology of the Old Testament* (ET London, 1961, 1967).

theological position, on these terms, ought to lie in the strengths of the particular model or imaginative construct from which it begins, and in the range of wider questions which it manages, perhaps unexpectedly, to illuminate. Eichrodt's selection of the concept of the covenant, for example, is successful to the extent that it can be grounded in certain key biblical texts, but it is also successful to the extent that it illuminates a series of further texts. The focus of debate among Old Testament theologians is therefore rightly on the question of the extent to which covenant is a key concern of the Temple cult, or of the prophetic proclamation, or of the Deuteronomistic history; where it misses the point is when Eichrodt's concept of the covenant is dismissed from these fields because particular texts, or even textual traditions, do not mention it. The latter criticism of Eichrodt depends upon such a crudely literalist view of the nature of biblical interpretation that the point should be obvious. The same argument, however, could be applied to the theology of Karl Barth, and, for example, to his selection of the concept of the Word of God as the starting place in theology. McIntyre, in his treatment of Barth's theology, admits the strength of this, but also observes that it leads to such great emphasis on listening to what God has to say that the expectation is heightened that God's Word will necessarily be verbalized.[27] While, as any reader of the *Theology of Prayer* in the present volume will discover, McIntyre is by no means opposed to such an expectation in the general sense, it can be overstated, if for no other reason that it leads to the expectation that God does not speak through images or events in history, which is patently not a sensible theological position to hold, and which not even Barth can be said to hold. While, therefore, the model of Christ as the Word of God in Barth's theology is immensely illuminating, not only in Christology but also in such fields as ethics, its strengths as a theological model must be set alongside its limitations. Of that other great Barthian model, the model of revelation, McIntyre is much more critical. This too is a theme which appears in the writings included in the present volume, and most particularly in *The Humanity of Christ*.

Thirdly, the role of imagination in religious epistemology involves something more than simply providing analogies or models for something already known; as has previously been said, the models are rather

27. McIntyre, *Faith Theology and Imagination*, pp. 140ff.

the sole media of our knowledge, so that it is possible to say that we know God in terms of fatherhood, for example, rather than that we describe a God otherwise known by means of the image of fatherhood.[28] Or, to put the matter another way, we know what the kingdom of God is, according to McIntyre, in terms of the variety of images used by Jesus in his teaching, which, taken together, build up a picture through a whole complex of complementary ideas which mutually connect with and correct one another. The relation between the model, or the image, and the object known, therefore, is much more immediate and direct than might otherwise be supposed. McIntyre openly refers at this point to John Baillie's idea of the "mediated immediacy" lying at the heart of our knowledge of God, for just as, for Baillie, God is immediately present through those finite media by which he communicates himself in a sacramental way — whether human words or a human embrace, a visible Church or bread and wine — so, for McIntyre, God is immediately known through the medium of our theological models, or images. The role of imagination, however, and so of the human subject, is here highlighted in a way which refutes the Barthian insistence upon the gift of faith as pure miracle, for God makes use of the human capacity to imagine, to create models, in communicating himself to us, and does not, as it were, simply speak directly from on high, or "vertically from above" in dialectical fashion. Here too, McIntyre's sympathetic assessment of the work of that other Baillie, Donald, the theologian-brother of John, can be seen. For in his theological masterpiece, *God Was in Christ*,[29] Donald Baillie argued that a realistic assessment of the nature of faith, of incarnation, of revelation, and even of forgiveness and atonement requires of us a realization that life in relation to God is not simply a question of grace alone, for the grace of God comes as something which establishes the self in its proper place, and which does not annihilate it; the experience of God's grace is, in truth, a question of all of God and all of me, rather than one of all of God and nothing of me.

Fourthly, and finally, in his exposition of the role of models and imagination in religious epistemology, McIntyre relies on a sophisticated analysis of the teaching of Jesus in parables, an analysis which is too

28. McIntyre, *Faith Theology and Imagination*, pp. 155-56.

29. Donald Baillie, *God Was in Christ* (London, 1948).

significant for us to pass over without further comment.[30] The parables of Jesus are rightly taken as the illustration *par excellence* of imagination's role in theology, but the crucial observation is made that they actually constitute the sole content of Jesus' teaching on a range of questions; they are not illustrations of some theme found elsewhere, which he stated in nonparabolic fashion. Jesus' technique is "to heap image upon image, in rapid profusion," so that we "run from particular image to particular image and so to the conclusion that Jesus wants us to see," a conclusion which is specific to us and particular, both in the original setting of the parable and in its contemporary application in the reading of the Bible or in prayer.[31]

Thus far there is little that is particularly original in McIntyre's treatment of the parables, for, as he himself makes clear, the same themes can for the most part be found in such standard modern expositors as Bultmann, Bornkamm, and Jeremias. From it, however, he draws the conclusion, particularly with reference to the work of theology and to the life of the Reformed Churches in particular, that the tendency towards a "de-iconizing" of religious and theological language, not to mention of Church buildings, involves something mistaken to the point of "the impoverishment and even barrenness of our teaching and preaching and writing."[32] More importantly, McIntyre goes on to argue a theological case for the unity of the image with the imaged, or the parable with its object, or the model with what is modeled, both on the grounds of his treatment of models as such, and by way of a consideration of the problems of sacramental theology. According to McIntyre, the very distinction which theologians introduce in sacramental theology between the sign and the signified, and which is basic to so much Christian theology, is actually evidence of theological misunderstanding, since the original unity of the two in the parabolic imagination, as we might put it, is only obscured by the variety of sophisticated and perhaps incomprehensible attempts that have been made historically to draw the two together. According to the nonparabolic, and seemingly unimaginative, tradition of thought on the subject, the two are separated by a great gulf. At the Last Supper, however, Jesus' words of institution did

30. McIntyre, *Faith Theology and Imagination*, pp. 19ff.
31. McIntyre, *Faith Theology and Imagination*, p. 27.
32. McIntyre, *Faith Theology and Imagination*, p. 32.

not start from an assumption of separation between sign and signified, with the result that an elaborate metaphysical, or for that matter linguistic-philosophical, theory was somewhere or somehow in his mind, "in intention," as it might be said by some, as to how the two are one.[33] Rather, it is Jesus' own realistic imagination, evidenced also in the parables which constitute his teaching about God, which we see at work; McIntyre can speak in this context of an "immediacy of identity," or of an immediacy which need not be mediated by such secondary, and ultimately misleading, sacramental concepts as "symbolizing" or even "revealing." His account parallels that of John Baillie, as noted above, in his notion of the "mediated immediacy" of all of our experience and knowledge of God. McIntyre's unique contribution is to perceive the central role of imagination in the sacrament, as in the rest of theology, in grasping the content of Christian faith.

The great question which arises in connection both with McIntyre's use of the concept of theological models and his related dependence on human imagination in theology concerns the status of our knowledge of God: Is it objective knowledge or "merely," as we might put it, subjective? The debate between "objectivity" and "subjectivity" in theology is, of course, a key concern of the Barthian tradition, particularly as interpreted in the Edinburgh context, but the question posed does not relate immediately to the Barthian thesis only. Rather, it raises a more general question concerning McIntyre's relation to a more pervasive tendency and problem in mid-to-late nineteenth and twentieth century thought and culture. For it is possible to construe the whole history of the philosophy of our own era in terms of a crisis of *meaning,* and not only of truth — a crisis, that is, of the precise status of *all* human ideas and values, of their origin and content, of their reference and their authority. This is a crisis which is integral with the so-called "death of God" in modern culture, for the death of God is to be understood as part of a wider death of absolute meaning in the modern world. The death of God, therefore, cannot simply be seen as if it were a question of interest or relevance only within the walls of the Church, or within the circle of those who are religious in a more general sense; rather, it is to be seen as part of a more fundamental crisis in modern thought, a deeper crisis of which it is itself a

33. McIntyre, *Faith Theology and Imagination,* pp. 35ff.

function. This crisis of meaning derives from the conviction that human beings themselves, and not God, or even, in the end, the ultimate nature of the physical universe, are the source of meaning. Human beings, in short, or, to translate the question into more familiar terms, their histories, or cultures, or societies, or even their particular psychologies, give rise to those ideas and values which we designate by the phrase "what is meaningful." Our ideas, therefore, since they have their origins in us, and not in the ultimate source or nature of things, are ultimately as finite and relative, as historically and culturally determined, as we are ourselves. The question of Pilate, "What is truth?" has been translated in our own day into a more fundamental question, "What is meaning?" If all meaning is finite and relative, deriving from sources which are by definition changing and conditioned by finite events and experiences — by a history, in short — then the question of truth too is made much more radical than even Pilate himself, the politician and pragmatist, could have foreseen.

This is not the place to labor this point, which concerns the pervasive relativism of modern thought and culture, but rather, and more simply, to raise the question whether McIntyre's theology of imagination, and his treatment of the theological model as the medium of our knowing, relies on or is explicitly or implicitly committed to, the relativist position. Are his models, in other words, versions of the view which asserts that all human knowledge, all our "meanings" in the sense outlined, are merely perspectival? Are they just "ways of seeing," creations of a particular human psyche or of a particular human culture, which might just as easily be replaced by a different series of perspectives or constructs, none of which ultimately take us to the heart of any objective reality, but which are rather simply functions of the subjective perspective of the person or persons whose imagination creates them? For if this is the case, then it becomes difficult to fathom how it is any longer possible to speak of God at all, beyond speaking of God as simply another imaginative creation of certain individuals or cultures. This is a question which is relevant to the work of many contemporary theologians, and which might well be asked of them, but in the case of McIntyre, the implication of relativism, of a purely perspectival doctrine of meaning, and of subjectivism, does not hold, and this for the following reasons.

First, and perhaps most importantly, the context within which McIntyre's doctrine of the theological imagination operates is a doctrine of creation on the one hand, and a doctrine of revelation on the other. Although this does not fully answer the problem, or the question which a thoroughgoing modern relativist himself or herself would raise, it does indicate that the accusation of a pure subjectivism is inappropriate. It is precisely because there is an objective metaphysical order in which exist God and the world as his creation and as the object of his love that theological language of the sort McIntyre employs is possible. Secondly, McIntyre is well aware of the problem posed by the so-called death of God, and of its epistemological presuppositions and implications; he nowhere adopts that position, although neither, it would be fair to say, does he attempt at any point a *comprehensive* refutation of it. Rather, one is struck by a certain impatience on the part of McIntyre with the whole debate, and by what might be called his "commonsense" alternative — commonsense in the good Scottish philosophical sense — according to which such radical skepticism is something which is not to be taken terribly seriously, except, perhaps, as a logical extreme useful only as a counterfoil to one's own thought, or as a marker of what is to be avoided as *non*-sensical. Therefore, though a more extended treatment on McIntyre's part of the relation between the theological imagination at work and the thesis of the modern subjectivist might have illuminated points that are obscure in his own approach to theology, one must take account at this point of the philosophical tradition in which McIntyre was trained, and in which, in many ways, he situated himself throughout his working life. For the Scottish philosophical tradition as a whole, and not just McIntyre as an isolated figure, has never been sympathetic to the claims of subjectivism, whether in the form of Cartesian doubt or in the even more radical, and more consistent, form of modern epistemological relativism. No one once under the tutelage of A. E. Taylor and Norman Kemp Smith, certainly, would easily be attracted to such a superficial thesis, despite its present cultural status.

Jesus Christ

Although he regards the work of the philosopher as crucial to that of the theologian, and takes an active part in the task of constructing a philosophical approach to theology, John McIntyre is not, as I have stated above, to be construed primarily as a philosophical theologian.

In fact, of his six books, three are concerned specifically with the questions of Christology and soteriology — *St. Anselm and His Critics, The Shape of Christology,* and *The Shape of Soteriology* — while two of the others — *The Christian Doctrine of History* and *On the Love of God* — are concerned for the most part with the Christological question indirectly, and often directly. Among McIntyre's published articles, furthermore, Christology stands out clearly again as his major interest. In keeping with this, I wish to suggest, McIntyre is to be understood primarily in terms of his contribution to Christology, and ultimately as a Christological theologian in the widest sense, in that his position even at other points is developed expressly with a view to the question of the person and work of Jesus Christ. Given the scope of McIntyre's treatment of Christology, no full-scale account of his position can here be attempted, but as a bare minimum, the following must be briefly considered: the significance of history for Christology; the doctrine of the incarnation proper; the nature of the atonement; and what we might call the "horizon" of McIntyre's Christology in his doctrine of God.

The central significance of history in McIntyre's Christology and in his theology generally will be well-known already to those familiar with his work. Within the present volume, however, this theme emerges with particular clarity in *The Humanity of Christ,* where we not only find an extended treatment of the question of the historical Jesus in the context of modern historiography, but also find the open statement that the discipline nearest to theology is history; one might almost put into his mouth the words, *historia ancilla theologiae,* "history is the handmaid of theology." The problem, however, and perhaps even the reason why McIntyre did not coin this expression himself, is that in theology, the use to which history has been put in modern times has been almost exclusively skeptical and destructive, to the extent that it has not served the theological enterprise at all well. The well-known "ugly big ditch" between the Jesus of history and the Christ of faith, which dates from Enlightenment times, and which is still current, is here in view. According to McIntyre, however, the skeptical use of history in theology has been accentuated for reasons which have little to do with historiography and a very great deal to do, in fact, with theology itself.

Originally, of course, the division between the Jesus of history and the Christ of faith was postulated by the philosopher Lessing on the grounds that any divine revelation must answer to the canons of Enlightenment reason, as being something rationally accessible to all human beings, and as conveying universal and necessary truth — which is precisely what does not characterize the "accidental truths" available to the scholar through the study of historical texts and events. Lessing knew, of course, and indeed himself popularized, the skeptical theology of Reimarus, who denied that any miraculous or supernatural events took place in the life of Jesus, ostensibly on historical grounds, but mainly, it might be argued, in keeping with his own well-known Deist outlook. In our own era, of course, both Deism and the rational ideals of the Enlightenment have been left behind, and for the most part completely abandoned, but the Jesus of history versus the Christ of faith dilemma remains. As McIntyre presents the case, this is due to the influence of existentialism, and specifically to the historical skepticism of Kierkegaard, whom he effectively sees as the father of modern theology, at least in this respect, that Kierkegaard provides what many accept as a theological necessity for rejecting the notion that historical science can ever, or ought ever, to serve as an adjunct of faith. If the latter is pure miracle, in short, whether in the Kierkegaardian, the Barthian, or the Bultmannian sense, then the work of the historian is not only rendered redundant, but actually becomes positively unhelpful and misleading to the theologian. At best, the historical-critical scholar at work on the texts of the New Testament can only pursue a path which is deliberately detached from the question of the miracle or the existential commitment of faith, and might, indeed, better serve these interests by means of what to an ordinary historiographer, not to mention an ordinary believer, would appear to be an excessive, *a priori* skepticism concerning the reliability of the biblical documents and of the events which they relate to us.

McIntyre is not, of course, entirely averse to the activity of modern historical-critical scholarship on the New Testament; his theology is intended to be open at this point as well as at others to the insights of modern secular culture, and to modern secular culture even as it manifests itself within theology. His response, therefore, is neither fundamentalist nor obscurantist; he is able to admit, for example, that much of the content of the gospels may well be, in part, a construct of the early Church, written or at least edited from earlier traditions from the new standpoint of faith. At the same time, however, he is, one might say, a skeptic where the *excessive* historical skepticism of the modern exegete is concerned, and necessarily so, for his position is that without a grounding in history, the whole of the message of the gospel is effectively emptied of content. What this might mean will be addressed shortly, but for the present, we may note simply that the main importance of this response lies in the claim that is most basic to it, and which has already been outlined: that modern biblical scholarship is excessively skeptical for what are, in the end, theological reasons — that faith and history are incompatible — rather than for straightforwardly historiographical reasons. One of his own characteristic complaints is that philosophers have almost completely neglected the nature of historiography, and therefore have allowed the excessive skepticism of the biblical exegetes to continue unchecked, as it were; his call is for the Christian intellectual to take up the challenge, and to address this remarkable lacuna in secular scholarship. For the sake of Christian theology, in short, an adequate philosophy of history needs to be developed.

One example of the manner in which modern exegesis excessively antithesizes faith and history appears in the tendency to dismiss the possibility of a divine intervention in history out of hand, as if the whole idea were incompatible with the nature of historical science. In fact, McIntyre insists, there are many things on which the historiographer must or might well insist in his or her work which are analogous to the question of divine intervention. The best example of this is human freedom, which is by definition inaccessible to scientific description, but the possibility of which must be maintained in any acceptable doctrine of history. Similarly, the psychological motives of an individual from the past, even where letters and the like do not provide direct evidence, must often be surmised by the historiographer by means of an imaginative identification with his or her subject, since without *some* reference, at least, to the element of psychological motivation, no history involving that individual's actions can possibly be complete. In the same way, McIntyre argues, it is at least plausible that the historian should be open to divine action, even if only at the level of those spiritual influences which move us in a type of religion which is primarily ethical, if not also at the level of the overtly miraculous. Certainly, McIntyre himself is necessarily committed to the possibility of the miraculous at the point of incarnation as a bare minimum, but in practice, a general openness to the possibility of divine action in the world is characteristic of his whole theology, though sometimes this may be seen more in terms of a spiritual influence than in terms of straightforward physical events.

What is more important than this, however, in McIntyre's account of the importance of history for Christology and theology generally follows on from something said in the previous section, that is, that any hard and fast distinction between a finite reality such as a verbal promise of grace read in the Bible, or the historical humanity of Jesus Christ, and its divine referent cannot be sustained from the standpoint of theological epistemology. In the case of Christology specifically, therefore, the historical humanity of Christ *is* the medium of revelation in precisely this sense, in that, for McIntyre, it does not simply point us to the divine, which is somehow known independently — by faith, as it were — but rather of itself conveys the divine promise and presence to us. If he were to sacrifice the humanity of Christ as the medium of revelation, in other words, he would also have to sacrifice the theological epistemology which coincides with it, his notion of the theological model as providing access to the reality of God. In this context, one of the crucial theses of *The Humanity of Christ,* included in what follows, comes into focus: the thesis that while we may not have sufficient material for a proper biography of Jesus, we do have sufficient material relating to his moral existence on which to build up a theology of his human nature as revealing God, and which is "more than enough," as McIntyre himself puts it, for any of us to go by in this area. What he particularly objects to in the excessive skepticism of modern biblical exegesis, one might finally conclude, is that it makes such an integrating approach impossible, and therefore that it destroys, on putatively theological grounds, the very historical, concrete basis upon which all Christian theology must rest. We simply have no other means of access to God, as if we could dispense with that basis and find an alternative approach elsewhere. Rather, Christian theology must insist at this point upon the absolute irreducibility of that in which God in Christ exists and is found: the human nature of Jesus Christ, existing as a man in history.

We turn now to address more directly the question of the doctrines of the incarnation and the atonement, for if "God was in Christ, reconciling the world to himself" in the sense that he was and can still be found in this specific historical human life, and "in, with and under" the biblical record of his life, death and resurrection, then the question of its precise theological content must be raised. The main sources which will serve as the basis for our discussion at this point are *The Christian Doctrine of History, On the Love of God, The Shape of Christology,* and *The Shape of Soteriology.* In the first of these, the following reference for the term "incarnation" is provided: "By the Incarnation I intend those events which form the subject of the Four Gospels, of which we make profession in the second article of the Apostles' Creed, and which have been variously described as 'God's becoming man,' 'God's entering history,' 'God's becoming one with us that we might become one, or at one with Him,' and so on."[34] What is striking about this is how commonsensical it is, and in particular, how rooted in the concrete details with which the theologian and the Church are concerned. Although McIntyre points out in the context of the passage just quoted that the discussion he thus initiates will be concerned with the place of the incarnation in history, and with its significance for the Christian understanding of history, it is nevertheless indicative of a basic feature of his whole approach, which is to highlight the significance of the man Jesus in the doctrine of the incarnation.

The concreteness of McIntyre's approach to Christology, as I have chosen to call it, is further developed in *The Christian Doctrine of History* through a consideration of the category of fulfillment as the primary basis for and even the fundamental content of the doctrine of the incarnation. In Christ, the Word spoken by God through the prophets is brought to completion, to such an extent that it is possible and even necessary to say that "the Word became flesh and dwelt among us."[35] After an elaborate exposition of the concept of fulfillment as treated by a series of modern theologians, in the course of which the dominance of the concept of revelation as a Christological category in mid-twentieth century theology is rejected, McIntyre proceeds to argue for the conclusion that through the notion of fulfillment, even the distinction between secular and sacred history is overcome. The total significance of the incarnation does not appear unless and until we are able to locate the incarnation, not merely at the center of the "thin red line" of *Heilsgeschichte,* but at the intersection of secular history and salvation-

34. McIntyre, *The Christian Doctrine of History,* p. 45.
35. McIntyre, *The Christian Doctrine of History,* pp. 49ff.

history, so that the incarnation is the point of convergence here, as in Christ himself, between God and the world.[36] Any other view, McIntyre argues, amounts to docetism — and this, it must be said, is an error of which many of our contemporaries, on these grounds, would stand accused. Even the groaning of creation in Romans 8:22 is organically related to the incarnation, conceived in this way, for nature's travails are part and parcel of that secular history which the concept of fulfillment allows us to regard as basic to the Christological question.

Implicitly, therefore, McIntyre's Christology is open to the concept of the cosmic Christ, though this is a theme which is not developed in *The Christian Doctrine of History* or in subsequent works. The burden of McIntyre's argument is more simply that God in Christ has identified himself with history. In other words, there is more at stake in the incarnation than merely a divine stepping into and out of the historical process, though there are some theologies which seem to be content with such a view. According to McIntyre, however, "Once the Incarnation has taken place there is no question of God stepping out of history, or of His contracting out of this once-for-all identification."[37] The implication of this is that since God has so identified himself with history in Jesus Christ, there is no Christology worth the name which can ignore the hard questions of historical criticism, of the philosophy of history, and, as the title of the volume in question has it, of the Christian *doctrine* of history, for to know God as revealed in Jesus Christ is to know him as he is revealed *there*.

If one were to ask who the God is who is thus revealed in Jesus Christ, then the answer must be: the God who *identifies* himself with us in love. This is the theme which emerges most strongly in the second main Christological *locus* among McIntyre's publications, *On the Love of God*, but an indication of its importance in his theology can be found already in *The Christian Doctrine of History:*

> . . . in accomplishing the salvation of the world, and in fact as the means by which he does so, God effects the identification of Himself with history. "He that knew no sin was made sin for us" (2 Corinthians 5:21). It was not some other history with which He identified Himself,

36. McIntyre, *The Christian Doctrine of History*, p. 76.
37. McIntyre, *The Christian Doctrine of History*, p. 80.

> some *Heilsgeschichte* without the sins and shortcomings and ambiguities of this kind of history that we know and help to make, but with this history in all its fallenness. This concept of identification is becoming, for me at least, the dominant one in the interpretation of the Atonement. . . .[38]

In fact, this statement has almost programmatic significance for the later volume, in which the three main themes found in this statement are developed at length — the theme of the loving identification of God with the beloved, the theme of his identification with precisely the *sinful*, and finally the significance of this for the doctrine of the atonement.

On the Love of God is arguably one of the more remarkable theological books of the 1960s, though it has never received the attention it deserves. In fact the volume anticipates many of the developments which were about to become standard concerns in English-language Protestant theology, though primarily under Continental influence, and actually develops these themes more carefully, with greater attention to detail and to the questions that might be raised concerning them from a more traditional theological standpoint, than did these other sources. For our purposes, and since his account of Christ's baptism is central to his exposition of identification, McIntyre's analysis of the baptism of Christ will serve as our point of entry to the Christology of *On the Love of God*.[39]

Love is identification, supremely and decisively, according to McIntyre, and the love of God is revealed supremely in God's identification with the sinful, seen in the baptism of Jesus. From the standpoint of traditional Christian theology, however, a problem is raised by this episode in the gospel stories. This stems from the fact that John's baptism was a baptism of repentance — whereas Jesus has been understood from the earliest times to have been sinless. Against this thesis, and particularly in view of the historical linkage between high theologies of Christ's baptism and low Christologies of adoption, the baptism of Jesus has long been treated by the orthodox with a certain theological embarrassment. McIntyre, by contrast, presents Jesus' baptism of repentance under John as a great symbol of the nature of the gospel, of the righteousness of

38. McIntyre, *The Christian Doctrine of History*, p. 79.

39. McIntyre, *On the Love of God*, pp. 186ff.

God, and of God's love for the world. Furthermore, in God's identification with the sinful in Christ, something was done at Jesus' baptism which was done at no other point, something which emerges as a theme of great importance in McIntyre's overall theology: an identification with the sinful in their act of confession and repentance. McIntyre never commits himself to the view that the human nature assumed by Christ was fallen, though he entertains the possibility on several occasions. He does, however, unreservedly associate himself with the views of the nineteenth century Scottish theologian John MacLeod Campbell, who held that at the center of incarnation and atonement is the identification of Christ with the sinful in their act of repentance. McIntyre would later write warmly of Campbell, ten years after *On the Love of God,* as "our contemporary ancestor."[40] To the question, how can the righteous God identify himself with sinners to such an extent as to share their repentance, McIntyre responds by arguing that there is no place in Christian theology for a playing off of the righteousness or justice of God against his love or mercy, as if the former had to be "satisfied" before the latter could be fully realized. The truth, according to McIntyre, is rather that it is precisely in his loving and total identification with the sinner that the righteousness of God is expressed, for it is precisely in this way that righteousness justifies the unrighteous. Thus Christ, and God in Christ, is "found where self-righteous orthodoxy least expected to find anyone with pretensions to be the Messiah,"[41] in the Jordan with John, and later, with the publicans and sinners, with Zacchaeus the tax collector, and supremely and finally upon the cross.

According to McIntyre, this perspective on Christology and soteriology sheds light on a number of important questions in Christian theology.[42] First of all, it is inappropriate, in view of the theme of identification thus understood, to understand the event of atonement as occurring solely in the death of Christ, or as consisting solely in what much Protestant theology has traditionally spoken of as bearing the consequences, or even the penalty, of sin. Rather, the identification with the sinful characterizes Jesus' whole existence, so that it is possible to

40. John McIntyre, *Prophet of Penitence: John MacLeod Campbell, Our Contemporary Ancestor* (Edinburgh, 1972).

41. McIntyre, *On the Love of God,* p. 197.

42. McIntyre, *On the Love of God,* pp. 198ff.

say (with John Calvin, at one point) that Christ began to pay the price of our redemption from the first moment of his existence.[43] Furthermore, Christ took upon himself the sin of humankind as well as its consequence, i.e., rejection by God, and that to the extent of making the perfect response of contrition on our behalf (following MacLeod Campbell).

Secondly, what happens in the incarnation and atonement cannot be construed in any other way, or any higher way, than as the identification of love with what is other than itself. McIntyre rejects the well-known idea of a divine "self-communication" in Christ, not because it says too much or because it says something wrong, but because it says too *little:* the concept of communication does not do justice to the love of God. Furthermore, the idea is rejected that in Christ, or the cross of Christ, we have a "revelation" of the love of God, on similar grounds. The identification of God with the sinner in Christ is total, so that it is not possible, or rather legitimate, to speak of what happens in Christ as pointing to a divine reality beyond itself; as was the case with the theological model earlier, or with the humanity of Christ and his divinity, that identification means that the Christ-event, and supremely the cross, is in and of itself God's openness to bear and to forgive the sins of the world, and not simply a sign of it. Among other things, this has implications for the question often asked, if not in academic or Church theology, then at least in popular Christianity, "When were you saved?" McIntyre's answer to this question is absolutely unambiguous: in the life and death of Jesus. This does not preclude the necessity of a human response to God's love — indeed, the final chapter of *On the Love of God* is devoted to this question (and opens up the nature of this response brilliantly), but it does locate salvation in the concrete, historical event in which God himself has reached out to the world in love, rather than anywhere else.

The final theme of *On the Love of God* that might be highlighted lies in what it has to say concerning God's involvement in the suffering of his creatures, in a discussion which anticipates a great deal of more recent theological literature.[44] McIntyre's argument is first of all a correlative of the view that one cannot speak adequately of God in less

43. John Calvin, *Institutes of the Christian Religion,* II,xvi,5.

44. McIntyre, *On the Love of God,* pp. 203ff.

than personal categories, as if he were simply a metaphysical object. This does not imply any trivial commitment to the proposition that to be a person, God has to suffer — a thesis that is too simplistic to be admitted by any thoughtful theology or theologian — but derives from the observation that the identification with the sinful which took place in Jesus Christ, and which was an unfolding of the love which God himself is, was an event that took place in the history of a person, and which has the concrete dimensions of that personal history. It involved his baptism by John, for example, and finally, of course, the cross. Ultimately, however, the question of God's involvement in the suffering of creation is addressed from the standpoint of the problem of theodicy as an obstacle to faith.[45] To those whose objection to the existence of God or to the notion of the love of God is found in the terrifying proportions of evil in the modern world, the thesis that God's love involves his identification with suffering provides an answer. The sufferings of Jesus, McIntyre argues, were not simply private to himself, but have the same universal quality as his identification with the sinner. To those who suffer, therefore, it is possible to say that God too is involved in suffering, in that he has identified himself with it. The Christian response to the problem of evil, therefore, is found in the fact that God in Christ stands with those who suffer. Although these themes are not fully developed in *On the Love of God,* or subsequently in McIntyre's writings, they do reflect something important in his thinking on the questions of incarnation and atonement, something which reveals his concern to escape the dominant theological clichés of the day, and even of the Reformed tradition, and to recover what is essential in the biblical message and in Christian theology.

The main studies of these two related doctrines of incarnation and atonement are, however, the books which bear the titles *The Shape of Christology* and *The Shape of Soteriology.* It is to these that we must now finally turn. In both cases, the conception of a model as the medium of knowledge is regulative, and in both cases, the point is to attempt to present what might be described as a three-dimensional picture of incarnation and atonement through a consideration of a diversity of theological models pertaining to each field. A failure to grasp the significance of McIntyre's theological method, however, can lead to mis-

45. McIntyre, *On the Love of God,* pp. 217f.

understanding. John Macquarrie, for example, in passing judgment on *The Shape of Christology,* argued that, though it gives other theologians material to work with and thus provides them with a starting point for reflection, it had no special thesis of its own.[46] In fact, of course, the volume crystallized for McIntyre the significance of the theological model, and provides for us what is still his most comprehensive treatment of the range of models which we may legitimately employ in Christology, of their strengths and weaknesses, and of their basis in Scripture and tradition. The point is precisely to do what Macquarrie does not want to see done in Christology, which is to argue for what, on the earlier metaphor, we might describe as a one-dimensional Christology, developed by way of a linear argument from a series of premises to a fixed conclusion. It must be said, therefore, that while McIntyre's method has its weaknesses and will prove to be disappointing to those who seek such linear arguments in theology, this is not the point of theology as he conceives it, or perhaps more accurately, it is not always the point of theology. On the whole, McIntyre seeks, rather, to open us up to new possibilities, and to clarify the logic of the metaphors, analogies, and models that we use in developing our theological understanding. In fact, fully half of *The Shape of Christology,* and almost as much of *The Shape of Soteriology,* is devoted to an exploration of the methodological necessity of such an approach. Understood in this light, the former book takes on new significance.

I do not propose to elaborate further on the methodological question, since this has already been treated in detail above. What is required, however, is a treatment of the three Christological models McIntyre discusses in his theology: the classical model, which understands Jesus in terms of two natures, divine and human; secondly, what we might call the "liberal" or "psychological" model, according to which we understand Jesus as a man in psychological terms, and in some sense, therefore, in terms of his biography; and finally, the revelation model, which is, of course, normative in much twentieth century theology, and especially in the Barthian school. The models presented provide for us an anatomy of the Christological tradition, for in them, we have what amounts to a comprehensive overview of the most significant tendencies in the Chris-

46. John Macquarrie, "Recent Thinking on Christian Beliefs, I: Christology," *Expository Times* 88 (1976): 36-39.

tological tradition, each of which has at some point or other been developed in opposition to the rest. McIntyre, however, wishes to present them as complementary visions of Christ, and in many cases to attempt to preserve elements of each of them from unjust criticism; of the three, it is the revelation model which he himself criticizes most sharply. In each case, however, his arguments are original and instructive.

The two-natures model represents, of course, the Christological conception which emerged as predominant in patristic theology, and which is enshrined for us in the classical Christological definition of the Council of Chalcedon in 451: "one and the same Christ . . . acknowledged in two natures, without confusion, without change, without division, without separation." McIntyre rightly draws attention to the fact that the description of Jesus as both divine and human is so familiar to us that it is difficult to see the extent to which it *interprets* the basic "given" of Christology in the scriptures, where, it is clear, Jesus is at the very least a single person, as yet undifferentiated, as it were, into discrete "parts" or natures.[47] Nevertheless, the strengths of the two-natures Christology must be affirmed, for both divinity and humanity are seen in him, and proclaimed of him in the New Testament, while the power of the model to sustain devotion and to shed light on theological questions has also to be admitted.

McIntyre's thesis is that the two-natures model in Christology has its origins, not just in scripture or tradition, however, but also in the logic of Aristotle's *Categories*, and specifically in the Aristotelian distinction between primary and secondary substance.[48] In the language which comes to be employed in Christology, primary substance is expressed as *hypostasis*, or "person," and secondary substance as *physis*, or "nature." Although as a historical thesis this is not entirely convincing, since in fact many of the early Christian Fathers were openly hostile to the philosophy of Aristotle, and since few of them consequently make explicit use of his logic, there is a strong philosophical case to be made for the claim made. It is clear, for example, that in the conceptual model at stake in two-natures Christology, there is an assumed ontology which needs to be brought to the surface, an ontology according to which it is manifestly possible to speak of the same thing in different ways — to

47. McIntyre, *The Shape of Christology*, pp. 83ff.
48. McIntyre, *The Shape of Christology*, pp. 86ff.

speak of a primary "substance," to use the generic term, as somehow consisting of, or as containing within itself, two different and separate secondary "substances." In this case, of course, the one subject in question is the incarnate Word, whereas the two things predicated of him are divine and human nature.

Perhaps the question is less that of whether or not the logic of Aristotle is expressly in view in, for example, the Chalcedonian definition, than a matter of the virtually inescapable conclusion which must be drawn from an analysis of Aristotelian logic itself: Some version of the distinction of primary and secondary substance, which corresponds to the language of subject and predicate, or of substance and attribute ("Socrates is a man"), is virtually inescapable in human thought and discourse. Aristotle himself, of course, did not think that he had literally *invented* a new way of thinking and speaking in his *Categories*, but rather simply to have made plain something that is always and necessarily the case in our thinking and speech: in our propositions, we assert a universal of a particular (which corresponds, in Aristotelian ontology, to the presence of the universal *in* the particular). In the end, this is McIntyre's conclusion, for those who would attempt to criticize the two-natures Christology on the grounds of some modern philosophical critique of the doctrine of substance have, he says, to reckon with the fact that ordinary language and ordinary human convictions about the world seem to imply something very like the substance and attribute distinction highlighted in Aristotelian logic.[49]

The more serious issue for two-natures Christology, according to McIntyre, is actually whether or not it can adequately express the mystery of the God-man himself in terms adequate to the reality with which we are here concerned. Two specific sets of problems are addressed in this context: first, the internal logical difficulties involved in saying that the one *hypostasis* possesses two natures, divine and human, the human nature being in and of itself anhypostatic, or "impersonal"; and secondly, the difficulty raised concerning the traditional conceptuality from the standpoint of modern anthropology and theology, according to which it all seems far too abstract, logical, and therefore lifeless. To give a name to the reality of God, or to the reality of God in Christ, one needs to use what one modern writer has called

49. McIntyre, *The Shape of Christology*, p. 102.

"personological" language,[50] and not the language of primary and secondary substance, or of *hypostasis* and *physis*.

As to the first of these, McIntyre's position is clear: a variety of ancient Christological positions must be reckoned to be inadequate on soteriological grounds, especially those committed to the *anhypostasia* doctrine. The specific complaint made is that to suggest that it is somehow human nature which the incarnate Word was dealing with in his saving work, but not the human person — which is something unassumed, by definition, on the *anhypostasia* formulation — is profoundly unsatisfactory.[51] McIntyre goes so far as to suggest that a more rather radical version of two-natures Christology offers a superior alternative, a Christology according to which the *hypostasis* in question in Jesus Christ would not simply be the divine Word, as it was for Cyril of Alexandria, for example, and as it is for the bulk of traditional orthodoxy, but rather a fusion of the divine and the human *hypostaseis*, or in short, a composite subject.[52] The God-man would thus be the subject in question in the gospels and in Christian devotion, rather than the divine Word *simpliciter.* While McIntyre does not pursue this thesis further in the book, it may well be consistent with themes found elsewhere in his theology, to the effect, for example, that God has identified himself with history in Jesus Christ, and suggestive of further possibilities. For example, on such grounds, it might be possible to speak of the suffering of Jesus Christ in a way which does justice both to God's involvement in the dilemma of the world, but which yet does not commit us to the overly simplistic view that in Christ, God suffers in himself, properly, as it were, in his own nature.

In what was perhaps the most perceptive review of *The Shape of Christology*, however, E. L. Mascall claimed that this critique of *anhypostasia* is misleading, on the grounds that the correlative doctrine of *enhypostasia* makes good any apparent deficiency in it.[53] It is, in short, perfectly defensible to speak of Christ's human *hypostasis* as existing "in" the *hypostasis* of the Logos. Mascall's argument was that to say that there

50. Heribert Mühlen, *Der Heilige Geist als Person*, 5th ed. (Münster, 1988), *passim*.

51. McIntyre, *The Shape of Christology*, pp. 95ff.

52. McIntyre, *The Shape of Christology*, pp. 99ff.

53. E. L. Mascall, review of *The Shape of Christology*, in *Church Quarterly Review* 167 (1966): 499-501.

is no human *hypostasis* in Christ is not the same as to say, for example, that Christ has no human mind, for the human *hypostasis* is not part of human nature, whereas the mind is; therefore, the doctrine of *anhypostasia,* and the correlative doctrine of *enhypostasia,* do not commit us to any truncation of Christ's humanity, or to any kind of psychological deficiency in Christ as a human being. In a letter dated 20th October, 1966, McIntyre responded to Mascall's critique, and developed his Christological suggestion in *The Shape of Christology* more fully.[54] "I am," he stated, "probably inordinately sensitive to the enhypostatic theory because of the tremendously popular treatment which it receives in our Scottish Barthian circles," a point which he then immediately related to the rather inchoate views of students. He continued, however, by pressing the argument of *The Shape of Christology* further: if Christ is without a human *hypostasis* — and so is not, in other words, a "person" in the twentieth century sense of the term — then his humanity must be reckoned to be *ontologically* defective, even if it is not, on Mascall's account, *psychologically* so. This argument, he conceded, rests on the assimilation of the *hypostasis-physis* distinction to the Aristotelian distinction between primary and secondary substance, a view which "requires to be looked at again." Nevertheless, if this assimilation is justified, then there has to be in Jesus Christ "a particularization of the general human nature in a *hypostasis* which is human," since, *within the terms of this ontology,* a secondary substance with a primary substance of "a totally different genus or species or order of existence is a non-sense." It is this conviction concerning the weakness of *anhypostasia* which leads to the contention that the *hypostasis,* or "person" in the contemporary sense, with whom we are concerned in the Gospels is the *God-man,* so that while "the natures remain as the Chalcedonian adverbs say, . . . the *hypostases* are fused." To Mascall's charge that the Chalcedonian definition is thus misinterpreted, McIntyre responds that the Greek text is ambiguous as to whether the definition is "about" the Second Person of the Trinity, or "about" the Incarnate Son. Though his position is thus somewhat clarified, McIntyre's central point in all of this remains the same as in *The Shape of Christology* itself: The Christological ontology implicit in the notion of *anhypostasia* is defective, and thus jeopardizes

54. John McIntyre to E. L. Mascall, 20/10/66; the McIntyre Papers, New College Library.

the integrity of our Christology, and even the genuineness of Christ's humanity itself. Nor is McIntyre's criticism of the standard form of the older two-natures Christology unique; within Scottish theology, for example, essentially the same point is made by H. R. Mackintosh, while the criticism of Chalcedon's "impersonal" categories is standard fare in the older liberal Christology for which Mackintosh himself, and ultimately McIntyre too, have such high regard.[55]

As to the second issue raised concerning the necessity for using personal language rather than logical language, where the claim made is perhaps somewhat more conventional, one might say that the whole approach taken to Christology in McIntyre forces this conclusion upon us. For example, in order to speak of the human nature assumed in the incarnation as involved in history in any meaningful sense, and certainly as having a personal history, it is necessary to move beyond the abstraction of "human nature" into such concrete categories as human development, culture, psychology, and so on. The work on *The Humanity of Christ* which follows is an extended treatise on just this question, which attempts to show that there can be no adequate Christological conception without reference to just such categories. But the basis for this approach is already laid in *The Shape of Christology*, specifically in the account of the "psychological" model in Christology, to which we now turn.

In fact, apart from the development of the concept of the theological model generally, it is the treatment of the psychological model which constitutes the main importance of *The Shape of Christology* as a whole, and which makes it one of the more important and revealing of McIntyre's writings. The account begins with the following definition:

> The psychological model is a comprehensive description of those interpretations of the person of Jesus Christ which both hold that it is *possible* to speak significantly of the motivation, feelings, purposes, cognition and in fact of the mind of Jesus Christ; and go on to affirm that interpretation of this sort contributes insights in Christology which are obtainable in no other way and for which there can be no substitutes.[56]

55. H. R. Mackintosh, *The Doctrine of the Person of Jesus Christ* (Edinburgh, 1912), pp. 214-15, 222.

56. McIntyre, *The Shape of Christology*, p. 115.

McIntyre proceeds to a defense of such Christology by way of an attack on those who reject it, first of all, and secondly by way of a positive exposition of the significance of the humanity of Christ for theology. The argument is presented explicitly as an attempt to restore to its rightful place certain of the permanent contributions of liberal Protestantism to our understanding of Jesus Christ, though with eyes open, it should be added, to certain of its limitations as well.

The basic problem which McIntyre finds in the theology which rejects the psychological model in Christology is, once again, the rigid separation between faith and historical knowledge which it presupposes. Since practically the whole of contemporary Christology stands in this tradition, whether consciously or unconsciously, it is unsurprising that it does not succeed in bringing the two together again. The only way forward, McIntyre argues, is by way of a theology which deals seriously with the question "how faith and historical knowledge are related to one another, for related they most certainly are,"[57] and which does not simply retreat into the Kierkegaardian skepticism which infects so much twentieth century theology. The ultimate implication of the latter, when thought consistently, is that Jesus Christ becomes merely an "x" recurring in a series of kerygmatic pronouncements, about whom, as a human person, we know literally nothing at all.

In fact, as McIntyre observes, even the most skeptical of New Testament scholars have been unable to sustain such skepticism indefinitely, since it would literally cut them off from any real contact with Jesus, so that there is a lack of simple intellectual consistency, and one might even say, of honesty, at the heart of this tradition. The truth, however, is that we are not faced with the stark choice between pure conjecture as to the historical Jesus and a thoroughgoing historical skepticism in our approach to the New Testament, as we have already seen at length above. Furthermore, there are powerful theological reasons for a recovery of the psychological model in our Christology, according to which we ought to be able to say something significant about the mind of Christ. First of all, without such a Christology, we are again effectively committed to Christological docetism, for though the Word was made flesh, he was "made flesh in a manner which escapes all the ordinary psychological observations that one would make about a

57. McIntyre, *The Shape of Christology*, p. 121.

human personality."[58] Secondly, and more seriously (for this first point is not entirely fair to the intention of the historical skeptics), given the dominance of the psychological understanding of human existence in our era, Christian theology will fail in its proper task if it fails to address the question of the person of Christ from a psychological perspective. Here, and here uniquely, through a consideration of how he thought about the Father, about his neighbor, about his life and death, and similar subjects, together with a consideration of the socio-economic conditions of the time in which he lived (which can, on McIntyre's terms, legitimately be considered under the heading of a "psychological" Christology), we can fill in the detail of the abstract, purely formal notion of "human nature" which is embraced in the Christological tradition.

The rootedness of theology in the life of the Church is, for McIntyre, one of the factors which compels us to take such an approach to Christology: "Anyone who has attempted to expound the two-nature theory to a group of senior Bible-class members will know that one of the very first questions raised in discussion afterwards is that of how a two-nature person operates psychologically."[59] One of the typical responses just as frequently heard by the Bible-class members themselves, undoubtedly, is to the effect that one should not ask questions that are too lofty, and instead, that one should worship before the incomprehensible. But such a response fails miserably, not only because it begs a real question — a question, or perhaps, *the* question which classical Christology has never squarely or successfully faced — but because it fails to recognize "how completely our generation has come to think in psychological terms, particularly, and I may add, appropriately, when it is thinking about *persons*."[60] If therefore, we are to think today of Jesus Christ as a person, some version of McIntyre's psychological model will have to be invoked. For though it would be fair to say that some recent Christologies have attempted to structure themselves on the *Trinitarian* conception of a person, it has also to be said that the implicit presupposition of this, to the effect that we have greater knowledge of what it is to be a Trinitarian person than we do of Jesus Christ as a person, is quite extraordinary, to say the least. Further, such an approach would

58. McIntyre, *The Shape of Christology*, p. 124.
59. McIntyre, *The Shape of Christology*, p. 129.
60. McIntyre, *The Shape of Christology*, pp. 129f.

appear to wish to reverse the logic of the statement, "the Word became flesh, and dwelt among us." For surely the implication of an incarnational theology will be that we must do justice to the "fleshliness" of Jesus Christ, so defined, or to his humanity, in short, as precisely the whole point of the exercise, since it is the point of God's involvement with us.

Two further insights are of special significance. First, if an adequate psychological model in Christology is to be developed, then we require an adequate ontology of persons, for the former will necessarily invoke the latter. McIntyre points to a variety of possible sources for guidance at this point: for example, to Martin Buber, whose I-Thou philosophy of religion recurs as an important theme in McIntyre's writings, but also to John Macmurray, the Scottish philosopher of this century who wrote extensively on how the self is to be understood as a philosophical subject in its own right, and is to be dealt with in terms appropriate to it; for Macmurray, this involved a personalist ontology of the self as agent, and as intrinsically relational.[61] In McIntyre's theology, the ontology of the self might be said, in addition to these, to have the dimensions of historicity, of freedom, and most importantly, perhaps, of morality. Secondly, however, McIntyre argues that the Christological models, as independent ways of understanding the mystery of Christ, ought not to be confused, while the criteria appropriate to one ought not to be used to criticize the others. The psychological model, therefore, cannot be dismissed because it fails, in some of its versions, at least, the "Chalcedonian test."[62] To move from one to the other without adequate differentiation is to expose oneself to category mistakes, and inevitably to risk a loss of Christological insight. "Nature" and "person," therefore, are not equivalent, but parallel concepts; what one reveals to us, the other does not. The future of the psychological model, therefore, lies in its expansion on its own terms, and not in its justification on the grounds of some more traditional Christological conception. This insight, which derives from McIntyre's understanding of the role of models in theology, as well as from his treatment of a variety of modern psychological models and their critics, might prove helpful to those who wish to pursue the

61. *The Shape of Christology,* p. 131. For a recent account of Macmurray, see David Fergusson, *John Macmurray* (Edinburgh, 1992).

62. McIntyre, *The Shape of Christology,* p. 142.

path outlined in future — and ought to serve as something of a corrective to those who will, no doubt, wish to criticize aspects of the Christological position outlined by McIntyre in the present volume.

The treatment of the revelation model in *The Shape of Christology* is more straightforward, and, as much of it is repeated in *The Humanity of Christ*, need not detain us unduly. Basically, however, several criticisms are made against it. First, revelation is not a sufficiently central notion in the New Testament, or in Christian theology, to sustain such elaboration in Christology; for example, it does not feature at all in what is of any significance in classical Christological or Trinitarian discussion, and is, even in its modern exposition, unable to sustain an adequate theology of the death of Christ. The more significant criticism, however, is that the revelation model has tended to be elaborated in a philosophically unsophisticated form, with the result that, in certain versions, it tends to imply that the divine Word is so uniquely the medium of revelation that the humanity of Jesus becomes an incidental inconvenience. This would be true of both Brunner, on McIntyre's account, and of Bultmann, whom, however, he does not mention. It is also, he claims, at times characteristic of Barth.[63] Since these themes are, however, as I say, taken up in the present volume, I shall not pursue them further. A third, important criticism of the revelation model is that it begs the fundamental question which it purports to answer, and the interest which it purports to serve. According to McIntyre, to say to an unbeliever that God is revealed in Jesus Christ is meaningless unless the term "God" already means something to him or her; claims to revelation presuppose some knowledge of a revealer, in other words, so that in conversation with total unbelievers — which is effectively the position of men and women in the Barthian anthropology — the revelation model can have no apologetic significance. Its sole function therefore appears to be in a context in which there is already some acceptance of belief in God.[64] The contrast between this negative exposition of the revelation model and the extremely positive assessment of the significance of the psychological model — which is openly associated with the older Christological tradition of liberal Protestantism — could hardly be more telling.

To round off this account of McIntyre's theology of the person

63. McIntyre, *The Shape of Christology*, p. 169.
64. McIntyre, *The Shape of Christology*, p. 171.

and work of Jesus Christ, reference must obviously be made to his most recent book, *The Shape of Soteriology.* This is an important study, drawing together into one whole a number of themes in his theology; the significance of theological models, once again, is elaborated in a fresh way, while an overview of the whole field of soteriological theory is provided, an overview which, along the way, provides us with an understanding of McIntyre's own relation both to Reformed soteriology and to the development of modern soteriological theory. Once again, a full treatment of these themes is out of the question, but two of special importance will be addressed. The first of these is the development of the idea of models in soteriology, and the contribution McIntyre thus makes to theology in this field. The second is a rather more difficult theme to handle, but goes under the heading of "incarnation, atonement and forgiveness," so that the question to be answered concerns McIntyre's understanding of the relation among the three. This provides us with an ideal place at which to bring this part of our discussion to a close, for of all the theological questions that are posed by Christians, this is surely the greatest, so that the shape of the answer provided by any theologian at this point will always be revealing.

In *The Shape of Soteriology,* what must be on any account a comprehensive list of interpretative models of the death of Christ is mustered; the ideas of ransom, redemption, salvation, sacrifice, propitiation, expiation, atonement, reconciliation, victory, punishment, satisfaction, example, and liberation are all pressed into service in the cause of conceptual clarification.[65] As in the case of Christology, so here the point is to provide what might be called an anatomy of soteriological theory, and the intention in this case is to provide a complete anatomy. In fact, the list is incomplete, for by "soteriology" McIntyre means only theories of the saving significance of Christ's death, whereas in the New Testament, and arguably in Christian theology too in the widest sense, the doctrine of salvation, which is the strict translation of "soteriology," involves eschatological conceptions to a very considerable extent. Thus, a complete list would have also to include such biblical concepts as adoption, resurrection, perhaps even regeneration, and so on. However, if for the sake of argument we admit that soteriological theory should be restricted to the interpretation of the death of Christ, as technical

65. McIntyre, *The Shape of Soteriology,* pp. 29ff.

discussion of "soteriology" frequently is, then the list of models provided can be taken to be complete.

In the end, however, this is not the primary issue; rather, the real question of interest concerns how all of these models can be said to pertain to the one event of the death of Christ. In and of themselves, it would appear, many of the models conflict, a fact which leads to considerable theological confusion, particularly at the popular level. For example, among those predisposed to interpret the death of Christ in strongly biblical terms, on the basis of a rather literal understanding of Scripture, the concepts of sacrifice and ransom, or of propitiation and redemption, are frequently used as if their reference were the same. In fact, the metaphors involved in these cases are quite distinct: One pays a ransom to a slave owner, or to thieves or kidnappers, and so redeems someone or something, whereas one sacrifices to God, or perhaps makes a sacrifice for someone whom one loves. The two fields of reference cannot be conflated without this resulting in theological confusion. This is the reason why, strictly speaking, the older patristic understanding of the death of Christ as a ransom paid to the devil, which is said to stem from Origen, but which has become since the time of Anselm so offensive to our ears, is actually a simple and consistent reading of the significance of the idea of ransom as applied to Christ's death. Clearly, one does not offer a ransom to God, but only to some *hostile* power who has taken someone prisoner, or made someone a slave, so that if a ransom is paid by Christ to someone, then it cannot but be to the devil, or to the powers of evil, personified in a more metaphorical sense. So the question becomes, "Which is it — sacrifice or ransom?" Or, if we draw on McIntyre's longer list, we might ask which of these is, in the end, the definitive interpretation, against which the rest are to be measured, or under which subsumed?

McIntyre, however, resists this approach, not because he fails to see the point, certainly, but because he regards the plethora of models or metaphors available as an aid to theological understanding rather than as an impediment to it. In his development of this theme, McIntyre argues that the great advantage of the diversity of models available is that they lend a certain "constellational richness," or "nuclear profusion" to our theology.[66] In other words, such unity as there is in soteri-

66. McIntyre, *The Shape of Soteriology*, p. 82.

ology is a unity-in-diversity, or a unity in which there is three-dimensionality, to use an earlier metaphor. To develop a single soteriological theory on the basis of one of the models, isolated from the rest, would lead to an impoverishment of our theology, and would amount to a misunderstanding of the nature of theological language and of proper theological method. The event of the death of Christ is, therefore, properly understood only when it is understood as multidimensional, and therefore only when we resist the temptation to tie together all of our conceptual loose ends in a single, unified — and largely sterile — theological conception.

This approach to the theology of the death of Christ is of interest for a number of reasons, the most obvious of which, perhaps, is that it provides a basis for a multidimensional approach to preaching the cross. As a preacher, one might do well to assume not only that there is more to preach about on this basis than, let us say, penal substitution as developed in Reformed scholasticism, but also that the likelihood of actually communicating with the different members of one's diverse congregation, with their different religious needs from week to week, will be increased to the extent that one is able to speak of Christ's death as example, sacrifice, satisfaction, and so on, rather than in accordance with a single soteriological theory, however neatly it is conceived. One might even say that this will be particularly true if the single, unified theory in question is as theologically and morally problematic as that of penal substitution.

Of particular importance, however, in this whole account is McIntyre's thesis that the models of soteriology are not simply interpretations laid on top of the primary fact of Christ's death, as if the given in this case were the death of a criminal under Roman law, and the theological interpretations purely secondary. Rather, the fact we have before us is itself the multidimensional event described through the models of soteriology.[67] One way of understanding this is to say that the historical event and its meaning cannot be artificially separated, as if the one were primary and the other secondary. The argument McIntyre actually offers in defense of this thesis, however, is that the theological model, if it can be sustained at all, must reflect something of the inner structures of the reality in question, the reality which is modeled. Thus the models are

67. McIntyre, *The Shape of Soteriology*, pp. 83ff.

all "involved in, and part of" the death of Christ, rather than "afterthoughts" contributed by the Church.[68] It is not the case, therefore, that Jesus died the death of a criminal, the primitive Church having later interpreted his death as a sacrifice, but rather that the category of sacrifice reflects what was and is the case about the death of Christ; if it did not reflect the reality to which it refers, it would never have become a successful theological model. In other words, as "The Cliché as a Theological Medium" in the present volume clearly reveals, McIntyre's theology at this point is committed to a version of epistemological realism, a realism, in short, in which it might be admitted that the models are the products of the human imagination, as we have already seen, but according to which such models are only possible in the first place because of the basic meaningfulness, and in this case the extremely rich meaningfulness, of the event of death of Christ on Calvary. The event in itself is rich in meaning, and this provides a basis for the richness of theological interpretation. Again, therefore, we find that McIntyre's epistemology is anything but subjectivist.

The relation between incarnation, atonement and forgiveness in McIntyre's theology was the second and final question to be addressed, and to this we now turn. We might begin by observing that, though the bulk of his theology is concerned with this question in an indirect sense, since the focus on history is intended to serve the interests of a doctrine of incarnation, while the atonement is the explicit concern of two major studies, McIntyre does not explicitly address it at length in any one work. The closest we do come to such an account is in *The Shape of Soteriology*, in which the question of how, or of the extent to which, the death of Christ comes to have universal significance is a major theme. What are called there the "media of universalization, relation and contemporanization"[69] include the various "soteriological prepositions" of the Greek New Testament, such as *anti*, *hyper* and *peri*, but extend, more significantly, to the more substantive concepts of imputation, recapitulation and identification, those concepts which have been frequently used in systematic theologies to refer to this relation. But of these, significantly, it is the concept of identification which underlies all the rest, and which "becomes the basis upon which the whole of the

68. McIntyre, *The Shape of Soteriology*, p. 83.
69. McIntyre, *The Shape of Soteriology*, pp. 88ff.

atonement rests."[70] We have already seen the importance of the concept in McIntyre's theology, so that there is no reason to press the point further. We need only summarize the position again: The Son of God has identified himself with sinful humanity in the incarnation, and ultimately in his death.

In McIntyre's soteriology, however, as earlier in his Christology, the attempt is to state the basic content of Christian teaching in terms which can bear the *personal* character of the subjects to which they relate, and to move beyond a merely logical, or in the case of salvation perhaps, a merely forensic description. In the opening chapter of *The Shape of Soteriology,* the importance of the move away from traditional accounts of the attributes of God, such as omnipotence and infinity, and towards the more moral attributes of love, mercy, goodness and justice is highlighted as the great decisive development in soteriology over the past two centuries.[71] Indeed, McIntyre goes so far as to suggest that this development ranks with the work of Anselm and the event of the Reformation as marking a paradigm shift in Christian thought about the nature of the atonement. This "ethicizing" of the attributes of God, therefore, which is consistent with the Buberian I-Thou philosophy, and with the general contours of McIntyre's own wider theology of God and his theological anthropology, we might reasonably expect to be developed in his own positive assessment of the relation between incarnation, atonement and forgiveness.

The final soteriological position which emerges in *The Shape of Soteriology* comes in the form of a response to the classical question, "Could not God have saved us by an act of sovereign will?" In other words, why was the incarnation and death of Christ necessary for the forgiveness of the sins of the world? This is a classical theological question, posed many times in the course of the Christian theological tradition, for example, by Anselm, who responds simply that it would not have been fitting for God to have acted otherwise than the way he did, in order to forgive. In his own account of Anselm, McIntyre rejects the view which posits a rigid necessity in Anselm's conception of the atonement, deriving from God's character as infinitely just, according to which Christ *had* to die in order for us to be forgiven. Anselm's

70. McIntyre, *The Shape of Soteriology,* p. 108.
71. McIntyre, *The Shape of Soteriology,* p. 22.

conception of the necessity for the atonement, McIntyre maintains, is rather a recognition that God's grace in Christ was an overflowing into the lost world of the love which God himself is, and therefore a self-determination proceeding from his own character.[72] The divine justice had indeed to be upheld, for it was not "fitting" for God, as the upholder of the order of the universe, to act unjustly, but more tellingly, God's justice in the atonement is entirely subordinate to his love. Furthermore, there is no question in Anselm of a wrath of God against sin needing to be vented. The argument, rather, turns on God's honor and on the situation of sinful humanity in relation to divine honor: It would not be fitting for humankind to come to God without making satisfaction for sin. In considering the question in *The Shape of Soteriology*, one might say that McIntyre's instincts are still to side with this moderate Anselmian approach. While the thesis that God simply pardons, without further ado, is rejected as overly simplistic, no hardline doctrine of divine justice or wrath is set up as the alternative.

McIntyre's position, it might be said, is that the seemingly infinite depth of sin cannot be easily disposed of *from the human side,* even if it *were* possible for God simply to forgive. Such forgiveness would invoke the specter of "cheap grace," and would therefore not be grace at all. Furthermore, the idea of cheap grace does not take account of the fact that forgiveness is precisely a costly thing to give, and often the costliest thing that one can give. This is not to say that in God's case, there is a divine justice which must be satisfied, and which could only be satisfied in the death of Christ, such that the atonement was the purpose of the incarnation and such that the incarnation made atonement theologically possible, but rather that in the death of Jesus, we see what reconciliation with God costs God himself. The point is brought out through a consideration of the soteriology of Donald Baillie in *God Was in Christ,* who argued that the forgiveness of God is to be compared to the forgiveness of one friend for another; in the latter, human situation, to forgive a friend's betrayal is a costly business indeed. It requires a sacrifice of oneself, a relinquishing of one's legitimate claims on the friend, and a willingness to embrace the pain which results from reaching out again to him or her. One need only consider the situation of a wife or husband who forgives the unfaithfulness of the marriage partner to

72. McIntyre, *St. Anselm and His Critics,* pp. 117-21.

see the point in all its force. The one forgiving, therefore, in a very real sense, *bears* the sin of the friend. Baillie compares this situation parabolically to God's forgiveness, and argues that his forgiveness too will involve no quick fix, but must be the sort of forgiveness borne of anguish, and which will be willing to bear suffering in order to be realized. McIntyre's response to this analogy is basically positive, and though he criticizes Baillie for not extending the point explicitly to take account of the cross, the fundamentally *moral* contours of Baillie's account of forgiveness are explicitly embraced.[73] What is lacking, however, must be supplied, and what is lacking is an adequate conception of the fact that the anguish borne by God in forgiving sin is not something that can be posited as existing in God "internally," as it were, apart from Jesus Christ; rather, it is something that is found uniquely in the cross of Christ, in history, and so in the concrete detail of the gospel proclamation.

What we might say, therefore, of incarnation, atonement and forgiveness is that in the cross, the love of God is revealed, a love which reaches out to the sinner so as to reconcile, but a love which is willing to bear the consequences of forgiveness to the full. We have seen on several occasions the importance of the concept of identification in McIntyre's theology, and here again the concept is indispensable. "God with us," the incarnate one, must be thought through to the full, as the event in history which has these consequences — or, to put the matter another way, as the event in history which we know through the models of soteriology. McIntyre's approach is not so much to ask why such a thing was necessary as it is to attempt to fathom it now that it has taken place, or like Anselm, to grasp why and in what sense it was "fitting" for God to act in this way in the cross of Jesus Christ. His answer, finally, is that it was fitting for God, in love and as a moral subject, to bear our sin in this way. On the human side, the recognition of this leads to the double response of faith and love: a faith which embraces repentance and which promises obedience, and a love grounded in who God is and what humanity and the world are known to be in the light of God's gracious outreach in Christ.

The theology of John McIntyre is thus, finally, a theology of the love of God, and a theology which has at its center God's love as known

73. McIntyre, *The Shape of Soteriology*, p. 111.

in the God-man, Jesus Christ. It provides for us a challenge to many of the prevailing theological "orthodoxies" of our day, "orthodoxies" such as our excessive historical skepticism, not to mention our tendency to slip into alternative moods of dogmatism or of political activism when the word "theology" is mentioned, rather than to carry out the true theological task of *thinking* the faith, of making it intelligible to our generation, and then, finally, of living it in a life of love in the Christian community. It further provides something of a program for future theological and philosophical reflection, most notably in the area of the philosophy of history, and of its theological implications, but also with respect to such questions as the strengths and weaknesses of the general movement of twentieth century theology, with all its unexamined presuppositions. In the final analysis, it will only be when theology in our era takes on such hard tasks that our secular culture will begin to listen to what it has to say. It is certain too, however, that in such an event, our theology will also be enriched along the way.

A Note on Works Included in this Volume

The material included in this volume derives from an extensive manuscript collection of McIntyre's work, representing his work over a period of three decades, which the present author happened upon over the course of the summer of 1994; it was a literary find, complete with unassuming cardboard box in the disused corner of a dusty room, of the sort of which dreams are made. I am grateful to Professor John McIntyre for permission to edit some of this material for publication, and to the publishers, who have supported the project financially.

The two main works which follow, *The Humanity of Christ,* and *Theology of Prayer,* date originally from 1970; the basis of the former is a series of lectures delivered in August of that year in Melbourne, Australia, while the latter is based on a parallel series that same month in Sydney. The material has been revised and updated, but on the whole, required only modest changes; I have judged that the arguments are sufficiently important and often enough sufficiently timeless to warrant a minimum of interference. Professor McIntyre has, however, occasionally been asked to revise some of the material, generally in view of later developments in his own theology. The whole then finally passed under his eye and pen. The shorter essay, "The Cliché as a Theological Medium," is a new piece which has been specially commissioned for the volume.

The significance of these works for an understanding of McIntyre's theology, and for an understanding of the shape of theology in our era, is considerable. One area of obvious interest which has already been highlighted is the theology of the humanity of Christ, which, apart from the recent attention of historians working on Jesus' Jewish roots,[74] or some of the work of the liberation theologians,[75] has still not progressed beyond the basic Jesus of history *versus* the Christ of faith dialectic which has been normative in much of Christology since the eighteenth century; the neo-orthodoxy of the mid-twentieth century, for the most part, was content simply to ignore the question as a "liberal" preoccupation. McIntyre's approach to this issue is of great interest precisely because it is so unique, cutting across, as it does, so much of modern Christological debate. Neither the historical-critical approach, especially when allied to a theological existentialism of some kind, nor the neo-orthodox approach, which simply asserts the priority of the divine revelation in Christ over its human medium, represents, for McIntyre, a viable Christological alternative. There is for him, in short, no way forward except by way of a basic shift in our thinking, a shift which must be both philosophically grounded in an adequate epistemology of history, and rooted in a theology which gets beyond many of the theological paradigms of the nineteenth and twentieth centuries. Although much of *The Humanity of Christ* is suggestive of future possibilities for theological reflection rather than conclusive in its arguments (a fact which reflects its unfinished character), the fact that it presents us with such an alternative vision nevertheless makes it a work of real importance. For if we accept McIntyre's thesis, first, that Christology must be concerned with Jesus as a *person,* and refuse to allow his "personhood" to remain an ontological abstraction; and secondly that, to be taken seriously in our time, Christology itself must take Jesus' real humanity seriously; then the exploration of what we today understand human nature to be, in relation to Jesus Christ, must surely become one of our major theological

74. E.g., Geza Vermes, *Jesus the Jew* (London, 1976).

75. E.g., Jon Sobrino, *Christology at the Crossroads* (ET Maryknoll and London, 1978); and *Jesus the Liberator* (ET New York, 1993).

concerns. McIntyre's Christology is unique in its exploration of these questions. Along the way, furthermore, *The Humanity of Christ* helps to fill in the detail of McIntyre's own theology between *The Shape of Christology* and *The Shape of Soteriology*.

The Theology of Prayer is in itself a less important work, to the extent that it is concerned with less fundamental questions in theology. It provides, however, a classic example of how a theology can be developed and articulated by means of the Anselmian method of adopting the position of the skeptic. Indeed, it would not be too much to say of it that McIntyre is here deliberately imitating the method of Anselm in the *Cur Deus-homo*. For in this work, McIntyre stands shoulder to shoulder with those who have difficulties with prayer in the contemporary world, whether intellectual or "religious," to face those difficulties himself, and to try to find a way through them, both for himself and for others. The range of problems thus faced is impressive: the clash of the "scientific" and the "religious" worldviews; the philosophical problem of the relation between God and the world; theodicy; and the death of God. McIntyre goes on to offer a detailed treatment of the theology and practice of prayer, through a consideration of the prayer of Christ, a defense of the notion of God's answering of prayer in the form of speech and a critique of the prominence of the notion of self-disclosure in the modern theology of revelation, and, among other things, an analysis of the role of symbolism in prayer, both individual and corporate.

Although the work is less seminal than that on the human nature of Christ, the *Theology of Prayer* is of special interest, for two reasons. First, one of the frequent deficiencies of conventional systematic theology, whether in the form of dogmatics or apologetics, is the consistency with which theologians appear to ignore the hard questions that come to such clear focus in the theology of prayer. In one sense, prayer is so basic to religious life that one would assume that it would be a major concern of theology and theologians in their work, but in fact, only a minority of theologians deal with it in any detail; the chapters on prayer in most of the standard textbooks in systematic theology, for example, are often among the weakest in them. In some cases, this would appear to suggest more than that the theology of prayer has been overlooked, for, as McIntyre himself suggests at the outset of his study, prayer, when raised as a *theological* problem, takes us to the heart not only of our theological method, but also of our understanding of God and of our relation to him. The neglect of prayer, therefore, will at times reflect a deeper series of problems in a given theology. Conversely, however, a theologian's treatment of prayer is, by the same token, likely to be revealing, and this is clearly the case with McIntyre.

Secondly, the *Theology of Prayer* is of particular interest because of its robust defense of the view that God can rightly be conceived of as "speaking" to those who pray, as a basic function of what prayer is, of its theological structure and of the Christian experience of prayer. Although a great deal of theology in the twentieth century has made much of the concept of revelation, and specifically of the self-revelation of God, such theology has frequently been hostile to the concept of propositional revelation, whether in the form of biblical or creedal statements, or those of the ecclesiastical hierarchy. The idea of propositional revelation has been dismissed, not because it is denied that God has spoken, but rather because God's primary "word" in the world is actually Jesus Christ, and because all statements about *that* primary word are secondary, and derivative. Theology as a science, therefore, while grounded in revelation, cannot be grounded in revelation conceived as a series of propositions which can then be elaborated upon in scholastic fashion, according to the older methods of both Protestant and Catholic theology. Rather, the science of theology must be concerned with the fact of revelation as the gift of God himself to the world, i.e., in the incarnation, as in the theology of Karl Barth above all, or in the gift of grace, as supremely in the theology of Karl Rahner. Almost all recent theologians, including those who have worked in the same theological traditions as those of Barth and Rahner, and excluding only those who have continued to maintain crude theories of plenary biblical inspiration, or of the inspiration of the *magisterium,* have tended to agree.

In the *Theology of Prayer,* however, John McIntyre attempts to reassess this tradition, and its claims. His argument rests on two foundations. First, it might be said that he presupposes that something, at least, of the linguistic turn in modern philosophy is entirely justified, in the sense that anything that is meaningful and that can be understood is also something that can be verbalized. If, therefore, there is any sense at all in saying that God responds to prayer, and this is certainly the position McIntyre wishes to defend, and that he responds in an intelligible way and not simply in a way which defies comprehension of any sort, then it is necessary to say that God's response is of a kind which can *rightly* be expressed in propositions, statements about what is the case, about what ought or ought not to be done, and so on. Secondly, he argues that to say this is not, *ipso facto,* to commit oneself to thinking of God in a crudely anthropomorphic way, as if God himself literally used language to speak to us. Rather, the point is simply that if all knowledge is in accordance with the capacity of the knower, which is certainly the case, and if all human knowledge takes place by means of the medium of language, as is arguably the case, then, to that extent, all divine communication, to be capable of being understood, must be capable of being verbalized. In this way, McIntyre seeks to defend the place of prayer in discerning the will of God, for in the context of worship, whether privately in the reading of the Bible, or publicly in the liturgy of the Church or in listening to a sermon, a person's prayer opens him or her up to what God has to say. McIntyre also, however, emphasizes in this connection that what God "says," or what he appears to say, must be carefully weighed, and must be open to theological investigation, since it takes place precisely through the human, and therefore finite and fallible, medium of language.

Since prayer, for McIntyre, is of particular theological interest, a number of his short prayers have been appended to the *Theology of Prayer,* in order to provide a rounded picture of his thought. Some of these were used originally to open meetings, but they are applicable to a variety of situations, and reveal something of the man who wrote them which perhaps nothing else could. For if, in prayer, one reveals what one worships, and in offering oneself in service, shows what one values, then in any real prayer we can discover much about the person praying, of how he or she thinks of God and of the human relation to God. McIntyre's prayers may also provide for us a set of religious symbols, as he calls them, to help us to express our own prayer, in some situations at least, more adequately and completely, in keeping with "the universalizing role of symbols" highlighted in the final chapter of the *Theology of Prayer*.

The essay, "The Cliché as a Theological Medium," attempts to provide a critique of some of the unexamined presuppositions of much recent theology. It deals successively with theological statements concerning faith and history, religious language, the contemporary relational concept of the person, ecumenism, pluralism, and peace and justice, raising the question whether our unexamined presuppositions about these issues do not make for obscurity rather than clarity of thought. The essay, as such, is self-explanatory, and needs no further comment, except to indicate the relevance of the section on religious language to an overall understanding of McIntyre's theological method, and the importance of the section on persons as relational, not so much because of the theme of relationality itself, but because of the extension of the category into Trinitarian theology. The Trinity is seldom discussed in McIntyre's publications, so much so that the treatment it receives here is virtually unique. In the course of the discussion, he supports the social doctrine of the Trinity, but is characteristically reticent about how far such Trinitarianism can be extended from the level of God's outreach to us, to the level of the immanent being of the Father, Son, and Spirit. The argument adds little to the sum of his theology which could not already have been surmised, but one statement, found at the end of section III of the essay, is of special interest. McIntyre suggests here that "the economic Trinity is the outward and perceptible form of the immanent Trinity, which is the eternal and inward being of the God who is Immanuel, with us from the beginning of time until its end." In the account of his Christology given above, I argued that Donald Baillie's understanding of the atonement is of great importance to McIntyre, both because it embodies the idea of identification which is so central in his theology and because it provides for us a model by which we may come to understand why it is that God does not forgive without or apart from the anguish of the cross. What one might now say is that the cross of Christ is to be conceived as an "outward and perceptible" expression of who God is in himself, as the God who loves — so that he is not only the God who is *in himself* "Immanuel," in the abstract sense, as it were, but is also the God who truly and concretely identifies himself with his world in love, in the person of Jesus Christ. The whole history of Jesus, and supremely the cross, is in this sense a realization in time, and in our world, of the being of the God who is love.

John McIntyre's contribution to theology may well be something which has still to be fully realized. What is clear, however, is that he provides a unique perspective on the theology of the twentieth century, a perspective can liberate us from an uncritical acceptance of some of the more common, and more problematic, of contemporary theological prejudices. In the context of Scottish theology, finally, McIntyre's central achievement — and it is one which ought not to be overlooked in view of the frequent presumption of a prevailing Barthianism — is to have continued on in the great tradition of liberal evangelicalism synonymous in Scotland with the names of John and Donald Baillie two generations ago, and which can be traced further back again into the work of such distinguished theologians as Hugh Ross Mackintosh.

The title of the present volume, *Theology after the Storm*, is taken from one of the unpublished manuscripts found among the McIntyre Papers at New College, a paper read at the centenary celebrations of Westminster College, Cambridge, in 1967. The essay speaks of the necessity of picking up the pieces after the work of the theological giants of this century — Barth, Brunner, Bultmann, Niebuhr, and, we might now add for good measure, such figures as Rahner and von Balthasar — and of attempting at last to assess their abiding contributions to theology, together with the direction of modern theology generally, in a wider theological and philosophical context. Since such a task has been taken on by McIntyre in the works which follow, the title *Theology after the Storm* has again been adopted.

Gary D. Badcock
New College
University of Edinburgh
Easter, 1995

The Humanity of Christ

CHAPTER 1

Human Nature as a Theological Problem

Introduction

In the classical periods of Christological controversy, the subject which commanded most attention was that of the deity of Christ. The controversy surrounding the subject tended to take two forms. On the one hand, it was concerned with whether Jesus Christ was to be identified with God, whether he was "very God of very God," *homoousios,* of one substance with the Father; or whether he was only of similar nature to God; or as the semi-Arians maintained, as regards all the essential attributes of deity he was dissimilar to the Father; or, as Arius himself is thought to believe, he did not coexist from all eternity with the Father, but originated in time by the Father's will, though as his first and most glorious creation. This whole cluster of questions provided the context within which the Church gradually hammered out the specific detail of its statement of the fact of the deity of Christ. Over against all attempts to reduce his status either to that of an ordinary creature or even to that of some intermediate existent, orthodoxy came out firmly on the side of the consubstantiality of the Son with the Father.

On the other hand, even within the limits of the affirmation of the deity of Christ, there was and still is room for controversy. The manner of the incarnation of the eternal Son of God was in its turn the subject of varied interpretation. For example there was the full-blown, uncompromising statement that "in him the whole fullness of deity dwells bodily" (Colossians 2:9). But there have been modifications of such a statement in the theory known as Kenoticism, according to which at the incarnation the Logos laid aside some of the attributes of deity (omniscience, omnipotence and omnipresence) while retaining others such as love, mercy and goodness — and even that he laid aside the whole of the divine nature *(physis)* retaining only the divine person *(hypostasis)* as the authentic marker of his deity. Obviously therefore, within the area laid down by the definition of the deity of Christ there was ample opportunity for disagreement, and it was an opportunity which was rarely lost.

If, therefore, there has been much controversy both in the period of classical Christological foundation, and we must add, frequently since, over both the fact and the character of the deity of Christ, it is equally clear that there has not been the same amount of controversy by any means over the fact and nature of the humanity of Christ. Admittedly there did take place at a very early stage in the development of doctrine the heresy of docetism, the theory, that is, that Christ only *seemed* to be human. At the end of the New Testament era itself, in the First Epistle of John, we are given the impression that there existed people who were prepared to deny that Christ had come in the flesh; they were anathematized as anti-Christ. Under the influence of Neo-Platonism, however, docetism remained for quite a long time an intellectual temptation to Christian theologians, for that philosophy identified the material and physical order as evil, and some of its exponents regarded the human body as a subject of shame. The docetists thought that a genuine incarnation, and therefore a genuine humanity in Christ, would involve God in disgrace and contempt; they therefore presented the incarnation as if in Christ, God only seemed to take human form. Clement of Alexandria drifted close to this position when he held that Christ knew no pain, or grief, or emotion, and ate not to restore physical energy, being empowered with spiritual energy, but only lest his disciples should misunderstand his nature. A subsequent controversy arose over whether the human nature of Jesus Christ had a separate will, or whether he had only one will, the divine will. There was, too, a prolonged controversy which extends even into modern theology about the character of the human nature which Christ took: Was it sinful human nature or was it sinless? A good case is, in fact, to be made on either side. If it was sinful human nature that Christ took, how could he possibly avoid sinning, at times, or even being a sinner? If he did sin or was a sinner, how then could he achieve the salvation of humankind? On the other hand, if it was sinless human nature that he took, how justly could we claim that he entered genuinely into the human situation, and if he did not take our sinful human nature, how then could he redeem it? "What he did not take, he did not redeem," is an old patristic saying which carries a lot of truth. That controversy therefore over the sinfulness of Christ and whether he took sinful human nature is one which is not entirely academic, but it never has reached the bitter proportions achieved by the controversies associated with the deity of Christ.

In modern times, controversy over the deity of Christ has continued, no longer perhaps in the language of the Greek Fathers who debated the concept of *homoousia,* but with the same purpose in mind. It was, for example, the point at issue in Donald Baillie's classic, *God was in Christ,*[1] and particularly in the reviews of that book which challenged the orthodoxy of Baillie's position by asking whether by his use of the paradox of grace he had established that God was in Christ in a way in which he was and is not in every believer who is inspired by the Holy Spirit. It was the point at issue in Emil Brunner's, *The Mediator,*[2] where under the rubric, "Through God alone is God known," he argued that God can be revealed positively only through God a second time, his very self repeated. The issue reappeared in Karl Barth's monumental constructions throughout the length and breadth of the *Church Dogmatics,* where he repeatedly defended the Word of God incarnate against all attempts to present Christ as less than the Word issuing from the very heart of God, unveiling the true and ultimate being of God. To some extent also, the suspicion which attaches in some circles to the Christology of Teilhard de Chardin arises over whether his concept of the Omega point can be genuinely identified with Christ, because the Omega point appears to be an emergent from the evolutionary process, and not to derive from a source beyond the process (as does the Son who is begotten of the Father and sent by him into the world).

1. Donald Baillie, *God Was in Christ* (London, 1948).
2. Emil Brunner, *The Mediator* (ET London, 1934).

There has been, then, a great deal of continuing controversy over the deity of Christ, and the controversy in relatively recent years has been aggravated through its association with a yet more fundamental controversy, namely, that of whether God is dead. It is absolutely pointless to be discussing the deity of Christ if at that very moment the whole concept of deity is under savage attack, to the point of denial. It is interesting that many who (somewhat prematurely) withdrew from the discussion about whether God is dead sought refuge in Christology, in the person of Christ, who perhaps because of his historicity or his real-life character appeared to escape the strictures to which a being is exposed who is transcendent, "up there" or "out there." Unfortunately, however, the demand for a God cannot be simplistically met with the reply that Jesus is God, for as a reply it begs the question: Either it is an admission that Jesus is wholly human, which the predicate of the sentence seems to refute, or it is a tacit reintroduction of the concept of deity from which escape was being sought in the assertion that God is dead. The Christological problem *par excellence,* therefore, still seems to be that of the deity of Christ, and the problem appears to be rendered doubly troublesome by the controversy over whether God exists or is, as Nietzsche said, dead.

That assessment of the situation, it might at first be thought, is reenforced by the fact that there is little controversy over the humanity of Christ. There are no theological banners bearing the slogan, "Christ had no human nature," or, "The humanity of Christ was a theological construct of the primitive Church." Christ's humanity has been accepted as fairly self-evident. He was born, he walked among people, worked with them, talked to them, healed them, cared for them, and died in a patently human manner, enduring all the agonies of an extremely inhumane crucifixion. It may not be possible for some to extend credibility beyond the point of the death and the burial to include the resurrection appearances and disappearances, but at least the credibility does extend up to the burial; some who believe little else are happy to subscribe to the notion that a life of transparent integrity and love was lived in the midst of ordinary, not too likable, not too unlikable, people, and that this life ended in a death of heroic courage and self-sacrifice. Theoretically, then, we ought on reaching the concept of humanity to have reached solid ground.

The trouble is that we have not, for one or other of two things happens. On the one hand, we are compelled to deify humanity, in the sense that if Jesus is the only God there is, and if Jesus is no more than a man (and we cannot say he is more than this if God is dead), then, paradoxically, we have made a man (even though it is this "man for all men") into God. But we know that a human being was never made to bear the strain of being God. If we try to make it so, the humanity breaks up, for it is flawed and finite, and our latter case is worse than our first. We would be better off with a God that is dead, than with a man as God when he can never possibly be God. Alternatively, the truth begins to dawn on us that humanity is far, very far, from being the self-evident concept we thought it to be when first began our deliberations on the person of Christ. I am reminded in this connection of Amos 5:18: "Alas for you who desire the day of the LORD! Why do you want the day of the LORD? It is darkness, not light; as if someone fled from a lion and was met by a bear; or went into a house and rested a hand against a wall, and was bitten by a snake." Those who surrender the notion of God, and even that of the deity of Christ, and take refuge in the humanity of Christ are, in my judgment, in a not dissimilar position, for the concept of humanity which has for many, many centuries been assumed to be translucent has now in our generation suddenly become opaque. Such opacity is even a partial explanation for a revival of a different kind, the revival of belief in the God of Deism, the strictly monotheistic God, who derives nothing from Trinitarianism or Christology, but who is the Spirit of the universe, though the revival is admittedly assisted by a certain *ennui* with the sophistications of some Christologies. What I wish to examine is the circumstances surrounding the difficulty of saying what humanity is, and therefore of using the concept without more ado in the construction of a Christology.

Two things are certain. First, we cannot now employ the concept unthinkingly in anything that we have to say about the human nature, in the assumption that everyone will know immediately what we mean, any more than they will know in some immediate way what we mean when we speak of the deity of Christ. The one is under attack and clouded in obscurity as much as the other. Secondly, in view of the critical approach which we are now obliged to adopt towards the concept of humanity, we shall not only require to take a fresh look at what has traditionally been said about the humanity of Christ in the past and at how it was said and why, but we shall also become aware that the greatest care is necessary in re-presenting the humanity of Christ in our day. The long-term prospect of our study has there been defined, of assessing the role of the humanity of Christ in past Christologies and of defining ways in which that humanity is being, and can be, expressed in our day. Lest, however, we be thought to be shouting "wolf," it is a prior task to demonstrate how confused the concept of humanity has become in present-day culture and theology.

Humanity Under Reassessment

What we are not prepared for in proceeding to this demonstration is the extent to which the concept of humanity is not only extensively variously interpreted in our day but also brought under severest criticism and therefore pejoratively interpreted. Let me begin with a discipline in which the concept of humanity has long been under discussion in the form of the idea of the self, that of philosophy. John Macquarrie has written of the serious problems confronting philosophical theology in the area of our conception of selfhood. "There are," he argues, "many areas of dogmatic theology such as the doctrines of salvation, of grace, of judgment and of a life to come, which assume that man has or rather is a soul, and that this self is somehow unitary, responsible and abiding. . . . The problem has become serious in the case of the self because the traditional philosophical description has broken down in the face of mounting criticism."[3] Now admittedly Macquarrie is here speaking specifically of the self, but in modern philosophy "the self" has either doubled in discussions for human nature, or has been certainly regarded as the essential part of it. "The self" is never intended to exclude the bodily element; the notion of "the embodied self" is representative of the views of most people in this field. Macquarrie goes on to illustrate his theme by showing how for almost two thousand years the self was conceived of as a substance and finally defined by Descartes as consisting of a *res extensa* (material, "extended" substance) and *res cogitans* (immaterial, "thinking" substance). The use of the word *res* (thing) indicates clearly the *thinghood* character of the self, and we would add, of human nature. Macquarrie mentions how Gilbert Ryle in his book, *The Concept of Mind,* severely criticizes the notion that the term "mind"

3. John Macquarrie, *Studies in Christian Existentialism* (London, 1966), p. 59.

signifies some special kind of thing, a "ghost in the machine." He moves from Ryle to someone who is much more sympathetic to the notion of self, namely, the Scottish philosopher John Macmurray who, in his book, *The Self as Agent*, similarly rejects the kind of substantiality associated with such "thinghood" as being in no sense an adequate model for the description of such a delicate and intimate construction as the self.[4] The flight from substantiality is pursued also, Macquarrie says, by recent Biblical theologians who claim to find nothing of the Cartesian dualism of two substances in the Biblical picture of humanity, but rather a unity which resembles much more the "embodied self" of modern thought. The writers whom Macquarrie mentions as variously destroying the old notion of substantiality as the basis of thinking either about the self or humanity are all drawn from the second quarter of the twentieth century, but he could have illustrated the point even more forcefully with a reference to David Hume, who among the many reflections he has to make upon personal identity says, "I cannot compare the soul more properly to anything than to a republic or commonwealth in which the several members are united by the reciprocal ties of government and subordination."[5] There is here no notion of some identifiable and continuing substance which one can examine introspectively, nor is there any other evidence for its existence. The uniform commentary upon our problem of the nature of humanity or of the self which derives from this sample of writers is that we cannot nowadays expect any agreement to the theory that there is a single substance called "the self" which has specific attributes of thinghood — a single substance which, if we transfer the reference to Christology, Christ could be thought to have taken at the incarnation.

It would be wrong, however, to leave the impression that modern philosophy has made only negative critical contributions to the modern analysis of the self, for there is another strain which solves the problem of the self or perhaps avoids it, by attempting to equate it with one aspect, or mode of itself. The result is a variety of what might be called perspectival analyses of the self. John Laird, who makes a still useful study of the subject, shows how the self has been taken to have feeling

4. John Macmurray, *The Self as Agent* (London, 1957).

5. David Hume, *A Treatise of Human Nature*, ed. L. A. Selby-Bigge, 2nd ed. (Oxford, 1978), p. 261.

as its dominant feature.[6] One prominent view makes the feelings of pleasure or displeasure, of striving or resisting, which accompany all other modes of psychical life the real kernel of the self. This view is expanded by other psychologists to include the feelings associated with such physical activities as respiration, sex and mobility. We are not particularly concerned with the merits of such a view of the centrality of feeling, the manner in which it seeks to make the essential self something immediately accessible to introspection, and not some metaphysical, mystical somewhat or other, or yet with its demerits, its ignoring of the other features of conscious life which all feeling necessarily presupposes. The reason for noting this view that the self is feeling is simply its concern to give an ancient metaphysical reality some kind of empirical basis in human existence.

The same motivation is to be found in two other views. The one seeks to equate the self with will — classically expressed in Kant's allocation of primacy to the practical reason, the will to act according to the universal moral law, as the key to the true self: "Only a rational being has the power to act *in accordance with his* idea of laws — that is, in accordance with principles — and only so has he a *will*."[7] A similar point of view can be found in Macmurray, who writes that, "The Self that reflects and the self that acts is the same self; action and thought are contrasted modes of its activity. But it does not follow that they have equal status in the being of the Self. In thinking the mind is alone active. In acting the body is indeed active, but also the mind. Action then is a full concrete activity of the self in which all our capacities are employed."[8] Macmurray would not himself wish his view to be regarded as one which selected a segment of the self, or of human nature, and falsely equated it with the whole. Activity in his view is totally inclusive of all that the self is and does. The doubt is still left, however, as to whether activity can be so comprehensive as to include basic attitudes, presuppositions, complexes and the like which *prima facie* at least have a claim to inclusion.

The second view motivated similarly to the view that the self is

6. John Laird, *Problems of the Self* (London, 1917), pp. 82ff.

7. Immanuel Kant, *Groundwork of the Metaphysic of Morals*, trans. H. J. Paton, 3rd ed. (London, 1956), p. 80.

8. Macmurray, p. 86.

feeling is that which equates the self with knowing. The outstanding representative of such a position in modern philosophy was Lotze, who sees in the capacity of the conscious self to compare ideas, to relate them to one another, to construct and arrange a manifold texture of such interrelating ideas the key to essential being and its substantial unity. Again there are philosophical inadequacies. Some of the unity of interrelating ideas must surely derive from the objects known as much as, if not more than, from the integrating mind, nor is it correct to equate self-cognition with the knowledge of interrelated objects. The point to be illustrated still stands, though the adequacy or inadequacy of each of these views of the self as feeling, as will, or as knowing is debatable: namely that they are all in their different ways attempts to impart meaning, tangible, empirical, non-metaphysical meaning, to what we label a "self," essential humanity, and that there is such considerable difference of opinion about what human nature really is as should cause us to hesitate before hastily making any declarations about God being made man, with queries concerning his humanity as have always been made concerning his deity.

The problem is not confined by any means to philosophy, for it exists in what is perhaps an even more acute form in psychology, in particular in connection with the mind-body problem. There is a chaotic confusion which ensues when we attempt to give values to the mental states and processes with which each person's body is associated. Classically, psychology has spoken of the modes of consciousness, cognition, of volition and affection, and has added the basic instincts and drives to complete the picture of ordinary human nature, but it is often now more concerned with such problems as the physiology of perception, or of learning, with the functioning of the central nervous system and with cortical localization. The study of personality carried out in the context of abnormal psychology has yielded a great variety of views on that subject. Freud classifies certain groupings of psychological functions into a permanent organized system, called the Ego, the Id and the Super-Ego. The Ego exercises adaptive functions such as perceptual, motor, and glandular coordinations, and enables more effective social and environmental relationships on the part of the personality. It also has integrating functions to secure the personality in the face of intrusions from outside and from within itself. The Id consists of the primitive, loosely coordinated and potentially disintegrant forces, which are insistent in their demands for expression or satisfaction, regardless of the inhibitions or restraints of external reality or of social convenience or convention. The Super-Ego takes as its most familiar form conscience, the part of us which condemns, judges, criticizes, assesses or alternatively approves or praises. The Super-Ego is largely unconscious, the Id is "totally unconscious." The energy for the functioning of the personality is derived from instinctual drives which are chiefly sexual and aggressive. With Jung there came an additional emphasis upon the notion of the complex, the distinction between introvert and extrovert personality traits, the importance of racial heritage as embodied in myth, art and symbol, with less significance being recognized in unconscious sexual drives than in the will to wholeness of the individual. Adler drew attention to the drive to power over others, as well as to the inferiority complex. It is not necessary to pursue the history of the concept of personality on into most recent times, for the original Freudian, Jungian and Adlerian structures have since been radically modified, for example, by the introduction of existentialist philosophical concepts; in addition, there has been much independent development along the lines of Gestalt theory by W. Kohler and K. Levin, and in many other directions by such writers as C. Kluckhohn, H. A. Murray and D. N. Schneider.

Three comments suggest themselves when we examine the relevance of these psychological theories to our Christological problem of the humanity of Christ. First, it becomes increasingly clear that when we use such a term as "human nature" or "human personality," we speak of a subject which, among psychologists as among philosophers, is a center of quite radical disagreement. There is no single "thing" to which we can be assumed to be referring in this context. Any deductions that we try to make from this concept, any light that we may seek from it upon the circumstances under which Jesus Christ led his life upon earth, are bound to be strictly limited in character and range. Secondly, we may quote a statement of Jung's: "The Christian God-image cannot become incarnate in empirical man without contradictions — quite apart from the fact a man with all his external characteristics seems little suited to representing a god."[9] Jung himself solves this contradiction with his theory that "God" and "man" are reconciled to one another as opposites which exist within the God-image itself. But in Jung's own

9. Carl Gustav Jung, *Memories, Dreams, Reflections* (ET London, 1967), p. 370.

statement, if we keep to the traditional concept of God, we become aware of the great difficulty encountered by any Christology which thinks of that God entering human nature as described in Freudian or Jungian terms. The difficulty would be threefold — of indicating how a Divine psyche (whose meaning in Freudian or Jungian terms baffles the imagination) could relate to a human personality in one person (the content of which is certainly not unproblematic); of showing whether or not Jesus Christ was a victim to the repressions, complexes, drives, aggressions which are so instinctual to normal human personality; and finally, of coping with the task of demonstrating how anything remotely approaching revelation could take place in such a context. Thirdly, there is a short way through all of the difficulties. It is simply to say that it is a category-confusion to suggest that the human nature which the Lord assumed at the incarnation can be construed in psychological rather than logical terms. The history of the subject suggests certainly a logical history and a logical context. The trouble is that the thrust of contemporary interest in human nature is in the direction of psychology. We want to know what his human nature was like. If it was like ours, then it must be open to Freudian or Jungian or Gestalt or existentialist-psychological analysis, unless we can demonstrate the general invalidity of such analysis or its inappropriateness to his specific human nature.

A further difficulty of our understanding of human nature in general and of Christ's human nature in particular arises in another discipline, that of biology. For many centuries it has been known that the particular form which human nature takes in any one case is considerably influenced by circumstances located in the ancestry of that instance. It is only in our own day that we have become aware both of the complexity of that hereditary conditioning and of the precision of its effect upon the nature of the person concerned. In times of greater ignorance we were prepared to allow that the color of skin, eyes and hair was completely determined by genetic factors, but human freedom was allowed enormous scope in forming the traits of personality for which we became distinguished and by which we are peculiarly identified in a company of similar but dissimilar persons. Now, however, because of the emphasis on psychosomatic unity, we are less sure of the range of that freedom, and more aware of the extent to which personality traits have their origins in genes and chromosomes. Even if we still cling resolutely to a voluntarist position, believing in some form of freedom of the will, we have to admit that human freedom operates within a much more tightly knit structure than was thought to be the case before more recent developments in genetic science. Two problems then arise when we make the cross-reference to Christology. On the one hand, unless we believe in a stupendous miracle (a belief which it is out of line with any willingness to go far with the geneticist's analysis of the origin and character of human nature) which produces an occurrence of human nature which is in fact totally atypical, then we have to allow that the human nature which the Lord adopted at the incarnation was simply a random sample from the mass of humankind. Any other would have served as well. On the other hand, it becomes difficult if not impossible to see how the Divine nature of Christ could operate to express either itself or the purpose of God, in and through such an intractable medium. If there is a built-in determinism in the genes and chromosomes structure and arrangement in the body, and in their influence upon character and development, then the role which the human nature of Jesus Christ is to play in the incarnation event is not the outcome of God's immediate action but of hereditary circumstances. In that context, it becomes impossible to press further with any combination of such a conception of the origin or the character of human nature with a traditional account of the union of human nature with the divine in the one person of Jesus Christ.

A similar point may be made from the disciplines of biochemistry and pharmacology, which between them have demonstrated the enormous changes which can be effected not only in a human body but in the whole personality by the disturbance of the biochemistry of the body and brain through the administration of drugs. Once again in a general way it was well known that drugs could reduce the inhibitions of a patient to certain kinds of activity or experience, or could produce in him or her conditions of euphoria or depression. But more recent drug experimentation has shown that character can be radically changed, scales of values turned upside down and patterns and standards of behavior altered beyond recognition. The whole development is such an extension in degree of former possibilities that it amounts almost to a change in kind of control and determination of human personality. There is admittedly a certain amount of panic in evidence over the development of such drugs. This panic is in no way reduced when the reports from centers allegedly studying the defensive medication required to combat chemical and biological warfare techniques are included to stress the dangers under which modern humanity lives in face of uncontrolled scientific-medical research. The emotion generated by Porton once inflamed and inevitably distorted any discussion about the influence of drugs upon the human body and personality. Emotion apart, however, there still remain three changes in the conception of human nature here involved which must give us pause. First, we are apprised in a fresh, alarming way of the vulnerability and destructibility of human nature. We should have known it before for we had heard the words of Second Isaiah often enough: "The grass withers, the flower fades, when the breath of the LORD blows upon it; surely the people are grass. The grass withers, the flower fades: but the word of our God will stand forever" (40:7f.). Somewhere along the line, the comforting assurance of the Platonic doctrine of the immortality of the soul had intervened to cheer our hearts. Today, however, we are being warned in uncompromising terms that the human personality is destructible. Even when we read in the Gospel of Matthew, "Do not fear those who kill the body but cannot kill the soul; rather fear him who can destroy both soul and body in hell" (10:28), we think that people can kill only the body, and only God can kill the soul. Perhaps that is what the text means, but we are learning a hard lesson in our day, namely, that we *can* kill the souls of others, at least in the sense of destroying their personalities and taking from them what is recognizably human in human nature.

The torture of the Inquisition for all its brutality and sadism was theoretically at least based on the assumption that it acted as a catharsis for the human soul in error. There was no intention to destroy but to save. We, by contrast, seem to have learned how to kill the soul, three thousand years after it was discovered. The second change in our conception of human nature which results from experiments with drugs upon the human psyche is, therefore, a new doubt about its stability. Here the evidence cuts across the deterministic conception associated with the geneticist's account of the influences operating on personality, and shows to us that even short of total destruction the human person may vary within a wide range of extremes. We have to surrender all notions about some unchanging quantum discernible at all times and in all places, something which Christ might have assumed. The third change is one which is given popular exposure in the presupposition behind the question, "Can drugs make you good, so that you do right actions?" Once we grant that drugs can change a scale of values, then it is a possibility that virtue may be drug-conditioned, though the correlation between drugs and any response so precise as virtue is perhaps a very long way off. The possibility is there but it does not in itself reduce the value of virtue which is done without medication; more importantly, unless and until it is done without medication, we can never be sure that it really is virtue.

The theme of the anti-human elements in contemporary culture and the difficulty which they create for a theology which claims the taking of human nature by the Son of God as the focus of salvation can also be pursued by means of certain theories in modern sociology. It is quite a number of years now since a very competent sociologist of my acquaintance drew my attention to the way in which in the social field the idea of social continuity of human personality had virtually disappeared — at least on a phenomenological level. He traced briefly the several situations in which a man would find himself in the course of a day: at the breakfast table in the silent, behind-the-newspaper, non-relation to his wife who is trying to attract his attention to induce him to pass the marmalade; in the car, on the crowded commuter road to the city, hurling anathemas at all and sundry as they cut in and turn right without warning; in the office, with the secretary who wants to retail the office gossip to not unwilling ears; in the board room with the rather suspicious, not so gossipy directors; in the bar before lunch, slightly expansive because delighted with a successful deal; on the golf course, a little earlier than the terms of contract allowed, and therefore schoolboyish with the glee that goes with truancy; at church on Sunday, with face of proper length and trousers of proper gray. My friend did not have great difficulty, in a slightly exaggerated way, in making the points, first, that it was difficult to trace any real continuity of standards, behavior, reactions, even humor, bearing and mannerisms in these different situations; and secondly, that the so-called personality was very much a function of, or a variable with, the social setting. If you add to this semi-serious analysis a hard dash of Marxist economic determinism, you have a very powerful mixture, which can be seen to be operative in quite a number of contemporary situations. Obviously, there has to be a limiting point for such a theory, for the social and economic pressures must have a fulcrum, they must have a center upon which they exert their force. Equally, the parallelogram of forces does not operate in vacuum, but has to act upon a moveable object. When this object is the human personality or human nature, and when the forces operating are social, economic or political, both the movement of the object and indeed the very character of the object are much more seriously influenced by these pressures than we appreciate if we think of human nature as a constant, recurrent identically in all its instances. The forces of relativism are unleashed in no uncertain fashion, and we have to modify our views accordingly of what is to be included in the definition of human nature as its inalienable content, and what is dispensable. Once we are aware that these same social, economic and political pressures were operative upon the human nature of Jesus Christ, we have to recognize that the contemporary doctrine of human nature carries the most serious difficulties for those of us who conscientiously endeavor to relate the Christian faith to modern culture.

Christ, Human Nature and Theology

The problems created for the doctrine of the person of Christ, with its two natures, human and divine, by attitudes in contemporary culture toward the concept of human nature, and of human personality, are in my opinion, therefore, extremely serious. What I find most disturbing of all is that we seem not to have any sufficiently convincing solutions on hand to offer to such problems. Maybe even to realize that they are problems is in itself a sufficiently important discovery, since the issue at stake is so seldom discussed. There are, however, at least two points in theology where the question of theological anthropology has been raised in a way which is relevant to our Christological question about the humanity of Christ. I want to take first of all what looks like a very clever piece of theological reasoning, deriving from the school of Karl Barth. The objection might be made to what has been put forward in the earlier part of this discussion, that it is based upon the quite false assumption that anything which is asserted in secular culture about humanity is relevant to what we have to say about humanity in Christ. This objection is held to be valid not only when these secular accounts of human nature make it extremely difficult, even at times impossible, to maintain the humanity of Christ together with his deity; but also when this humanity is presented in such fully idealistic terms as would be quite compatible with Christian belief. The mistake in the presentation lies in the failure to realize that it is a totally wrong procedure to look first at humanity as it exists in general and then to look to Christ to see how he has assumed it and what it consequently means in his case. The proper procedure is to examine first the humanity of Christ, absorb as fully as we can its full character, its qualities and attributes, the behavior in which it expresses itself, and only thereafter to approach human humanity, if I may use the phrase, in the light of that vision. Theologically, such a procedure may appear to be impeccable, but it has all the characteristics of what might be called a "piologism," a holy and therefore an uncritically accepted doctrine.

It is, in fact, questionable whether such a view is quite as unimpeachable as it first appears to be. For example, when we recall the patristic principle which I have already mentioned, "What he did not take, he did not redeem," we are obliged to say that the human nature which Christ bears must reflect something of the inadequacy, the imperfections and the sin which are the marks of human nature as it is in us. It is this humanity which he took, one is tempted to add, with all the ambiguities and ambivalences, repressions and complexes, drives and aggressiveness, which modern culture has discovered within it. If, on the other hand, the humanity which is attributed to Christ is so totally different from that which we possess, it is going to be extremely difficult for anyone to establish even an intellectual relation between the two, quite apart from the deep, soteriological and moral relationships which are the purpose and motive for the incarnation. Moreover, unless some kind of connection is seen to exist between the humanity we ascribe to Jesus Christ and the humanity which we have been so variously describing in our earlier analysis, then the difficulties arising from that analysis may in the end prove disruptive of any serious attempt to present the humanity of Christ in contemporary terms. In any case, it is difficult to resist the reply to this theologically impeccable view (that we see what our humanity is in Christ) that it looks circular because it is circular. Humanity is something which we identify in ourselves because we are human, and which we consequently can identify in Jesus Christ. That is not to say that the quality of his human life will not far outstrip anything that we can ever hope to achieve, or that we shall not find in him the ideal and the perfection which we shall long to emulate. But the very fact of incarnation presupposes that the Word of God assumes something which is by definition *ours* and not his, to perfect it, to redeem it, and to give it back to us again; unless that order is retained in theology, the whole logic of the doctrine of the incarnation is threatened.

The second point at which theology has come very close indeed to the problem of our discussion, namely, the nature of humanity, is in its lengthy deliberations on the concept of the *imago Dei.* Here, it might well have been expected, the problem will have been solved, and we shall be furnished with a definitive anthropology. Our expectations, however, do not survive even a short reading of the subject in most popular text books. Here there is disagreement as sharp as any to be found in the secular context. The *humanum,* which is for the purposes of the discussion equated with the *imago Dei,* is described in three ways. First, it may be taken to include such qualities as intelligence, ability to communicate in articulate thought, moral capacity both for evaluation and action, sociability, and the knowledge of God, implying love for and obedience to God. The definition is very much of a conventional nature, conforming to a logical pattern. Secondly, human nature has been equated in fallen humanity with considerably less than was included in the previous definition, chiefly with rationality and moral capacity, the others having been lost through the Fall. The question of how much was lost at the Fall has been the storm center in the theological controversy over the doctrines of sin and human nature, and has rather tragically diverted attention from the real issue of what is fallen humanity and what is redeemed humanity. The controversy has at times been reduced to a process of point-scoring — and while the doctors have quarreled, the patient has died. I would lay much of the blame for the confusion in modern conceptions of human nature, both in the Church and outside of it, on this prolonged and futile controversy about the relic of the *imago Dei,* about how much was left after Adam fell. The controversy was, I believe, futile because it began from two postulational positions, two prior definitions, the one saying that a set of attributes bearing the stamp of the *imago Dei* remained after the Fall, the other that only some of these attributes remained while the rest were lost. When the original positions were postulated, defense of them began. Neither side captured the other's garrison, and the result was stalemate.

A possible third definition, which has little to do with the first two, and is in no way a result of the conflict between their respective exponents, attempts to explain the *imago Dei,* the *humanum,* not in substantialist terms at all, but relationally. Both Barth and Brunner were to be found supporting it, when they were not attacking one another. According to this view, the *imago Dei* is not something that exists in us, but is, rather, the relation created by God when he addresses us. One could call it the "addressability" of humankind by God, although one must be careful to note that the *imago,* defined in these terms, is not an inherent capacity in human nature, for it is not a quality that exists prior to God's act of addressing us. This view has affinities with the sociological view which analyzed human nature in terms of a series of social, economic or political situations in which it was to be successively found. It does not, however, provide a sufficient answer to the question of human nature posed, for the same problem exists for this theological anthropology as existed previously for the sociological anthropology, namely, that there has to be some thing or person which *enters into* such relations. It is, in the final analysis, always logically improper to try to define anything purely in terms of the relations in which it stands, for it must first *be* something in order to stand in relation to something else. It would seem, therefore, that the theological definition of the *humanum* as the human being addressed by God implies a prior account of who it is that is addressed by God, and we shall there have to fall back on fairly conventional terms. Even so, it may still be the case that an important point has been made: that we do exist in a certain specific relation, namely, a relation of love towards, obedience to, and worship of God, and that it is in being implicitly or explicitly sustained by God in that relation that our humanity comes to its fullest possible expression.

To draw this part of the discussion together, and to indicate the next stage of our investigation, let me summarize in the following way. First, we can not but be impressed by the sheer variety of interpretations which are offered in contemporary culture, both secular and Christian, of what constitutes human nature. This fact has many immediate consequences in the fields of social decision, political planning and international aid, as well as in the more mundane situations which require us to enter into moral relationships with our neighbors or with economic groups. Our actions in all of these areas will be most seriously affected by our presuppositions of what human nature is, how it is conditioned and when it can be expected to react. In fact, many of the things which are happening in the world today and are being allowed to happen, are directly the result of what certain groups, in power and in responsibility, consider human nature to be.

Secondly, and more seriously, human nature is, one might say, under attack to a degree quite unprecedented in human history. In the past, we have had philosophical theories which reduced the mental to material, psychological theories which were prepared to write human nature out in purely behaviorist terms of physiological reflexes and reactions, and economic theories which reduced it to a counter in the economic struggle. Today we have theories which can implement their pejorative assessment of human nature, showing how effectively drugs can reduce a person to a drooling idiot, or to a will-less automaton responding solely to external stimuli. We see how too in a less dramatic way a whole way of life can be conditioned by the "silent persuasion" of advertising and newsmongering, and how completely one can be conditioned into standardized patterns of behavior by the pressures of society and the economic system.

Thirdly, undoubtedly the whole ambiguity which attaches to the concept of human nature creates inevitable difficulties for a faith which makes as much of the fact of incarnation as does Christianity. The fact of the human nature of Christ is not being called in question, but what *is* at stake is what that human nature means, what content it has. It is not open to us to settle for a sophisticated theological analysis of human nature, for we are then left with a cultural credibility gap between that analysis and ordinary usage. So I return to my main initial contention that the humanity of Christ should be as much a matter for investigation and be recognized as being as great a *skandalon* to modernity as was and ever has been the deity of Christ.

Fourthly, I have no intention of driving a coach and four through the labyrinths of modern anthropological assessments, but propose rather to try a less direct approach. After looking, as we are obliged to, at the function which the concept of humanity played in the original Christological formulations, I want to take as my text for what follows the words of the Prologue to John's gospel, "And the Word became flesh and lived among us . . . full of grace and truth." Perhaps if we can rewrite what "living among us" means, relating it to what God purposed and achieved through it, we shall be able to live a little more easily with the violent disagreements of modern anthropology.

CHAPTER 2

Humanity as Universal

If we are to offer some basis upon which to reread or to give fresh interpretation to the humanity of Christ in the face of all the diverse interpretations confronting us today, it is perhaps necessary to appreciate fully what was the intention of some of the older conceptions of the humanity of Christ. One of the most important aspects of the classical Christologies was the way in which they presented the humanity of Christ in universal terms, so that on the one hand the whole of humanity could be regarded as comprehended within the redemptive act and on the other the redemptive act could be made available for the whole of humanity. The humanity of Christ is the medium of universalization of the redemptive role of Jesus Christ, and it is at the same time the medium of the redemptive act itself, for it is through his humanity that Christ offers himself in life and in death to the Father in obedience to the Father's will for him and for the whole of humankind. It is interesting and illuminating to examine the different ways in which the human nature of Jesus Christ is invested with the universal function.

Humanity the Logical Universal as a Class

The simplest starting point for this part of our examination is to take the notion of the logical universal as constituting all the members of the class and to see how this notion can be applied to the humanity of Jesus Christ. The equation of the term "humanity" with "all people" is an established logical device and a common linguistic practice, for on the one hand, the logical universal "humanity" can be taken as equivalent to the total membership of the class of people — "all people," and on the other, there is a good deal of evidence that that is how we often popularly employ the term. "Humanity" designates the whole class of men and women, set over against, for example, another section of creatures, such as the animal orders, or even nature as the vegetable kingdom, together with the geographical structure of the world and of the rest of the inanimate universe. When we talk of "humanity" increasing in numbers, so that it becomes a threat to itself in terms of physical space and nutriment, we are essentially thinking of the whole membership of the class of humanity, all men and women whatsoever, the term "humanity" then being a shorthand reference to them as a comprehensive group. There is no mystique intended, no curious something above and beyond the all-inclusive total, but simply "all sorts and conditions of people."

All of this is more or less common sense, but the question we must raise is how this equivalence of humanity with all of the individual members of the class "people" relates to Christology. The relation has been established in a number of ways. First, it has been held that Jesus Christ has in some mysterious way gathered all of us into himself in the process of incarnation, by his taking human nature. On this view, the *assumptio carnis,* the assumption of humanity, is the assumption of the whole of humankind. It is worth pausing to observe how comprehensive and specific our reference has become. We are not thinking of humanity generically, disregarding those features which distinguish us from one another, our color, creed, race and religion, or those aspects of our relationships to one another which heighten our differences, our wars and conflicts, class struggles and family feuds. We are affirming these differences one and all in their concreteness and offensiveness, and acknowledging their inclusion within the whole class which Christ gathered to himself in the incarnation. There are included there, too, men and women as they are in themselves, with all their inner tensions, doubts, anxieties, fears, and uncertainties, together with their longings, hopes, ideals, dreams and ambitions. The point here is that the assumption of humanity which takes place at the incarnation is itself an acceptance of men and women as they are, not idealized, transmogrified beyond recognition. The whole of humanity can therefore regard itself as included distributively in the assumption of human nature which took place when the Word was made flesh.

Two comments remain to be made. The first relates to a consequence that follows from such an inclusion of all men and women in the humanity of Christ, i.e., the fact of their oneness with one another. Paul stated it for all time: "There is no longer Jew or Greek, there is no longer slave or free, there is no longer male and female; for all of you are one in Christ Jesus" (Galatians 3:28). Incorporation in Christ is both the affirmation of all our differences from one another, for we have to be assured that they are real, and the rejection of them as ultimately making any real difference in our relation to one another or to Christ. It would not be enough were we simply told that they do not really exist, or that they were "in the mind" or "in the eye of the beholder." In order to be rejected, they have first to be acknowledged; then their rejection is real. It is *only in Christ* that the rejection takes place; only because they are gathered into him are they ultimately annulled. That annulment which was initiated in the original assumption of flesh by Christ remains effective for ever. Insofar as Christ assumed humanity into the Godhead and did not surrender it after death, the assurance continues valid that the differences that shatter our relationships with one another are rejected in him. For the Christian *that* assurance, and not some feebly supported command to "love your neighbor" or "treat others as you would like them to treat you," must remain the real foundation for belief in, and the motivation towards, the unity of human beings everywhere. The second comment on the role of the concept of the universal as applied to the human nature of Jesus Christ is that it offers a clear indication of the importance of human nature as the medium of the redemptive work of Christ. Humanity which might have been found to be some idealized, remotely perfect humanity, is rather presented as the down-to-earth, ordinary, confused, warring, embittered, good-hearted, hopeful, despairing, mixed-up humanity which we all know, which we all are. The redemption is effected through what we are, if you like, by including us. No one can self-pityingly complain that he has been left out. That is the disarming part of it.

A second way of establishing the relation between the universal and the members of the class in Christology and soteriology can be seen in those interpretations of a number of theological doctrines which use the concept of our new being "in Christ," and which lean heavily on the notion of incorporation, incorporation here being the process of "assumption" viewed from the other side. Clearly, in many of the doctrines, as we shall see, the reference is only to those who are full believers being incorporated, rather than all people, but for our purposes, the basic notion of a large group being gathered into Christ is substantially the same in both cases. There is the long series of theologians from Adolf Deissmann onwards who have employed this concept as their definitive description of the new relationship to Christ brought about by faith, sometimes as a status or condition, as an ontological relationship, as a mystical absorption of spirit within the Spirit of Christ, or as simply a way of life.[1] This account of the Christian's relationship to Christ reflects closely several parts of the High-Priestly prayer of Jesus himself in John's Gospel: "I ask not only on behalf of these, but also on behalf of those who will believe in me through their word, that they may all be one. As you, Father, are in me, and I am in you, may they also be in us. . . . The glory that you have given me I have given them, so that they may be one as we are one" (John 17:20, 22f.). The term which classical Trinitarianism has employed to denote this oneness of the Father with the Son is *emperichoresis,* interpenetration, which involves a very high degree of inclusiveness of the one by the other, though short of total assimilation and indeed with retention of integrity of being. In Paul, the theme of incorporation is used again in speaking of baptism, though this time the reference is to the death and resurrection of Christ rather than to his incarnation (though these can be only notionally separated), when he says, "Do you not know that all of us who have been baptized into Christ Jesus were baptized into his death. . . . For if we have been united with him in a death like his, we will certainly be united with him in a resurrection like his" (Romans 6:3, 5). In each of these cases, more is intended than some vague spiritual togetherness; incorporation, the word used above, brings out more clearly the ontological character of the relationship. The same notion is exemplified, of course, in the well-known metaphor of the body of Christ, equated with the Church, but when we move to that metaphor we introduce a rather different series of concepts, now substituting the members who together form the body and have an interorganic relationship to one another for

1. See the useful study by J. K. S. Reid, *Our Life in Christ* (London, 1963).

the more neutral idea of a logical class with all its members rather externally related to one another. The body metaphor is perhaps a proper correction of the earlier logical category, but to develop it takes us beyond our immediate purpose which is simply to show that there is endemic to Christian thought about the relation of humanity to Christ these features, namely that Christ through his assumption of human nature enters into a relationship with the group corporately (as well, of course, as with all of the individuals of the group separately), and that this relationship is an inclusive one.

What the different Biblical presentations all emphasize, we must carefully note, is that it is believers (in baptism, in confession of faith, in daily dedicated living and in the eucharist) who are incorporated in Christ, and so far they illustrate the notion of assumption by Christ of the group into himself. What is not illustrated, and this point is of great importance for all theory about the incarnation and the atonement, is that the Word of God, in assuming humanity, assumed the whole of humanity. The difference between these two positions may be variously interpreted. It may be taken as the area of clash between universalism and particularism, one view suggesting that it was the whole of humanity which Christ took and for which he died, the other affirming that he assumed unto himself only the elect and for them, and them only, was crucified and raised. There is another way of looking at the situation, namely, to retain the affirmation that it was the whole of humanity which Christ took, and for which he died, so that he thereby laid down the objective possibility, or more properly, the objective reality of all human salvation. Those who subsequently subjectively appropriate through the Spirit the objective work of Christ, are incorporated into him here and now, claiming their birthright for themselves. It is as unthinkable that Christ should assume only a portion of humanity as that he should through taking the whole of humanity automatically redeem them all, without their faithful participation in, and appropriation of, that act. What we do, then, in contending for the fact that Christ in assuming humanity at the incarnation gathered into himself the whole class of humanity is to state at one stroke the single broad base upon which the whole redeeming work of Christ rests. It is almost as if we said: "Come, the four corners of the world, in this and every other generation; there is salvation sufficient and more than sufficient here for all."

Humanity as an Adjective

No matter how comprehensive and all-inclusive we make the notion of humanity by equating it with the whole class of men and women, we still cannot escape the responsibility of providing some kind of account, some general definition of what a human being is. That was the logical problem which Socrates used to pose to all his young friends: How can you gather together all the righteous deeds which are going to constitute the class of "righteousness" if you do not possess some preconception of what constitutes righteousness? In the same way, to talk of human beings, to be able to separate them off from the rest of creation is already to be aware, to some extent, of what is common to them all. Theoretically that is so, and yet, it is when we come to define the *humanum* that we encounter the gravest trouble, as can be seen from our previous discussion of the variety of views of human nature that exist in common currency today. Without embarking upon an attempt to solve problems (which we could not then solve) or to ignore them, we must recognize that one feature of the universal character of the human nature of Jesus Christ is the way in which he shares in the characteristics of all people. In other words, the universalization of the humanity of Christ takes place not simply through a process of denotation but also through one of connotation, not only through class but also through meaning, not only through extension but also by intension, not just by distribution but also by description. To that connotation, meaning, intension, description we shall now return.

When we speak of the human nature of Jesus Christ and say that he was human, we intend that he had a physical nature like ours, a body of a certain shape and size, eye, hair, skin of a certain color; that he had an emotional nature like ours, becoming, as the Scriptures tell us, angry, hungry, tired, lonely, kindly and loving and on occasions suffering intense physical and mental pain; that he had a moral nature, with a capacity to judge between good and evil and to express himself strongly concerning both and to direct his life and actions in the light of his perception of the difference between the two; that he was intelligent and could make rational assessments and argue logically; and that like other people, he was socially inclined, and had a lively sense of their needs and great gifts of communicating his thoughts to them. So much is but a long-winded way of saying that when the Word became flesh in Jesus Christ, he had all the obvious qualities of human nature, being physical, rational, sociable, ethical, responsible and free. In fact, so completely and so obviously was he human, so genuine was the human nature that he possessed that he was often mistaken as being only a man: "Is not this the carpenter's son? Is not his mother called Mary? And are not his brothers James and Joseph and Simon and Judas? And are not all his sisters with us? Where then did this man get all this?" (Matthew 13:55f.) The last question might seem to imply that they were appreciative of the numinous character of his actions, but the fact of his humanity seemed to be fixed in their minds, obscuring his deity as so many Lutheran theologians were later to say, so that two verses read that he did no mighty works there "because of their unbelief."

It would be wrong, however, to leave the examination of what might be called the definitional aspect of the humanity of Christ without acknowledging that in this area some of the most long continued Christological controversies have taken place. Let us take two examples only. The first is one we have already noted in Chapter 1, which arises in connection with the moral character of Christ's human nature: Was it sinless or sinful? Strong arguments can be advanced for affirming that it was sinless human nature which Christ took, the most important being that if he were himself sinful, then he would not be qualified to effect the salvation of his fellow sinners. Only a sinless person could establish the merit required; for the sacrifice for the sins of the whole world, the victim must be innocent. The empirical argument also is often used that there is no sign whatsoever in the Gospel accounts of his ever having sinned — quite the reverse, it is maintained, there is everywhere transparent and inspiring goodness. On the other side, it is pointed out — though this argument is only of recent popularity in Christian theology — that if Christ intended to redeem human nature there was not much real point in his taking sinless human nature, which no human being had anyway. He had to take the sinful nature which required salvation. The patristic saying, "What Christ did not take, he did not redeem," has been given a totally new lease of life for the purpose of illustrating this theory. If he had not taken sinful human nature he would not have redeemed it. If we may revert just for a minute to the previous view of human nature, the universal, including all of the class, we could reinforce the contention that it was sinful human nature, the *massa damnata* that Christ gathered to himself in incarnation and atonement. This view, however, despite its considerable persuasiveness, is not without its difficulties. The chief perhaps of these is to conceive how, if Christ's human nature were sinful, this sinfulness did not show up in his behavior. Personally, I can see no solution to this problem. It is clear that if you wish to conserve certain points in your Christology, you declare respectively for a sinful human nature in Christ, or for a sinless human nature but I doubt whether any synthesizing theory will ever secure both sets of points. For my own part, I have on occasion asked to be allowed to say that Christ took sinful human nature without himself becoming a sinner or in any way evincing sin, but even that may be to ask for excess tolerance.

The second point of controversy to be mentioned is associated with the intellectual powers of Jesus Christ. If he were genuinely human, then his intellect would be subject to the limits imposed upon all other human beings. He would not be omniscient, at least in respect of his human nature. Are we then to say that his divine nature has an omniscient mind and his human nature an intelligence of limited scope? The obvious difficulty arises of facing the fact that Jesus Christ would then be said both to know and not to know the second law of thermodynamics. I have mentioned elsewhere the ingenious theory of E. L. Mascall, that there are two kinds of knowledge in the human mind of Christ: first, that which he has come by in ordinary daily experience as does any human being; and secondly, that which has been introduced into the human mind by the divine nature, which he also has, as circumstances require it, and according to the capacity of the human mind to receive it.[2] As theory it is clever, but it is doubtful whether it altogether escapes the problem of Jesus Christ both knowing and not knowing the same fact at the same time, and whether it does not fall into the heresy of Nestorianism, which ascribes two full persons to Jesus.

In case we be thought to be too simplistic in our brash disposal of the different interpretations of humanity, we might connect the present discussion to that of the previous Chapter by saying that they apply to the human nature of Jesus Christ if they apply at all to ordinary human nature. Jesus Christ is to be regarded as human if being human involves

2. John McIntyre, *The Shape of Christology* (London, 1966), pp. 136ff., with reference to Mascall, *Christ, the Christian and the Church* (London, 1946), pp. 53ff.

having a human psyche which is constructed in a certain way and is to be influenced in different ways by the pressures put upon it. His human nature obviously stands in a certain relation to biological evolutionary process, for example; how else could he be regarded as human? His attitudes in many cases betray evidences of sociological conditioning, of political coloring, of economic determinism. Without such evidences, we should have to revise our estimate of his humanity or face the charge of a new kind of docetism. This aspect of his humanity will be deployed in our study of the particularity of Christ's humanity in Chapter 3; in the present context we are still concerned with the universal aspects of the attributes which constitute the humanity and in which he is in the same position as we ourselves.

Humanity as Representative and as Substitute

We have been considering two of what we might call the traditional formal logical ways in which the humanity of Christ has been universalized in Christology: through the class concept and through the definition. There have been others equally famous, and to three of them in particular we now turn. The first of the three is contained in the notion of "representative humanity." Certain aspects of this concept require to be emphasized. First, it is important at the outset to see that the purpose of using the notion "representative" is to universalize the humanity of Christ — so achieving the double aim which we have already remarked upon, of connecting the humanity of Christ with all men and women and their salvation, and at the same time of securing for each and every one the assurance of a relationship to that salvation. The universalizing force of the representative humanity is expressed in the fact that the effectiveness of what is done through Christ's adopting this role is not limited by its having taken place in one place at one time, and through one man. It is available for all of us, because all of us are represented. Christ assumes a humanity which has a representative role for soteriological reasons, and a discussion of the term must explore these reasons, relating the soteriological purposes served by this term in this way to other terms adopted for soteriological definition.

Secondly, while the meaning of the notion "representative" is perhaps fairly obvious, there will be no harm in noting that it contains the following elements: the representative is someone who is speaking or acting on behalf of a group of persons who are bound by what he says or does; he also expects to be treated as they would were they present; he may not have exactly the same characteristics as they have — for example he may be sinless while they are sinful — but as long as he acts as their representative he must be treated as if he had; what happens to him may be regarded as happening to them. The notion of representative carries within it the implication of such a close relationship between the representative and the represented, that relations obtaining with the former are assumed to obtain with the latter and *vice versa.* In the case of Jesus Christ, the closeness of the relationship between the representative and the represented is brought out by the fact of the acceptance by the representative of the nature of those whom he represents. So when he stands before God, he bears humanity, not in his own name but in that of those he represents. All those intimate relations which we observed as endemic to the representative position are secured in this unique way.

Thirdly, while I have been emphasizing the closeness of the relation of the representative to those he represents, this relationship is to be distinguished from that of inclusiveness, which was a feature of the universal humanity as a class concept. The representative does not include those whom he represents; he may be looked upon as if he did, and they may be looked upon as if they were included in him, but in fact they are not. The relation is an external and not an inclusive one, and should not be given overtones of the idea of incorporation.

Fourthly, there is provided by Christ, through this representative role, to men and women, a subject of transference for guilt. Through his actions to which they are related in this represented way, they are given relief of their burden, not solely by some magical happening which preceded their existence by two thousand years (which is how some may regard the way incorporation in Christ works) but by a genuine psychological transference. This transference is evidenced by their mental and spiritual health and is based upon the representative terms in which the incarnation and the atonement have been presented. The representative concept has therefore grounds to commend it on psychotherapeutic grounds, which may give it an advantage over other soteriological concepts.

Fifthly, the notion of representative is a very fair copy of what the Bible says when it relates the life or death of Jesus Christ to ourselves by the preposition *hyper,* as I have written elsewhere.[3] It is customary at this point to introduce certain exclusive connotations; the word, we might try to say invoking etymological authorities, does not mean this or that. The evidence would seem to indicate beyond doubt that there is a comprehensive range of valid translations of the term; from "in the name of" through "because of," "for the sake of," "on behalf of," to "instead of" and "in place of." No one can deny, if he has the least feeling for language, that the word *hyper* carries one or other of these different meanings on the different occasions of its occurrence in New Testament literature, on occasion carrying as far as we can judge one or two of them at once. It may be that we wish on other grounds to set up Christologies or soteriologies which make more of one sense than of another, but we must not endeavor either to impose any one of these exclusive senses upon texts which cannot grammatically bear such a meaning or to present our Christology or soteriology as if all the occurrences of *hyper* meant the same thing and could be used without discrimination in the construction of a single doctrine of the person or of the death of Christ. My reference is, of course, to the subtleties involved in the distinction between representative and substitutionary theories.

Dorothee Sölle, in her study, *Christ the Representative,* has discussed this question at length.[4] Sölle claims that there is a quite radical distinction between the representative and the substitute. The representative takes temporary responsibility and makes decisions for the represented, but only in specified areas. Representation is very much conditioned by circumstances of temporality, which can take the ontological forms of weakness, immaturity, absence or sickness. The representative regards the other person as irreplaceable, and therefore does not put himself or herself in the other person's place completely or take it over permanently. There may come a day when the represented will resume responsibility, and the representative must then surrender his or her role, hoping that the represented will homologate whatever decisions have been made or actions taken. The substitute, on the other

3. John McIntyre, *The Shape of Soteriology* (Edinburgh, 1992), pp. 90ff.
4. Dorothee Sölle, *Christ the Representative* (ET London, 1967), p. 20ff.

hand, has an entirely different part to play. He or she treats the other as replaceable, in fact as dead. The substitution is permanent, absolute and unconditional, so that the replaced is obliterated and forgotten. The antithesis of the two concepts is summarized for us by Sölle in these words: "Substitution is a final exchange of dead impersonal or depersonalized being, whereas representation is the provisional intervention of persons on behalf of persons."[5]

It is not surprising that, when the difference between the two concepts is drawn in these sharp terms, Sölle should automatically gravitate to preference for that of representative in the description of Christ, and to the employment of it as a rather uncompromising means of separating soteriologies and Christologies into groups which are acceptable or unacceptable. Before going on to consider the validity of the distinction, we ought to note the light which she throws on the idea of *Christ* as the representative. She notes four distinctive characteristics of the Christian conception: historicity, universalization, voluntariness and suffering. (i) As against the representation which might occur in magical rites — the constant availability of some representative — in Christianity the representative occurs in a certain place at a certain time. There is historical concentration at a single point in space and time. "There is representation only in one name," as Sölle puts it.[6] (ii) Again, as against magical ritual representation, where each occasion requires separate facilities for representation, Christ as representative acted once and for all. The salvation achieved by him is not reserved for the members of one particular class or nation or race, but is effective for the whole world. Sölle sees the danger that this universalization may revert to that "error of magical thinking" as she calls it, known as substitution. (What she does not make plain at this stage of exposition is how representation of the kind she sets over against substitution *can* universalize its effectiveness. She does so later by means of the notion of identification.) (iii) The representation which Christ makes is a completely personal and voluntary act of association with ourselves and is not compulsorily imposed upon him by his divine nature. This association with ourselves rests, therefore, not on his identity with us in virtue of his previous being so much as on his act of identification with

5. Sölle, p. 23.
6. Sölle, p. 68.

us. Nor is this identification an act over and done with, objectionable and in the past. It is an unfinished and continuing relationship. (iv) The fourth element in the Christian concept of the representative is suffering. As against Jewish interpretations of Isaiah 53, for the Christian, Christ proves himself the elect representative by his suffering for the whole world.

Sölle's earlier discussions of the representative have left unsolved the problems of how the representative is related to ourselves and of how we are to be included in the representation. The rejected notion of substitution had rather drastically achieved this end by destroying the irreplaceable being of persons (or more precisely by assuming them to be replaceable because dead in sin). Representation has therefore to be supplemented by the notion of identification. Christ identifies himself with men and women, past, present and future, in his readiness to accept them without limits and without conditions. The pattern for this sort of identification Sölle finds in the Enlightenment's idea of Christ as teacher, which she endeavors to rehabilitate. In my judgment, since the idea of the teacher *illustrates* and does not replace the idea of identification, we may for our present purposes set it aside as at this stage perhaps creating for us more problems than it solves. The notion of the punishment which Christ as representative bears is cashed out in terms not of expiation of a God who is Nietzsche's "old oriental," or of penalties paid for indignity visited upon God, but of such an identification with those who are involved in the "deadly cycle" which is the hell of the consequences of wrongdoing, and its recoil upon the wrongdoer, as leads in the end to the restoration of a broken personal relationship. Christ's "sharing of the punishment, his identification with the botched cause of the other person, makes him into a servant who takes responsibility and suffers,"[7] who acknowledges his own guilt and accepts punishment.

Sölle obviously has made a very substantial contribution to the subject of our discussion, and it would be wrong not to attempt to assess its validity. First, on the critical side, I would have to say that the rather rigid antithesizing of "representative" and "substitute" is postulational rather than factual or etymological. Admittedly it may be a relief to come upon someone who can see the distinction in such a clear light,

7. Sölle, p. 122.

and, as drawn, it may serve certain classificatory purposes in expounding meanings of the terms. The term "substitute" has a meaning very similar to that of "representative" in ordinary parlance; the substitute is the person who stands in for, who replaces, the original person. There are perhaps two differences which may be noted. On the one hand, the substitute concept is more frequently related to the single substitution of one person for another, whereas the representative concept covers more the idea of a group being represented by a single person, though admittedly the representation of the single person cannot be excluded in the case of the representative — the Queen's representative, the Prime Minister's representative, to mention obvious cases. Almost never does the substitute stand in for a group. Imagine the supporters' reaction at a football match, if a substitute player were replaced by ten men. On the other hand, the term "substitute" used in the Christological context most frequently applies to the death of Christ and is associated with penal or satisfaction theories of the death of Christ, where the emphasis is upon the *passive* obedience of Christ. He bears our sins, carries our sorrows and on him are visited the iniquities of us all. He stands as our substitute at the point of condemnation, judgment and punishment. Alternatively, because he bears in his death the suffering which is the proper sequel to sin in a universe governed by a righteous God, he satisfies the demands of that God for justice to be done in respect of evil. In the idea of representative, there is emphasis more upon the active character of the work of Christ, upon *active* obedience. As our representative, he offers to God the total obedience to God's will, the total willingness to offer up his life to God for the salvation of the world, the total love for God, which we in our sin and guilt are unable to offer. God accepts that offering from Christ, since he is our representative, as from ourselves. In fact, Sölle has completely confused these two distinctions in her remark that "Christ as representative bears the punishment of sin," for the notion of punishment is associated with passive obedience and therefore with substitution.

Secondly, what Sölle does not fully appreciate is that the notion of representative by itself is unequal to the burden which she imposes upon it. It is only when it receives content from, or is spelt out in terms of, the idea of identification that it begins to function with any conviction. The idea of identification answers major questions which Sölle has left unsolved in the earlier parts of her book — namely, what does the representative *do*? How does he, in the particularity of his space-time existence, universalize his role so that he is properly related to those he represents? More embarrassingly still, what is it to be a representative? What the representative does is to become one with those he represents and to suffer and be punished on their behalf. That is what it is to be *this* representative. He universalizes his particularity by making his identification available to all men and women in all ages. This position is one with which I have a great deal of sympathy. In *On the Love of God*, I have argued that both vicarious satisfaction and penal substitution "imply a certain separation of the Subject from those for whom He is acting vicariously, or for whom He is a substitute. . . . Now, if we are going to hold that the concept of identification is the final category for the definition of love, then clearly we are obliged to pass beyond vicariousness and substitution to a description which eliminates the separation. . . ."[8] What I there said concerning vicariousness and substitution could equally easily be applied to representation.

Humanity as Identifying

Sölle's use of the concept of identification supports the conclusion to which we had been moving, that representation and substitution are not altogether adequate categories for the description either of the humanity of Christ or of the universalizing role which his humanity is expected to play in the redemptive situation. Let us elaborate that conclusion a little. The notions of representative and substitute, as indeed also that of vicariousness, all imply some kind of external severance of the two parties concerned. As representative, Christ is, almost by definition, in a different place from those he represents, having different characteristics from them. The substitute takes their place, and bears the agonies the sinners deserve. Vicariously, the Savior endures the torments of the damned, for were they to be subjected to them, they would perish. This kind of externality was absent from the class concept of the universal human nature, as we have just noticed, though in that case the inclusion was affirmed in such logical and even ontological terms that the whole compassionate element which certainly is

8. John McIntyre, *On the Love of God* (London, 1962), pp. 209f.

present in the representative or substitute concept and even in that of vicariousness, was in danger of being eliminated. The problem, then, is how to maintain the close internal nexus between ordinary human nature or humanity and the human nature or humanity of Christ, and at the same time to conserve the elements of compassion and tenderness without which we fail to do justice to what could be called the basic motivation of the incarnation and atonement. The one concept which fulfills that double qualification is the concept of identification. What, however, does it mean?

In ordinary usage, identification is a process in which someone makes himself or herself at one with the people in a situation, accepting their way of life and customs, adopting their problems, sharing their anxieties and sorrows, empathizing with their condition, feeling their condition, getting inside their skin. We have a sufficiently wide range of metaphor to hand to indicate that the experience is a fairly common one. It has been used in a wide variety of contexts: to describe the kind of life at which missionaries ought to aim, instead of regarding themselves as a community apart, within their own European compound, members of the tea-planting set; to provide bouquets for successful authors and playwrights who so master their subject and matter that they are able to project not only themselves but also their audience into the situation and characters of which they write; to set a standard for social workers that they may learn to bridge the social or moral or judgmental gulf which impedes progress in genuine assistance; to suggest ways in which we break the deadlock that is so often created by failures in mutual understanding and sympathy that are the most common causes of international tension, political unrest, economic and industrial dispute, marital disharmony and family quarrels. These are but a few of the contexts in which this theme will occur, but they are sufficiently wide-ranging to refute any suggestion that it is a sectarian or a religious fad.

The next feature of identifying which we should note is that it is to be clearly distinguished from absorption in the subject of identification. In fact, if absorption should take place, then identification has defeated its purpose by changing to another category. In other words, there has to be in all identification some kind of detachment, some holding back to conserve personal identity. This detachment, which is contained in all identification as a polar element within it, is in a sense the condition of the possibility of identification. The missionary who identifies with the people of another culture to the point of loss of detachment, that is, to the point of total absorption, becomes guilty of a degree of deceit, if not even of hypocrisy. No Westerner can be a "complete" South Indian, but can only pretend to be, and it is this pretense, implied or expressed, which in such a situation would rob the identification of its authenticity. Similarly, the social worker who identifies with the problems of the drug addict to the point of becoming one would by that very fact lose all effectiveness in attempting to deal with the social-psychological problems of the client's addiction. Or again, the author who over-identifies with the subject of a book or play soon loses the nicely balanced judgment, the right degree of approval or indignation or horror, which sustains the note of absolute accuracy. The pastoral counselor who "takes sides" as a result of involvement with a patient very soon finds that his or her counseling becomes interference, interference which is resented even by the person whose side is supposedly taken. Identification, therefore, is not absorption into a situation or with a person; it retains detachment as a center in its polar field.

These generalizations upon the notion of identifying are of great importance for our appreciation of that identification which is achieved by the Word when in being made flesh he assumes human nature. No ordinary human being can begin to achieve that ideal of identification which is the proper relation between human beings who know, understand and love one another. We repel each other too much — explicitly by the things we say to one another, and the things we do; less overtly by our attitudes to one another, our "huffs" and petulant reactions; and even quite unconsciously by mannerisms of speech or behavior which cause an irritation to others in inverse proportion to their magnitude. We do not ourselves have the degree of mental, emotional or spiritual perceptiveness which enables us to establish a properly empathetic relation with someone else. Such is the human nature of Christ that he does achieve that perfection of identification even when the subject is at its most offensive and repellent. Paradoxically, in his case the detachment is also at perfection. Were the identification to be total, then he would have changed into a man. In assuming flesh, however, he remains God. This detachment ultimately is the ground of his ability to suffer in our place and on our behalf. Without it, with total identification and no detachment, he would be dying on his own behalf. Thus interpreted, the human nature of Jesus

Christ has to be regarded as sinless. A sinful humanity could not fulfill the demands required by such a standard of involvement, nor could anything less than perfection in humanity bear the suffering and sorrow entailed by death for human sin. It has to bear it, know its deepest sorrow, be conquered by it — and in being conquered, be detached so as to conquer it and be raised from it. That demand, that degree of involvement, is one which only perfect humanity could achieve.

How then, do we describe the universalizing work of humanity in Christ when we have so cashed it out as identifying with humankind? The universalization takes place not in some class group fashion, not distributively through a logical universal, but rather differently. It is to be located in the fact that Christ through his human nature identifies with *every* human being no matter in what situation he or she is found. It is identification which is not limited even by death itself, for in the loneliness and sense of abandonment of death there is — for such is the promise of Christ's human nature — the assurance of his presence with rod and staff. With no limit in that the most soul-searching of all the directions which our lives may take, there is established the conviction that he is immediately and intensely present in every situation which can possibly overtake us.

So finally, I think that I should like to say that it is the way in which Jesus Christ through his human nature has identified himself with every circumstance which can befall humanity that is in the end the basis of all the forms of universalization which we have noted. We are all gathered into Christ as members of the total class of humanity because he has identified himself universally with us, regardless of color, creed, religion and race. He has acquired those items which the meticulous logician gathers under the rubrics of precise definition by positively identifying himself with humanity as it is; the consequence of such identification is that the logician "reads off" the terms of his humanity in definitional precision. He stands as our representative before God because he has made his own our nature, our case, our sin, our pride, our disgrace, our shame, while retaining the polarity to it through the detachment of his perfection. He can genuinely be our substitute, bearing in himself the stripes with which we are healed, because he has identified himself with the condition which deserved that judgment. In a simple sentence, he is who he is because he has identified himself with us. All else derives from that, our salvation, our life, our hope our destiny. It is all there.

CHAPTER 3

Humanity as Particularity

It is clear that much emphasis has traditionally been placed upon the universalizing role given to the human nature assumed by the Word of God at the incarnation. This universalization serves two purposes. On the one hand, it seems to ensure the inclusion of all humankind in the redemptive work of Jesus Christ. On the other hand, it relates that redemptive work subsequently to all situations in which we find ourselves requiring and asking for that redemption. No one, of whatever sort or condition, of whatever color, creed, race or religion, coming to know Christ in the Gospels and to hear of the crucifixion, can fail to realize that that life and death of Christ are directly relevant to his or her particular, unique situation. In both respects his humanity is the medium through which that redemption was executed by Christ. There has, however, recently been a considerable reaction to the idea of the human nature as being a universal, a questioning of it even at the cost of the many obvious merits attaching to it, and conversely, a determined attempt to do greater justice to the *particularity* of his human nature. I wish to begin in the first half of this Chapter by commenting on five immediate ways in which the particularity or at least the non-generality of the human nature taken by Christ has been described in modern times, proceeding thereafter to a sixth major form of the emphasis upon particularity.

The Fragmentation of Human Nature

One of the most obvious features of contemporary approaches to the problem of human nature is the break away from the notion that a human being is a finely balanced constellation of attributes, which are variously dispersed and varyingly dominant among the human race but appear in some form in all its members, and even from the notion that the human being is the subject of a tidy definition universally applicable to *homo sapiens* as such. We might have been tempted to characterize this development as exclusively modern had Aristotle not beaten us to the mark two and half thousand years ago with his famous remark, "Man is by nature a political animal."[1] Among the more contemporary expressions of this view can be numbered the following: economic, industrial, educated, ethical, religious, historical, and technological humanity. The intention of such definitions of humanity is to make the point that we do not exist in a vacuum, or in the form of a logical concept or definition. Human beings, rather, occur in a variety of situations, and our assessment of which of these situations is the more important determines how we describe them. If we share the Marxist concern, we can lay out human nature as a function of economic determinants, varying strictly in accordance with their variation. If we live in the ivory towers, it is not inconceivable that we should come to read human nature in terms of courses, tutorials, grades and degree classifications. If we are good religionists, then human nature will be that part of creation which bears the image of God as a stamp upon its features, not forgetting that that description is far from being an account of humanity in the round, and more a statement, as we have seen, of our relation to God. Religious description itself seems, therefore, to be as abstractive as any of the others which we have mentioned, which may not altogether please those who think of religion as recapitulating and comprehending all the components of human nature. Even if we were to argue that the category of the ethical covers the whole of human life, and that it may succeed where religion failed in comprehending the whole human being, we are in fact no more successful. The ethical, by itself, is a merely formal concept; it derives its concrete content from

1. Aristotle, *Politics,* 1253a.

outside itself, from such as the economic, political, social, and educational fields of human endeavor.

Two comments may be made upon this first direction of departure from universals towards particularity. On the one hand, there is enough of this kind of thinking going on today to make us realize that it is not simply a passing fancy, nor can we optimistically expect it to be overtaken by error, even though it is a patent instance of what Whitehead named as "the fallacy of misplaced concreteness." In thinking of humanity as economic, social, technological, educated, psychological, or religious, the specialists seem to achieve sufficiently satisfactory results to justify their assumption that human being is as they describe it. There is also a proper modesty in the confinement of attention to one aspect of human reality. On the other hand, it is perhaps equally clear that there is no single, synoptic or comprehensive view available to gather together all these different "humanities" into one single "humanity." The fragmentation is, if you like, a part of our culture, or a necessary consequence of the complexity of modern life. However we describe it, it appears inevitable that we cannot produce any compendious item which might answer to the title of human nature. This has obvious implications for how we conceive of the human nature which Christ assumed at the incarnation, implications which I have already outlined in Chapter 1.

Humanity as Relatedness

The second direction of departure from the classical conceptions of human nature is illustrated for us by Joseph Haroutunian.[2] According to Haroutunian, from the time of Augustine, theologians have spoken of "human nature" or "nature" as a fixed entity that can be discovered and defined by a study of the individual's particular characteristics and traits. Human nature, however, is for Haroutunian a function of communion among people. We come to have a human nature and to know it as such in that relationship to our fellow creatures that is called love. So radically different is the real conception of human nature from the traditional one that Haroutunian even suggests that, to avoid misun-

2. Joseph Haroutunian, *God With Us* (London, 1967), pp. 146ff.

derstanding, it would be better not to speak of human nature at all. "The apparently universal notion, at least in the Western world, that one man can be and that he can have a nature suggests an alienation that gives us, not a human ontology, but one from which the human manner of being is excluded."[3] The Western world should not have allowed itself to reach the point of forgetting what Aristotle said, "He who is unable to live in society, or who has no need because he is sufficient for himself, must be either a beast or a god."[4]

Once again the rewriting of the meaning of human nature, or more precisely its rejection as a universal, must carry very important consequences for Christology. Certainly on Haroutunian's terms, we could no longer think of Christ's human nature as a series of attributes or qualities. In the place of that account, we might find ourselves turning to the different ways in which Christ portrays human beings in their relatedness to one another — in their love for one another, their forgiveness, their concern, their seeking out the lost, their sharing of one another's joys and sorrows, their sacrifices for one another. To say that the Word "took human nature" is to say that Christ as a man entered into all these relations to others which we have just enumerated. This description carries no reference to "human nature" as some fixed entity or collection of inherited traits. "The Word was made flesh" means precisely that the Word as a man became variously related to men and women upon earth as one of themselves.

The Human Condition

The third deviation from the norm of the classical conception of human nature is represented by Jean-Paul Sartre. His rejection of the very idea of human nature is well-known, deriving primarily from his contention that "existence" is prior to "essence," that I am what I am not as some essential *res cogitans,* or embodiment of moral duty, or as any universal whatsoever; I am who I am, rather, as the one who exists, who is an upsurge of freedom into the world, and who thus wills to decide and to act, not on the basis of any preestablished rules, but with a sense of

3. Haroutunian, p. 150.
4. Aristotle, *Politics,* 1253a.

abandonment, of being on my own in a world without a God.[5] But Sartre obviously is not going to get far without some kind of transcription of the old notion of human nature. His substitute concept, one that appeals certainly to many, is "the condition of man": "It is not by chance that thinkers of today are so much more ready to speak of the condition than of the nature of man."[6] Though we have to be careful not to equate Sartre's anthropology with a pure individualism or subjectivism — for he succeeds in retaining a universalist emphasis in such statements as "freedom is willed in community"[7] — the emphasis is throughout on what I decide, upon my action, upon my existence, and not upon any predefined human nature.

When we attempt to relate this account of human nature — or more precisely, this rejection of human nature in favor of the notion of the human condition — to the incarnation, it would seem that the task is not a difficult one. The New Testament narratives of the events in the earthly life of Christ tell us of a man who acts, who makes decisions, who appears in a certain socio-economic and political milieu, a man who has taken upon himself the entire range of the human condition, to the point of meeting the loneliest abandonment of a death darkened by a sense of rejection by God and by betrayal by his own friends. The facility with which this adjustment can be made may tempt us to ask the question whether it might not be advisable to drop altogether talk of the humanity of Christ, and substitute such a phrase as "the human condition of Christ." I should myself be reluctant to do so, but prefer to continue to use the term, as it were, with my eyes open, recognizing, first, that this usage does not commit me to what Haroutunian called "a human ontology" or to any doctrine of a metaphysical substance of humanity; and secondly, that when I do use the term "humanity" I spell it out in Haroutunian, or Sartrean or fragmented senses, for it is in these ways that I think and talk of human nature. Not to make such acknowledgment is to be intellectually dishonest. To refuse to continue to use the term "humanity" in these ways is a quite unnecessary piece of self-sacrifice, for the term will more than earn its pension because of its advantages as a shorthand device.

5. Jean-Paul Sartre, *Existentialism and Humanism* (ET London, 1948), pp. 32ff.
6. Sartre, p. 46.
7. Sartre, p. 51.

Humanity as "This Man"

We turn for our next illustration of the particularity of the human nature of Jesus Christ to what must appear a curious quarter, namely, the theology of Karl Barth. There is no doubt whatsoever that Barth can be shown to favor the idea that the humanity which Christ has taken is universal humanity. He puts it clearly himself: "What God the Son assumed into unity with himself and his divine being was and is . . . not merely 'a man' but the *humanum,* the being and essence, the nature and kind, which is that of all men."[8] This statement when examined is, of course, seen to be an anti-statement, designed to dissociate him from any possibility of Nestorianism, the theory that Jesus Christ had a complete human personality, a *persona* or *hypostasis* of humanity as well as a *physis;* it dissociates him as well from the other conceivable charge of adoptionism, namely that the Logos adopted "this man Jesus" when it was obvious that he had the moral and spiritual qualities which were in highest harmony with the divine nature of the Logos. As an anti-statement, this remark of Barth's makes its point. The trouble is that Barth appears very suddenly to realize that perhaps the price is too high, for three pages later he seems to correct himself with the assertion, "God Himself is in the world, earthly, conceivable and visible, as He is this man. . . . God Himself speaks when this man speaks in human speech."[9] It is almost as if Barth recognizes that if the incarnation is to have any reality at all, it has to be presented not in conceptualist, universal terms, but with precise particularity, even if the price is some kind of implied heresy.

On this last question, it should perhaps be simply argued that if our choice is between some universalist, non-Nestorian human nature which nevertheless falls foul of docetism, and a particularist, non-docetic human nature which falls foul of Nestorianism, the latter must surely prove the more acceptable of the two. Even those Christologies which attempt to maintain the link with the universalist view do so while also attempting to secure the integrity of the humanity of Christ. In our kind of world, however, and in our kind of culture, human nature means not some ideal essence, as it may have done in Platonism, or a

8. Karl Barth, *Church Dogmatics,* IV/2 (ET Edinburgh, 1958), p. 48.
9. Barth, IV/2, p. 51.

logical universal as in Aristotelianism, or even a class as in symbolic logic; rather, human nature means for us what characterizes *this* man, or *that* woman. In one sense, there is nothing even peculiarly modern about this. For the Biblical writers who preserved the stories for us, as for the chief actors in their stories, any question about the humanity of Christ was a question about this man Jesus, who was the carpenter, whose brothers and sisters they knew, who said this and did that — all with a quite precise particularity, the particularity which is the stock-in-trade of stories passed from mouth to mouth, and eventually, in the folk lore of the group, from generation to generation.

Humanity as "the Scandal of Particularity"

The natural halting place in the transition to our lengthier discussion of particularity is the Kierkegaardian concept of "the scandal of particularity." I have written on several occasions of the way in which theological existentialism within the heritage of Kierkegaard has at times sat very loose to the detail of history, so much so that the criticism of dehistoricization is not an unfair allegation.[10] For the present, however, we are thinking of the particularity of Christ's human nature. Kierkegaard writes,

> That God has existed in human form, has been born, grown up and so forth is surely the paradox *sensu strictissimo,* the absolute paradox. . . . A relative paradox relates itself to the relative difference between more or less cleverness and brains; but the absolute paradox, just because it is absolute, can be relevant only to the absolute difference that distinguishes man from God. . . . But the absolute difference between God and man consists precisely in this, that man is a particular existing being (which is just as true of the most gifted human being as it is of the most stupid) whose essential task cannot be to think *sub specie aeterni,* since as long as he exists he is essentially an existing individual . . . while God is infinite and eternal.[11]

10. E.g., *The Shape of Christology* (London and Philadelphia, 1966), pp. 115ff.

11. Søren Kierkegaard, *Concluding Unscientific Postscript* (ET Princeton, 1941), pp. 194f.

This quotation brings out very clearly our theme of humanity as particularity. Kierkegaard here and throughout his work makes a great deal of the precise particularity which is the characteristic form of being of the existing individual. This particularity expresses itself in the concreteness of the responsibilities and duties which command his attention in the detail of his relations to his fellows in daily life. What Kierkegaard calls the absolute paradox is that the God who is from eternity to eternity, who thinks and acts and exists, in the ancient phrase, *sub specie aeterni,* is nevertheless incarnate, not in some general way, but by becoming this existing individual. This absolute paradox is what the Bible has in mind when it speaks of the Gospel being a stumbling block to Jews and foolishness to the Greeks. It is what Kierkegaard means by the scandal of particularity that the God of all eternity and of all space should be so particularized that revelation of his nature and purpose occurs in such a limited situation, in the life and death of Jesus Christ, and that the eternal happiness of each individual should be dependent upon his relation to this particular, historical phenomenon in the life of a very small insignificant nation in the Middle East.

Now Kierkegaard holds a very pejorative view of the nature of historical knowledge, one which has passed almost totally unchanged into modern existentialism both religious and secular; two points are noteworthy in what he has to say in this connection. They come from two quotations, both from the *Concluding Unscientific Postscript:* "nothing is more readily evident than that the greatest attainable certainty with respect to anything historical is merely an *approximation.*"[12] For Kierkegaard, the historical element in Christianity is something in relation to which the best knowledge attainable is merely an "almost." This skepticism he goes on to apply to the Scriptures and to show how the certainty which is aimed at in biblical criticism is a constantly retreating and unattainable goal. The point he made in this way has been accepted by biblical critics for the 150 years since he wrote, only being challenged by literal inspirationists who find certainty in the words dictated by the Holy Spirit to form the Scriptures. The second quotation completes the picture begun by the first: "Faith does not result simply from a scientific enquiry."[13] In fact, if any certainty were to be created by such enquiry (e.g., into the canonicity of the individual books of the Bible, their authenticity,

12. Kierkegaard, pp. 25f.
13. Kierkegaard, p. 30.

their integrity, the trustworthiness of their authors), then it would threaten to devour faith, which does not rest on some outward objectivity but is inwardness, subjectivity, passion, essential decisiveness. Out of this antithesis of knowledge (arrived at by research and criticism) and faith has arisen a distinction which has been used at times to suggest that faith is antirational, and that it has no foundation in historical fact. Neither of these consequences is necessary, for Kierkegaard is saying quite firmly that faith ultimately requires an intensely personal decision in relation to its subject, and that this decision is categorically different from knowledge of the results of historical criticism. What Kierkegaard does not do — and here is my reason for insisting on this matter — is deny either the essential humanity of Christ, which for him took the form of "this existing individual," or the historicity, as we normally understand it, of the incarnation. For him two distinctions will always obtain: first, the distinction between what happened and our knowledge of its happening — for our knowledge of its happening can be shot through with approximations without affecting the basic fact of its occurrence; and secondly, the difference between the two basic ways in which we may be aware of, or related to, what has happened — by knowledge, in a critical way, and by faith, in an existential, decisional way. In Kierkegaard, therefore, we have another and particularly influential form of the movement to define the humanity of Christ in terms of particularity.

Humanity as Historicity

One of the most important ways of describing the particularity of the humanity of Christ is that which defines it to be historicity, and which thus attempts to anchor Christology in the particularity of the "Jesus of history." This will be our main concern in the second half of the present discussion. It might appear at first sight that in selecting historicity for this purpose of defining humanity in the contemporary setting, we have made a most unfortunate choice, particularly because the questions of the historical Jesus, and of the historicity of Jesus, are still among the most hotly debated of our times. The areas of controversy are fairly well known. For example, there was the early debate which arose out of Harnack's *What is Christianity?* and which still has something to say to us. This debate examined the assumed antithesis between the Jesus of history and the Christ of faith, and the validity to be assigned to the view that Jesus of Galilee presented for us what must be regarded as the essence of Christianity: the message of the Fatherhood of God, the brotherhood of man and the infinite value of the human soul. On such grounds, a strong case has been made against the traditional, ecclesiastical conception of the atonement, which, according to Harnack and his followers, was developed by Paul but which in fact distorted the "essence" of the primitive faith as proclaimed by Jesus.

George S. Hendry pointed some time ago to three circumstances which in his opinion brought the Jesus of history movement into disfavor.[14] One was a recognition that Harnack's analysis of the so-called "essence of Christianity" was a form of reductionism and oversimplification which omitted major features of the faith. To probe into the sayings of Jesus and his actions, according to Hendry, is to be impelled towards basic Christological questions. The real Jesus of history, for Hendry, raises questions which cannot be answered within the compass of Harnack's theology. The second circumstance noted by Hendry was the rise of the form-critical movement, which assigned the New Testament material to certain specific purposes of the primitive Church served by brief confessions of faith, hymns of thanksgiving, wonder-stories and so on, none of which included the provision of a precise portrait of a historical person. The third circumstance which Hendry noted as inimical to the Jesus of history movement was the development of neo-orthodox theology, with its forceful representation of the classical formulae of the faith — incarnation, atonement, resurrection, and so on — in a most comprehensive manner.

In one sense what Hendry says is true: The Jesus of history movement, with its sharp antithesis between the Jesus of history and the Christ of faith, and its underlying assumption that the historical components which form the Jesus of history are easily accessible on investigation, has been brought to a sharp halt. However, it has to be quickly recognized that the kind of distinction which Harnack promulgated has in another respect become more defined than ever, of course for reasons vastly different from those contemplated by him. For whereas Harnack, having separated the Jesus of history from the Christ of faith, laid the stress of his theology upon the former, many of his critics came to lay

14. George S. Hendry, *The Gospel of the Incarnation* (London, 1959), p. 3.

the stress of their theology upon the latter, almost to the rejection of the former, to the consequent impoverishment of their theology and indeed of their religion. The movement in this direction had begun before Harnack in the thought of Kierkegaard. Once knowledge and faith are antithesized as they were in Kierkegaard, and knowledge reduced to an approximation while faith becomes the medium of religious immediacy, then inevitably greater attention has to be paid to the contemporary subject of faith than to the ambiguities of his historical appearance. That agnosticism which we have already considered in Kierkegaard runs through the whole of the theology written a century after his *Concluding Unscientific Postscript,* uniting thinkers so widely separated in all other respects as Tillich, Bultmann, Barth and Brunner, and including in its influence those existentialists who would reject any other association with Christian theology.

The flight from historicity — one might even call it a stampede — has taken a number of forms. It is necessary to bring them all out into the open as such, so that we may thereby assess the importance of the attempt to recover the historicity of Christ and to see the place of his humanity in this attempt. One form of rejection of the historicity of Jesus is more implicit than explicit. It insists that the New Testament contains essentially the *kerygma,* the Gospel which is to be preached here and now, and which in being preached, brings men and women into direct confrontation by Jesus Christ. The exact historical origins of that *kerygma* are beyond recall, because from the very start what was intended both by those who preached the Gospel in the first instance and by the New Testament writers who prepared the Gospels as we now have them was that their hearers should receive the Good News, be converted and believe in the ever-living Christ.

(One major omission I must mention from the lengthy discussion of the *kerygma* in the second half of this century is that of a clear definition of the content of the *kerygma.* If the kind of meticulous analysis had been given to *kerygma* as was given to its running mate in that celebrated theological vaudeville act, *Kerygma and Myth,* then I feel that theology generally and New Testament theology in particular would have been considerably better served than it has been by the demythologizers over that period. *Kerygma* has all too often been the residuum left after the scum of myth has been removed, and too little the positive, dominant criterion to decide what was inalienable to living faith and what dispensable. In fact, C. H. Dodd's *Apostolic Preaching and its Development* is perhaps still the best single attempt to describe what we can regard as the message with which the primitive Church invaded an alien, unbelieving, over-religious world. Moreover, had greater detailed attention been paid to the content of the *kerygma* and less willingness shown to accept Kierkegaard's reduction of the essential, irreducible content of the faith to the fact that Christ died for the salvation of humankind, then, I would argue, that more definite content of the *kerygma* might have led scholars along the path to the rediscovery of the historical elements of the faith, back into the territory which Harnack tried to take by direct assault and which the existentialists surrendered.)

The separation from the historical Jesus took other forms. It has been argued, for example, that the Gospels were not written as contemporary comment upon what Jesus Christ said and did, the sort of thing you get daily on the radio, or in the newspaper. They were all postresurrection documents, written from the standpoint of a faith which knew that the cross was not the end of all the earthly aspirations of Christ and his disciples, that the promises which he made were eventually fulfilled, and that even his sayings carried something of the color of the eventual victory which crowned the earthly life. Let me go farther and quote the words of a colleague of my own, Hugh Anderson, who does not subscribe to the view I am at present examining, but which as he so rightly points out is the premise from which it commences: "With all assurance we can say that, save for Easter, there would have been no New Testament letters written, no Gospels compiled, no prayers offered in Jesus' name, no Church. . . . [At] the very heart of the early Church's preaching stands the word about the 'Author of life, whom God raised from the dead. To this we are witness' (Acts 3:15). Even more emphatically does Paul confirm the cruciality of Easter: 'If Christ has not been raised then our preaching is in vain and your faith is in vain' (1 Corinthians 15:14). Easter, therefore, is no addendum to other factors in the story of Jesus Christ; it is constitutive for the community's faith and worship, its discipleship and mission to the world,"[15] and we would add, for the records of what Jesus said and did. As Professor Anderson continues: "When eventually [the apostles and disciples] left their accounts of

15. Hugh Anderson, *Jesus and Christian Origins* (New York, 1964), pp. 186f.

Jesus of Nazareth, based on memories of Jesus colored by experience of the risen Christ . . . these accounts inevitably contained the 'secret' which had been divulged in the Resurrection. . . . The Gospel 'story' of Jesus could accordingly be recounted henceforward only, so to speak, as a 'kerygmatic history.'"[16] Such enthusiasm on the part of the first believers in the risen Christ for the importance of the resurrection in interpreting the pre-Easter life and death of Christ cannot be questioned; without it we would not have had our Gospels. The question really is whether, if they had not in some way themselves been convinced of the importance of the pre-Easter Jesus for the understanding of Easter resurrection, they would ever have troubled to record in such detail, and without attempting any degree of harmonization, so much about Jesus' words and actions as they did. Their conviction about the importance of this relationship, about the significance of pre-Easter for post-Easter, was itself a fact of the post-Easter, resurrection faith of the Primitive Church. Had they not held that conviction, it would have been very easy, and tempting — for the memory of Calvary was still sufficiently vivid and horrific — to suppress the unsavory and the disreputable, and to present a triumphant, all-conquering Lord of all creation.

Another form which the attempt to minimize or even to eliminate the historical features of the life of Christ is what is thought to be a throwaway admission that, after all, the Gospels are not biography. Käsemann has put the point graphically: "We have now come to see that our Gospels, with the necessary exception of Luke, are not in the least interested in the composition of a comprehensive biography of Jesus nor in investigating what has been reported about him, to see how far it is reliable and how far it corresponds to historical reality."[17] One other comment from Käsemann connects closely with our concern in this Chapter: "A primary concern of the Gospels is unmistakably the particularity with which the eschatological event is bound to this man from Nazareth, to the arena of Palestine and to a concrete time with its special circumstances."[18] While Käsemann from this quotation is seen not to be likely to eliminate the historicity of Jesus Christ — *he* is

16. Anderson, p. 241.
17. Ernst Käsemann, *Essays on New Testament Themes* (ET London, 1964), p. 30.
18. Käsemann, p. 31.

obviously much too conscious of the significance of "this man of Nazareth" for the eschatological event intended by God through Jesus Christ to allow that to happen — there are some who likewise affirm that the Gospels are not biography who see that statement as equivalent to a denial that the Gospels are historical in any sense, and to the view that the whole question of historicity is irrelevant here.

When it is denied that the Gospels are biography, a number of different contentions are being made. First, it is claimed that the Gospels do not set out to present a balanced picture of everything that Jesus said and did from the cradle to the grave, but that they omit large sections of his life and deal with others at exceptional length. Secondly, it is argued that the picture is one which has been subjected to heavy interpretation in the manifold ways expounded by New Testament scholars. Thirdly, it is asserted that the Gospels were prepared as the *kerygma,* the Good News, which when preached was hoped to lead men and women not to factually accurate knowledge of a historical period, but to faith in Jesus Christ; the Gospels were from faith to faith. What is not implied by any of these contentions, however, is that the Gospels reject the notion that what they say contains historical material, or that they invent other nonhistorical material to serve as pseudo-historical foundation for what they have to say. Far too often an assumption of the nonbiographical character of the Gospels has been taken to be equivalent to their nonhistoricity, which is, however, a quite different affair.

These, then, are several different ways in which in our time there has been a perpetuation in obviously much more sophisticated terms of Harnack's basic distinction between the Jesus of history and the Christ of faith, the distinction being drawn now in favor of the Christ of the Gospel, and at the expense of the historicity of Jesus Christ. It is very interesting to observe how, almost in every case, there is implied by the emphasis upon the Christ of faith some kind of retro-reference to the historical Jesus. Those who antithesize the *kerygma* with the historical Jesus find themselves, in supplying some adequate content to the notion of *kerygma,* increasingly driven into the middle of the material of the Gospel sayings and the miracles and the historical circumstances of the crucifixion. This connection is greatly strengthened when we note that there ought to be a greater approximation of the content of the *kerygma* to that of the Gospels, which after all formed the basis of the message, and the literary medium by which the Church spoke of Christ to the world. Too sharp an antithesis of resurrection message with Gospel story thus breaks down in face of the realization that the risen Christ who was the subject of post-Easter proclamation was always declared to be one with Jesus of Nazareth. In fact, without that continuity being spelled out in sufficiently broad terms to be recognizable, the Easter message would have been a nonsense. So, too, while biography is the wrong literary category for the Gospels, nevertheless what they had to tell was regarded by those who wrote them, as by those who heard and later read them, as a faithful account of the life that was lived and of the death died in terms of their basic factual character and of their place in God's purpose of salvation. What we have been discovering in these readily accessible examples can be illustrated at much greater length by reference to the history of post-Bultmannian New Testament scholarship, for example, in the various "new quests" for the words of Jesus (Bornkamm), or for the eschatological message he preached (Robinson), or for the conduct of Jesus (Fuchs). But in each case the intention is the same: to do justice to the irreducible core of historicity in the situation which the older Liberalism had described as the Jesus of history, by extracting it through all the filters of modern criticism and by exposing it as the irrefutable historical antecedent to the *kerygma* as preached in the primitive Church.

When, therefore, I choose to equate the humanity of Christ with the historicity of Jesus, to use the jargon, I am buying a share in this very keen contemporary controversy about the historical features of the Christian Gospels. In order to show that that purchase was not after all so disastrous, I have been illustrating the ways in which already from within New Testament scholarship itself ways are being opened up into the historical situation of the incarnate Lord. But I should like to put the case yet more strongly for attempting to explore ways into that historical situation which is of such central importance to Christian faith. Let me make the case in three ways.

First, it looks as if an undue concession has been made to the degree of agnosticism which is to be assumed present in historical knowledge. Sometimes this skepticism attempts to find support from logical and epistemological sources. Historical knowledge does not have the immediacy of sense-perceptual knowledge, nor can it rely upon personal recall as can memory-knowledge; it is not simply a combination of perception of data and logical inference, nor can it readily be seen to involve direct acquaintance with the past. In the history of philosophy, where such questions as our knowledge of the external world, our knowledge of God, even our knowledge of ourselves and of other selves have been widely debated, the problem of the nature and validity of historical knowledge has never received adequate treatment. Not even its supposedly assured probability status has been adequately discussed. The result is that the half-thought-out, indeed half-digested critique of historical knowledge, which was given such impetus in philosophy and theology by Kierkegaard, has passed into the mainstream of existentialism and through it into modern theology in most of its forms in one way or another. The consequences have been a gross distortion in the assessment of the historicity of the Gospel records and of the authenticity to be attached to statements made by the writers concerning Jesus' words and actions. A virtue has been made of necessity; when reenforcing Kierkegaard's rather artificial antithesis of faith and knowledge with distinctions between the Jesus of history and the Christ of faith, theologians and New Testament scholars have comforted themselves with the theory that, even if the history goes and knowledge of it becomes totally problematical, no matter — faith will secure our relation for us in the here-and-now. If there is one service which philosophy can offer theology at this time to atone for the neglect of over a century, it is to conduct a careful examination of the nature of historical knowledge and to make a precise judgment as to the possibility, in the first place, and next, the true content, of such knowledge. There is what amounts to a professional agnosticism in respect of historical material in modern theological and biblical scholarship which requires to be exorcised. It is an agnosticism which rests on rather insufficient grounds, and until the grounds are reexamined there is a strong case for accepting some kind of *prima facie* authenticity for historical knowledge.

Secondly, the trouble with those who are skeptical concerning the knowledge we can have of the historical Jesus, and of the Gospels as reasonably accurate records of what he did and said is that they are never completely consistent. David Hume in his *Dialogues Concerning Natural Religion* demonstrated that no one is ever a consistent skeptic; if he were, he could never move from the spot on which he is standing. Skepticism is like dumplings and measles: it is spotty. Thus scholars who are skeptical in their judgment of the value of the Gospels as records concerning Christ are by comparison almost credulous in their approach to what these same documents have to say about the mind of the primitive Church. In this connection, the records may not be untrustworthy in quite the same sort of way, but the genuine skeptic will not be able to resist a question about their authenticity in other ways. The high degree of emotion attaching to their subject matter, the obvious concern of the writers to establish the status of their hero, their anxiety over their own position in the world, these and other factors could readily distort their accuracy of report — even if it is taken as a report *on themselves*. "They that take the sword shall perish by the sword," nowhere more surely than where the sword is the sword of the skeptic. Clearly, then, once the illogicality of "here a little skepticism, there a little skepticism," the fatuity of a kind of theological old Macdonald's farm, is properly grasped, and once it is acknowledged that we have to trust some of the records some of the time, then it becomes immediately clear that the way is opening up for reentry into the area of the historical Jesus. This entry will be effected, not because we believe that such knowledge as we are granted will make faith any easier, for it may make it more difficult, but because without it the Easter message, the resurrection faith, the kerygmatic proclamation will float away untethered to the ground of historical occurrence and of the human condition.

Thirdly, attention must be drawn to what is another unstated but genuinely assumed consequence of the historical skepticism endemic in most theological and biblical scholarship over the past half-century, namely, that if we have skeptical views about the *records* of the historical life of Christ, then we thereby disprove his historical existence. Usually, the point is made by the critics of the historical skeptics when they begin to fear that the erosive effect of agnosticism is destructive, finally, not only of the believer's faith in the historicity of its Lord, but even of the very fact of his earthly existence. It is made so much of by the critics that the historical skeptics who are also theological and biblical scholars begin to believe it themselves. They can have faith whether Christ lived or not *then*, for he is alive *now*. In the hands of a writer like Schubert Ogden, such a position has been taken to the logical conclusion of maintaining that the authentic existence of the life of faith can be not only formulated and described but lived apart from the historical phenomenon of Jesus of Nazareth.[19] While one admires Ogden's con-

19. Schubert Ogden, *Christ Without Myth* (London, 1962).

sistency, one can only wonder how such a position could be regarded as Christian. There is then, so I have said, a basic epistemological misunderstanding operating here. Granted that our knowledge of the historical Jesus is dependent upon records which may at points not be historically accurate in the sense of providing a carefully balanced portrait or biography; granted that we may have our historical inconsistencies; nevertheless, so long as we are prepared to make some statements about historical elements in the Gospels, we have tacitly acknowledged that the inadequacy of our knowledge does not rob the subject, whom we know, of his existence. Being and knowledge are two different things, and though we would have the gravest doubts about the existence of some being of whom *all* our knowledge proved to be totally unreliable or self-contradicting or just fantasy, yet so long as we attach some authenticity to our knowledge we are implicitly affirming the reality of the being we know. Such an affirmation commits us to the further exploration by means of historical science and textual criticism of the texts of Scripture, full in the face of the bluff of the historical skeptics who have worked their confidence trick on the rest of us far too long now.

How, then, does this discussion of the historicity of the historical Jesus and the authenticity of the Gospel records as witness to his life link up with our central theme of the humanity of Christ? The connection is, I am convinced, direct and immediate. The discussion of the historicity of Jesus is *eo ipso* a discussion of his humanity. Alternatively, the argument concerning the historical structure and content of the incarnation is the modern form which the argument about the humanity of Jesus Christ is taking. As we build up the historical material, we are in that process constructing the detail of the humanity of Christ. Accordingly, the concern for that historical material yields support for the theme of the humanity as particularity. The humanity which we reach through historical research is that of "*this* man of Nazareth," even when, with the Gospel writers and the theological interpreters of the Gospel, we add that "this man" is the bearer of the revelation of God, the medium and mediator of the divine purpose of redemption. The particular, the individual we have always been told, is the category of the historical, and Jesus Christ is no exception. His historical particularity, in so far as it is human, he shares with the rest of us. To except him from that condition would be to place his humanity once again at risk.

Given our situation today, separated by two thousand years from the event of the incarnation, relying as we must so heavily upon the records which mediate that event to us, then the only way in which we can explore the humanity that constitutes the core of that event is to direct our minds and hearts to these records. There is no short cut, nor dare we ever be deceived into thinking that there is by those who say that historical knowledge is not faith. Two points are clear. First, if the historical knowledge finally goes, then faith rapidly becomes a mysticism with little substantial basis to support it and ultimately with no soteriological message to relieve the way of its own oppression by the One, or Perfection, or whatever the object of contemplation is going to be called. Secondly, it still remains the case that for those who wish to know God through Christ, the one way is through the Bible and the records of Christ which it has preserved. The historical question, with its implications for the humanity of Christ, is still the most central problem which our faith has to face. In a sense, God has gambled on the historicity of Christ as on his humanity. He is only "dead" when that gamble is lost, for he is placing stakes nowhere else.

So far, I have been presenting the humanity of Christ in this section as if it were a rather reluctant partner in the association with the historicity of Christ. In fact, we may with profit present the roles in the reverse order. It is perhaps an immense help to those who are fighting the battle of historicity to be aware that it is also the case for the humanity of Christ that they are advancing. The two have been allowed to separate. Yet every reduction of the historically permissible minimal core of the Christian faith is to that same degree a dehumanization of Christ. If the humanity of Christ is only the tangential contact of the Divine nature with the human in the conception of Jesus or the crucifixion or the Resurrection, then the human nature becomes insubstantial, wraithlike. If that humanity is to be genuine, then it has to be part of the historical process, and the efforts to recover the historical matter of Christ's existence are in fact efforts to find the true dimensions of the humanity of Jesus Christ. In a sentence, the dehistoricization of the faith which is thought to be implied by existentialist theologies as critical theories is the docetism of the twentieth century, because by its skepticism it takes humanity out of the only milieu in which it can possibly exist, namely, historical process. It is, of course, wrong to use names, or worse nicknames, as big sticks to frighten people with. Yet existentialism, which has contributed so much in our time to the understanding of what it is to be human — *this* person at this time in this place with responsibility for this future — must not allow its insights when applied to Christ to be snatched from its grasp and ours, by that problem component within it, namely, historical skepticism. Theological existentialism will have to make a choice here, and my forecast is that it will in the end surrender its skepticism if its entail is docetism.

These are the considerations which sway me when I am asked what I consider to be the discipline closest to theology in matter and purpose, and I have to reply: "history." In that discipline there is concern with records, their authenticity, their composition, their clues to the mind and character of their authors. There is in history preoccupation with human beings in all their uniqueness and particularity as well as in their togetherness with one another; in short there is concern with humanity. All of these items occur in theology and are handled in theology in ways not at all dissimilar to historical method. If our theological historians for reasons of pseudo-piety outstrip their lay fellows in their enthusiasm for skepticism, they may be brought back from their excesses by the reminder that to question as they do the historicity of the records and ultimately the historical Jesus is to put the very humanity of Christ in question. So, too, to pursue the historical question is not so much to seek to substitute knowledge for faith, or research for obedience, but rather to seek the humanity of Christ which remains the only foundation of faith either in the deity of Christ or the reality of God.

CHAPTER 4

Humanity as Morality

Why Morality?

The dangers which seem to arise from any attempt to define the humanity of Christ in terms of morality are immediately obvious and all too familiar. For example, it seems as if by even suggesting such a possibility we have automatically presented the incarnation as no more than the provision by God of a moral example for human beings to follow. Any mention of an ethical quality in relation to the incarnation has the immediate effect of calling up specters of a now dead and gone Liberalism and of seeming to turn the wheel of theological development back through 180 degrees. Or again, it may be thought that it entails a reduction of the significance of the incarnation, the entry of the Word into the Flesh, on the one hand, and on the other of the atonement, as the twin pillars supporting the cause of salvation. To try to link the pillars by means of the morality which is seen in Christ's humanity is thereby to diminish their responsibility in the divine economy of salvation. Between them they must be seen to bear the load of the redemption of humankind. Further, if it simply has to be acknowledged that the moral being and behavior of Christ are of importance and value, these are so not in relation to any part this morality plays in the work of salvation, but by way of illustration, say, of how we must live.

In view of the many questions which can be placed against the role of morality in interpreting the humanity of Christ, it is not surprising that in a good deal of modern theology and Christology the moral content of his humanity has been minimal, for example, in those treatments of his humanity which minimize its importance by describing it almost exclusively in functional or mediatorial terms. Thus, the humanity sometimes appears in the role of Logos-bearer, as the earthly manifestation through which the Logos is enabled to make his presence known in human society and history, providing the physical arena as it were for the incarnation. In such a conception, the weight of interest and attention must obviously fall on the Logos, while a great deal is made, as we have noted already, of the problem of how far he retains in this incarnate context the full powers and attributes of his preincarnate existence. His humanity merely supplies the occasion for the incarnation, sometimes without contributing anything of its own to the event. Secondly, when emphasis is to be laid upon the atoning death of Christ, or upon both his life and death in an atoning capacity, once again the humanity has been regarded as the instrument through which the atonement is effected. It exercises a mediatorial role, but once more the value which the occasion has, the results it effects, derive from the real agent in the situation, which is the Logos. Thirdly, we have ourselves in the recent discussion of Christ's humanity as particularity and as historicity fallen into the same kind of trap, in so far as we have given the impression that the humanity of Christ is, as it were, an index to historicity, the sure and certain indicator that the *kerygma* cannot be dehistoricized. Conversely, by arguing as we did that historicity is the mode in which the humanity of Christ is now to be discussed and defended, perhaps we ourselves conformed in great measure to the fashion of formalizing that humanity, categorizing it, and so reducing it to an abstraction. It is most important that we for our part should correct the imbalance by supplying a *content*, including a *moral* content, to the form. Fourthly, for genuinely laudable theological reasons, others have made what must be regarded as a similar error by presenting the humanity of Christ as a kind of revelation-window, the means whereby the believer perceives, beyond Christ's humanity, the divine Word. John Robinson stated this view — without, of course, being committed to some of the implications I would draw from it — when he wrote, "Jesus is a window through the surface of things into God."[1] The idea here was that the human nature should be in some way transparent, whereas, as we shall argue here and in the next chapter, it ought to be seen in its own light, as having its own

1. John A. T. Robinson, *Honest to God* (London, 1963), p. 128.

significance, its own filling. There is at stake here, of course, the whole question of the nature of revelation, which need not meanwhile detain us; for the present, what is of note is that the view of revelation which pictures the human nature of Christ purely as a window to the divine empties that human nature of intrinsic significance and reduces any interest that we might wish to have in its moral character. Fifthly, it is difficult at times to avoid the criticism that in many of the classical Christological controversies, as in many of their modern revivals, the human nature of Christ has appeared almost like a metaphysical counter in a complicated game, or, to change the figure, the result reached after a complicated arithmetical calculation in subtraction or division. The whole exercise, one feels, could have been carried out with a proper set of symbols and without anything so full of flesh and blood as humanity. That description may well be partly caricature, but it does carry truth so long as we fail to look at the humanity of Christ in the round, as a true human nature like ours, and therefore as a nature which can and must be characterized in terms of morality.

P. T. Forsyth stated what I have been saying, though in his own more forceful language:

> The modern moralization of religion prescribes a new manner of inquiry on such a central subject as the person of Christ. It plants us anew on the stand point of the Bible, where all human ethic is pointed, transfigured and reissued in Christ's new creation of the moral soul. . . . Was it by a moral way, by moral conquest, that Christ came to his final glory? Then it must have been by a moral way that he left it. Is the end of our salvation a moral glory? Then the origin of it must have issued from moral glory. Is it an eternal salvation? Then its moral glory rose in a moral Eternity. Did the Eternal come by a transcendent moral act? Then that act began in Eternity. A final salvation means a saving act eternal and absolute. Some metaphysic is here involved, certainly, but it is a metaphysic of the conscience. It starts from the conviction that for life and history the moral is the real, and that the movements of the Great Reality must be morally construed as they are morally revealed. The spiritual world is not the world of noetic process or cosmic force, but of holy, i.e. moral, order, act, and power.[2]

2. P. T. Forsyth, *The Person and Place of Jesus Christ* (London, 1909), pp. 222f.

The point of Forsyth's protest must be taken, for the metaphysical categories of theology, such as omnipotence, and of Christology, such as the concepts of *hypostasis* and *physis*, have not traditionally been given clear moral connotations.

From the point of view of our present discussion, and by way of introduction to what follows, I should like to make two comments on what Forsyth has said in this quotation. First of all, what he is interested in is the moralizing of general theological categories, for example, relating goodness to omnipotence, omniscience to love, absoluteness to mercy and the introduction of moral categories within the great centers of faith, incarnation and atonement. But he seems to do so in a way that is doubly defective. On the one hand, he appears totally insensitive to the problem of how the moral categories (which are part of our own experience) are not only applicable to a transcendent reality but also serve to modify those other attributes which do not exist in us but do characterize that reality. Part of the problem which he ignores is the problem of analogy, but part also is that of how attributes condition, limit, define, even moralize one another within God's nature. On the other hand, he does not notice that there ought to be a moralizing not just of God's attributes and actions but also of those of the humanity of Jesus Christ. In fact some efforts in that direction would serve as a proper introduction to moralizing in the direction of the divine attributes, if we genuinely hold, as Forsyth did, to the fully Christocentric approach. The second comment which I have to make is that, despite his concern for the moralizing of the religious categories, Forsyth does not offer any extensive analysis of them or what is meant by them. He seems to take it for granted that it is totally sufficient to name the process of moralizing without indication of what it implies. Yet the concepts of morality in general, and what constitutes moral behavior, in fact what religious status is to be given to moral behavior are subjects of hot dispute in theological circles. It is important therefore to provide some kind of analysis for the term, some filling which clearly indicates areas of connotation and does not leave all to the imagination. For our present purpose, at least, that must be our remit, for with the theme of Christ's humanity as morality, we are committed to exploring this controversial territory, controversial in itself, but doubly so in the Christological reference.

In answer, therefore, to our opening question, "Why morality?" we can now give our answer: The humanity of Christ is in danger of becoming a metaphysical concept in a complex conceptual game, and is also at times regarded solely as a meaning-bearer, rather than as something meaningful in itself, or as a bracket or an occasion and not a thing in itself. The most effective single way of meeting these several dangers is to supply the concept with content, there being none more adequate than that of morality — which is itself life, behavior, motivation, act, and decision.

The Structures or Patterns of Morality

It might be thought that the most obvious way to approach this whole question would have been to launch at once into a catalogue of what could be called the classical Christian virtues, to detail them all and apply them to Christ's human nature as the supreme perfection of all goodness. In spite of its obviousness, and maybe too its traditional simplicity of treatment, that approach does not altogether commend itself to me. It suggests too much that the virtues are quasi-labels which attach to Christ, he being the whole set and we being only some, or he having large ones, we having small and rather tattered versions of the same. I want to propose that we look at what are normally called the Christian virtues as structures, constructed of relations into which we enter with other persons and other things and above all with God, or alternatively, as patterns which govern the behavior of a person in the situations in which he or she is found. The virtues, that is, are not static attributes or qualities; rather, they are behavioral patterns, structures of action, relationships and attitudes and value systems.

Before proceeding to the detailed discussion, let me draw attention to what has become a widely agreed feature of morality, namely, the sociality of morality. The sociality of morality is affirmed not primarily because it is a peculiar quality of morality as such, but because it is a derivative from the sociality of human existence. In the I-Thou philosophy of Martin Buber, where the *inter*-personal nature of the basic structure of our existence prescribes not only the relationships in which we find ourselves but also the attitudes and intellectual reactions we are obliged to adopt, morality is involved in this network of personal relationships and so shares with them the quality of sociality. A similar definition of the sociality of human existence is found in Karl Barth's doctrine of creation in the *Church Dogmatics*.[3] He begins by quoting Genesis 1:26f.: "Then God said, 'Let us make humankind in our image, according to our likeness; and let them have dominion over the fish of the sea, and over the birds of the air, and over the cattle, and over all the earth, and over every creeping thing that creeps upon the earth.' So God created humankind in his image, in the image of God he created them; male and female he created them." Barth uses the passage to establish the point that the image of God is not to be construed in solitary terms, but rather in terms of man in relation to woman — "male and female he created them" — as if the basic human unit were not a man or a woman solo, but "man-and-woman." I do not wish to draw further attention to the idiosyncrasies of such exegesis, but simply to take the valid point which Barth is making, namely, that a man or a woman always exists in relationship to other people, and is only properly human in such relationships.

What began in the likes of Buber and Barth as a philosophical and even an exegetical analysis subsequently became a commonplace of human thought, namely, the sociality of our existence, our awareness of the relationship not just of sympathy but of responsibility which we bear to others throughout the world. Not least of all, when distance separates us widely from those who are in distress, when the presence of such distress in our own homes by means of television serves only to increase our impotence to help, we are nonetheless acutely aware of our responsibility towards such people in distress because of our deeply human solidarity with them. Bonhoeffer makes the same point: "Man is not conceived of by God . . . as an isolated, individual being, but as in natural communication with other men. . . . God does not desire a history of individual men, but the history of the community of men. Nor does he desire a community which absorbs the individual into itself. . . . In his sight the community and the individual are present at the same moment, and rest in one another. The structures of the individual and the collective unit are the same."[4] It is a short step, therefore, for Bonhoeffer to take when he goes on to think of Jesus Christ as "God in human form, not, as in other religions, in animal form — the monstrous, chaotic, remote and terrifying — nor yet in abstract

3. Barth, *Church Dogmatics*, III/1 (ET Edinburgh, 1958), pp. 184f.

4. Dietrich Bonhoeffer, *Sanctorum Communio* (ET London, 1963), p. 52.

form — the absolute, metaphysical, infinite, etc. — nor yet in the Greek divine-human of autonomous man, but man existing for others, and hence the Crucified."[5] But this man-for-others notion has to be seen, not as an extra dimension added to human nature by Christ at the incarnation, but as a dimension of humanity as such. It is an oversimplification to think of human beings as selfish, self-centered, and of salvation through Christ as involving our being turned outward to others, so that redeemed humanity learns, following Christ, to be "for others" too. Natural humanity is already Bonhoeffer's "man-for-others"; our sin consists in the distortions which we introduce into these constitutive relationships with others — for our deceptions, betrayals, lies, insincerities, and crimes all depend for their very occurrence upon our already being in relationships. The redemption involves the renewing of these distorting relationships so that our being-for-others is a being-for-their-good. To sum up then, the sociality in morality is not something which morality *adds* to some nonsocial character of human existence. The sociality is a *function* of that humanity, a form which it may take to ensure the well-being of our relation to one another.

The Structure of Love

To return now to the discussion of the patterns of morality, the examination of the sociality of morality being the demonstration of the substantial pattern of all morality, may I begin at the most obvious starting place, the *love-structure.* By stressing the structural element in love, we endeavor to draw emphasis away from the idea that love is a feeling, a warm inner coziness, a spiritual electric blanket, an idea which made it easy for Brunner to say that it is paradoxical to give the command "Love thy neighbor," because an emotion can never be summoned up. "Thou shalt love" interpreted as an imperative to enter into a number of specifiable relations to your neighbor and to your enemy, carries no such inherent paradoxicality. What I have called the love-structure becomes a vast complex of different structures which I have elsewhere specified and need not repeat here at any length, namely, the structures of concern, communication, commitment, community, involvement, identification, response and re-

5. As quoted by Robinson, p. 76.

sponsibility.[6] Concern is our sensitivity to the plight in which our fellow human beings exist and our anxiety to be related helpfully to them. Communication is our success in making known to them our intention to help, our sympathy with them and our understanding of them. Commitment is our specific decision not to stand outside of their situation as observers, but to be actively engaged to take action of some sort or another. We have made the decision; we have crossed the Rubicon. Community is the close relationship of togetherness achieved by the abandonment of all self-separation from the plight, the need, the difficulty, the hunger, the fear or others. Love is now side-by-side with the other person in his or her distressful situation. When involvement is reached, then one person has taken on responsibilities within that situation, acts on behalf of the other person, and has begun to move the situation around to achieve a better result for the friend. Identification is the final step in this process, which is one of increasingly close relationship between the two persons concerned. Identification is close to absorption of one person in the purposes, hopes, fears, anxieties, joys of another, but it stops short of a loss of the self in the other, for through all of this we must still remain ourselves.

Three comments occur to me concerning that rehearsal of the structures which together make up what I have been calling the complex love-structure. First, they represent what might be called "stages in love's way," a progressive deepening of the relationship which at any stage is to be regarded as the love relationship. These stages not only define for us what love means, in an age in which this relationship has many imitations and substitutes as well as total misrepresentations, but they chart out for us a kind of route to follow in the development of the relationship, a kind of practical counterpart to the medieval mystic's ladder to the beatific vision. That practical charting enables us to assess the degree of sincerity of our own love for our fellow men and women.

Secondly, since compiling these "stages in love's way" some years ago, I have asked myself whether the list was adequate and complete. Two modifications have occurred to me, both of which I think are admissible, though one after qualification. The first addition is that love is *imagination.*[7] So much of our unloving, or cruelty to one another, or

6. McIntyre, *On the Love of God* (London and New York, 1962), *passim.*
7. Cf. John McIntyre, *Faith Theology and Imagination* (Edinburgh, 1987), pp. 65ff.

insensitivity, is due to sheer failure in imaginative appreciation of the stress under which other people live, the temptations they have to face, their fears and anxieties. Clearly, if love is to operate at all, it must be permeated with a strong element of imagination. But positively, it is imagination that transports us into the situation of the other, enables us to feel what it is like to stand in another's place, and to begin vicariously to experience something of his or her emotions, and through that empathy to be reenforced in the motivation which will lead to the processes of commitment, involvement and identification. It is imagination, also, which turns bare statistics and factual reports into the personalized terms of starving children with no hope of life beyond three months, of homes broken up forever, or of career ambitions reduced to shreds. Imagination, therefore, fulfills the double role, cognitively of enabling us to think ourselves into a state of affairs from which we are removed by physical distance or by the manner of its presentation to us, and emotionally of providing the spur to action in relation to the situation so understood. The second addition to the catalogue of the constituents of the love relationship which has occurred to me is the idea of *acceptance.* Acceptance is obviously a necessary feature of love, the willingness to take a person as he or she is, without enquiring into their "background," to use a slanderous term, without asking whether there is an intention to improve habits or abandon grudges, without laying down any conditions for the future continuance of the relationship. Acceptance is a key feature of any pastoral relationship, implying as it does rejection of any judgmental attitudes to the other person. It is at the root of all forgiveness, both preceding and following it. The objection might be raised by those professionally involved in pastoralia that the notion of acceptance is somewhat too passive, and that it must be replaced by, or at least implemented by, a process of participation in the situation which is accepted, or with the person who is being accepted. The point is a valid one, for such acceptance could well entail taking the person on his or her own terms to the extent of compromising with the situation which is intolerable or hopeless or plainly morally wrong. By advancing beyond acceptance into participation in the situation, the love felt begins to take action, to show caring in deed and not just in word. In fact "participation" I should read as a synonym for "involvement" and "identification," so that to some extent the participation element is already covered. If, therefore, the passive elements can be eliminated from the idea of acceptance, and it is closely related to participation, involvement and identification, then we could perhaps adopt it.

Thirdly, once again, I should like to draw attention to the fact that we have here been speaking of human love as a structure in human morality, always with an eye ultimately to the fact that it is this human nature, with this morality, with this love-structure, which Christ takes. If we are to remain within the terms of our claims for Christ of the genuineness of his humanity, then it must be so. At the same time, all of these constituents in the morality which he evinces, the love which he shows to men and women, will be heightened, intensified, purified, but they will be essentially the same components, and that is the important point.

The Structure of Hope

One frequently ignored contribution of the Christian Gospel to the Roman Empire of the first century was a promise of hope. Looking backwards, we have seen in the concept of love the major emphasis of the primitive Church, and our own Reformed training has led us to make much of the notion of faith. But in a world in which an ordinary member of Roman society had nothing to look forward to, because of the absence of any belief in afterlife, and in which a philosopher could contemplate an endless, repetitive cycle of events in history, it was reassuring to learn of the realities of resurrection in Jesus Christ and of the consummation of all history in a final act of God in Jesus Christ. At a time when the notion of hope has been revived from within Christian theology by writers such as Jürgen Moltmann[8] and by liberation theology, I should like to offer now what could be called the *anatomy* of hope, indicating its main structural features. First, hope begins by affirming the reality of whatever causes despair. It looks at hunger, at underprivilege; it looks at bad housing, unemployment, biological and chemical warfare; it looks at the drug situation, child abuse, terrorism. It looks at them all, and it acknowledges their dark reality with open eyes. Hope here stands opposed to the banal, rosy-spectacled rubbish

8. E.g., his *Theology of Hope* (ET London, 1967).

about the clouds all having silver linings, and about the darkest hour of night being just before the dawn. Hope does not begin until you really come to terms with the facts that the clouds have no silver lining, that the night is unendingly dark, and that the road ahead sometimes has no turning. If you do not come to terms with those facts, then you spend the rest of your life running away from them. Hope, in other words, is the sharpest, the most acute, the most perspicacious kind of realism. We reject the image of hope as the blindfolded woman playing the last remaining string on her harp. The image is wrong, because hope is not blindfolded. Its eyes are wide open — to the truth, to reality, to things as they are, however squalid, revolting, or heartbreaking. Hope affirms the facts.

Secondly, hope recognizes the impossibility of any rational or imaginative escape from the situation. Hope, in other words, is still going along with despair. It has faced the facts. It has assessed them, and measured them, this way and that; it has probed and pushed them, and tried over and over again to extract from them some grain of explanation, some iota of justification. It has all failed. There is no rational structure to what has happened. This aspect of hope — its failure to impose any kind of rational interpretation upon the despair-creating facts — has nothing less than canonical status in the book of Job. There, as disaster after disaster hits Job, he rejects the religious and high-sounding explanations of his fairweather friends. He throws them all back in their teeth as failures to account for the tragic dimensions of the evil that was beginning to break him. Hope recognizes, too, the total failure of any imaginative escape from the hard facts of the case.

Thirdly, hope refuses to accept the situation — of hunger, misery, sorrow, unemployment — as final. Hope still believes in the future. It is at this point that hope categorically breaks with despair. For despair, the present is the end. Everything has been shattered. There is nothing left to live for, nothing still to be expected from life. We have come to the end of the road. Despite its realism, despite its open acknowledgment that there is no rational or imaginative escape from the situation, hope still declares that there is a future. It is interesting that it is often at this point that communists have shown their keenest interest in Christianity. It is almost as if they had begun to see that determinism, like patriotism, is not enough. They have preached for so long and so much that men and women are caught in the enslaving toils of the economic machine that they have almost entirely destroyed the very possibility of hope by denying the future. If you are a slave to the machine, if you are literally enmeshed in its gears, then you have no future. All you have is a past. It is all locked up there, and if you insist that you have a future then it is just your past over again. The fact that intellectual communism in Europe reached this stage, the full awareness that its own teaching severs the possibility of change by denying the future, has proven to be crucial to its downfall.

So to the final structural feature of the anatomy of hope: Hope looks to the future, not as to a vague shapelessness or emptiness, but in the confident expectation of some sort of delivery, redemption or salvation. But its evidence is hard to find. It is not found in rational justification, or in imaginative projections. One piece of evidence which St. Paul mentions is that "the love of God has flooded our hearts." The hope, in other words, does not rest on our own private convictions, even upon our faith, which by some subtle metamorphosis could be transformed into hope. The evidence for the hope is implanted in us by the love of God. It is his assurance that nothing can break the bonds with which he has bound us to himself. Put in another way, the hope is grounded in the fact that the God who has in Christ undergone the solitariness of Gethsemane and the agony of Calvary is not likely to allow anything which this world can do to us, finally to pluck us from his grasp. That is the dynamic of Christian hope. That is what gives it the confidence that it can change the future, change the world, change society, make history. To the communist, then, we shall have finally to say that you cannot have that drive, that dynamic, that will to change, that possibility of change, without the ground on which it all rests, the love of God shed in Calvary's profusion and now flooding our inmost heart. In a word, you cannot have our hope without God.

Finally, to relate this discussion of hope to our interest in the humanity of Christ, we observe that these same structural features were apparent in Christ's own view of his human life in the world: He was realistic about his own future, the death he must die at the hands of the authorities. Nevertheless, he was confident that the God whose will it was that he should be incarnate would not finally desert him, and that beyond the crucifixion there would be for him as for all his disciples a fullness of real, radically different life.

The Structure of Trust

We come next to that aspect of the structure of morality which derives from the creaturely status of humanity with the world and nature. This feature of human morality is particularly worthy of mention in reference to Jesus Christ, because its presence is an indicator of the authenticity of his humanity. He analyzed with accuracy the anxious condition in which people ultimately find themselves, who are constantly giving thought to the morrow, to the provision of more and better goods for themselves, forgetting the degree of their dependence upon God for everything that they have and are. Such trust, like love and hope, has certain structural features. First, it springs from an awareness of human finiteness, which does not, however, pass over into either despair about that finiteness or conviction of its sinfulness. Humanity is finite, but is so with that mature finiteness which can find security in a reality which does not show in the finiteness and instability of its own being. At the same time, such finiteness as humanity has is not to be equated with sinfulness; to be a creature is not to be a sinner. Finiteness becomes sin when the creature forgets its finiteness and ignores the insecurity of its position, and its own insufficiency. It is not difficult, nor is it unjustified, to universalize this particular aspect of the analysis, to draw attention to the ways in which such finiteness and what humanity does about the limitedness of its existence lie at the root of so many contemporary psychological, psychiatric, social and political evils. That Jesus Christ should have shown himself so sensitive to this situation is for me a clue to the extent of his involvement in our human situation.

Secondly, the analysis of this basic condition, the diagnosis of the human situation, is not in itself, however, part of the moral structure of trust, though trust happens in that context. Trust is what the moral-religious person does about his or her finiteness. Such a person recognizes it — there is no alternative for a creature — but then sets it against one who is the Creator, in whom are made good the deficiencies, the uncertainties, the inadequacies and the sin of the forgetfulness of finiteness. This trust may cover a wide range of intensity — from the recognition that worry will make no difference anyway to the outcome of our present distresses or limitations; or from the quiet self-assurance which, admitting to its own limitations, endeavors to live within them, to the simple acceptance of the fact that "the Lord will provide," or the courageous affirmation that "in everything God works for good with those who love him." Such total abandonment of his own life and destiny to the care of God was again a mark of the genuineness of the humanity of Christ, and an indication of how our lives should be oriented in similar situations of insecurity and finiteness.

Thirdly, such trust has obviously had to be described in religious terms, though I should prefer to say that the terms were ethico-religious. Essentially, trust is the relation to God, but it has to work itself out in the complexity of our precarious relation to the world around us and to our friends within it. Some excerpts of the total structure of trust may be maintained in isolation from the rest; some of the ethical attitudes which recognize human finitude but do not affirm the need for dependence upon God may be noticed in Stoicism. But whether such ethical attitudes can be maintained in an altogether stable position, without toppling over either into a pessimism which is hard-shell subservience to anything that happens by saying that it certainly will happen, or into an indifference which does not care what happens, is very much a moot point.

Stewardship as a Moral Structure

It is difficult to resist the judgment that the trust which accepts its dependence upon God and does not allow itself to become too anxious about tomorrow might, if carried to extremes, result in a degree of irresponsibility. It certainly has on occasion resulted in a degree of indifference to the natural order which has had harmful consequences for the natural environment. It is not possible to develop a Christian ecology at this stage of our discussion, but I should like to note that the responsibility to God for what happens in nature has now become a major part of our moral purpose in the world. The concept of stewardship is written into the New Testament itself, above all in Jesus' parables of the faithful and unfaithful stewards (Luke 12:42ff.; 61:1ff.) — though the New English Bible, by an unforgivable lapse, translates the word *oikonomos* first of all as "steward" but later as "bailiff," a word of unusual offensiveness to most Scotsmen. In this gross mistranslation it actually comes close to doing what Calvinism never quite succeeded in doing, namely, to destroy the whole concept of stewardship. Calvinism had, with its notion of the *dominium* of humankind over nature, done a great deal towards fostering the idea that human beings can make the lesser orders in creation serve their own purposes. Humankind is not bound to them by any lines of responsibility or care. The idea of a "bailiff," whose role seems to be more that of keeping trespassers off the master's property in a somewhat negative way than of positively developing it, does not do much for the concept of stewardship. Here we have, not only a piece of literary ham-fistedness, but a theological omission of considerable magnitude.

Over against this tendency, our use of the concept of stewardship is a recognition of the fact that we are in a world which was, like ourselves, created for a purpose. If this purpose is not carefully fostered, if we use and abuse it solely for our own purposes, nature will have its revenge upon us. It may be possible to argue for a responsible ecology purely on the basis of our responsibility for future generations, that is, to people who are as yet nonexistent. However, selfish considerations often enter in at this point as a deterrent to genuine ecological responsibility, such as a realization that we ourselves have had to accept the world as we got it, with its slagheaps, human waste, and air pollution, and that just as we have had to make the best of a bad job, so should our descendants — especially those who are not *our* children or children's children. My own judgment is that little short of a fully religious acknowledgment of the fact that God has placed us in the world as his stewards will supply adequate motivation for a complete ecological concern. That judgment has to be made in face of all the religious evidence showing how intemperate religious people have been in the past, with Calvinistic fury squeezing the last penny of profit out of the mines, the soil, the miners and putting nothing back, or with other worldly unconcern leaving the natural world to its own devices, unguarded and untended. Against this, a Christian sense of ecological stewardship is perhaps the greatest single moral discovery of our time. It may even prove to be the single good byproduct of nuclear power and weaponry, which have made us aware, as nothing else could, of our supreme responsibilities within nature and to nature.

Service and Self-Sacrifice in the Structure of Morality

One of the interesting features of the moral structures which we have been examining is the way in which ordinary everyday situations are accepted as paradigmatic of moral and ethico-religious situations. This fact is nowhere in greater evidence than in the case of self-sacrifice and service. "Unless a grain of wheat falls into the earth and dies, it remains just a single grain; but if it dies, it bears much fruit. Those who love their life lose it, and those who hate their life in this world will keep it for eternal life" (John 12:24-25). Dying to live is a feature of everyday existence. The seed falls into the ground and dies, but from it springs the new life of the wheat. This natural, recurrent process is made by Jesus into a symbol of the life of total service, not only to God, but also to other people. "No one has greater love than this, to lay down one's life for one's friends" (John 15:13). A structure of subhuman existence is first taken as a structure for human morality and then in its turn for service both to Christ and to God. The transference from the natural order to the moral structure may seem like a category-mistake, but it conceals the imperative which can with little difficulty be exposed. In the natural order there is no choice before the grain of wheat thrown into the ground. If it falls upon the right soil it will germinate. As another parable reminds us, if it does not, it will either be choked with weeds or trodden underfoot. But the person does have the choice which is denied the grain of wheat. One may elect to lose one's life to save it, or elect to give up one's life for one's friends. What is a natural sequence in the natural order becomes a choice, a promise, a sanction in the moral order. For our present discussion, the significance of this structure of morality is that, not only does it show that at this point, too, the humanity of Christ receives content and character from the morality of the humanity which it adopts, but that through this humanity, and more particularly, through this moral structure of self-sacrifice and service which is part and parcel of the humanity he assumed, Christ effects the salvation which was the purpose of the incarnation. Christ died to live — he was crucified, dead and buried; the third day he rose again from the dead. The self-sacrificial dying and living was adopted, exemplified, fulfilled and its purposes demonstrated for all time.

Openness

At this point it would be normal to proceed to the analysis of the structure of freedom, but I would prefer in the present context to speak of openness rather than freedom. The two concepts are slightly different, but it is hoped that we can accept what is contained in freedom and move on from it. Freedom is presented so often, almost to the point of boredom, in terms of freedom from and freedom for; it has regard to those circumstances from which the agent has been liberated, whether social and economic pressures, the hidden persuaders, the not-so-hidden pressures of friends or political agents or the like, as well as to the opportunities for the fulfillment of which the agent has been freed, such as service to others, an education, a career in the army or a life as a writer. A certain amount of this material "brushes off" on the concept of openness which I shall be using in its place. Openness is very much a directional concept and it may be defined in that way. First, morality is openness to the claims of other persons, and of the situations in which they and we find ourselves in relation to one another. It is sensitivity to the ways these claims affect us, disturb us, inconvenience us, and morality is determination to remain open to these claims in spite of all such contrary circumstances. Immorality occurs when openness is replaced by closedness, by total rejection of the claims of others in the circumstances of their presenting themselves to us. It occurs when we see the hungry, the homeless, the underprivileged, the dispossessed, and find in ourselves no response, to the point of even rejecting all of their claims by a total refusal to do anything about them. Christ had a single sentence for it: "A Levite when he came to the place and saw him, passed by on the other side" (Luke 10:32). It is the sin which has increased a thousandfold in our day through the capacity of need to come starkly before us by means of the mass media. We no longer have ignorance as excuse. The openness of morality, then, is not simply perceptiveness of the claim of others, but feeling for them and being motivated to action on their behalf. It is the whole cycle from recognition to final succor.

Secondly, the openness of morality is openness to the future, to the possibilities that may develop out of a situation, and which therefore to some extent have already begun to affect the present character of the situation. Genuine morality is sensitive to these possibilities in order to ensure that the most favorable of them is actualized, or at least that its possibility is safely guaranteed. When the claims of the present and the future are set against one another, it is often to the disadvantage of the latter, as if it were in some way less real than the present, being not yet existent. Nothing could be farther from the truth, as we have seen in examining hope. The future is in its own way as real as the present, and the influence which it exerts upon any moral situation is often far, far more pressing than the present. We have not learned to live morally until we have shown that we can forego some immediate pleasure, for the sake of some future, as yet unrealized but nonetheless real, good. Mature morality is such complete openness to these future possibilities as allows them not only to govern the demands of the present, but also coordinates them into some kind of coherent system. "Faith," says the writer to the Hebrews, "is the assurance of things hoped for, the conviction of things not seen" (Hebrews 11:1), and he could equally easily have been writing of morality and *its* openness to see things hoped for.

Thirdly, having said so much of present and of future, we can now safely add that morality is openness to the past. It is so in a number of ways. For example, it recognizes that every situation, with all of its claims, has not been created *ex nihilo*. It has, rather, developed from a whole series of previous states and conditions, which have in their several ways contributed to its complexity. They must all enter into the assessment of the situation, not as prescribing its outcome, but as circumscribing the possible solutions that can be offered, making some even impossible. Openness to the past, while recognizing the claims of the past on the present, will refuse to allow that the past has deterministically settled beforehand everything that can be done in the present. There is an element of decision required in the present which can mold these claims of the past upon the present, and from them resolve something new, fresh, creative. Openness to the past rests ultimately, as we shall see, upon the fact of forgiveness. It is through forgiveness, the forgiveness of God and the forgiveness of one another, that the paralyzing effect of past on present and on future can be broken. One can immediately see the importance of and the necessity for this element in openness in situations of civil war — in Northern Ireland, for example, or in the Balkans, but it applies just as much to any situation in which mutual forgiveness is needed.

Conclusions

With the mention of forgiveness, however, we come to the end of the analysis of the structure of morality and proceed to three themes with which I wish to conclude. The first is the *tensions of morality.* The tensions of morality have been variously described at different points in the history of ethics. It was before Christ that the statement was made, "*video meliora proboque; deteriora sequor,*"[9] which receives an almost literal translation in Paul's epistle to the Romans 7:19: "For I do not do the good I want, but the evil I do not want is what I do." Tension appeared later in the history of Christian ethics, though this time through the setting of the temptations of the flesh against the will and purpose of the spirit. In Kant the presence of inclinations was recognized as the condition, if not of the morality of any action, then at least of our assurance that the deed was done from the right motives. A good deed done because we wanted to do it might certainly be good and we might still do it, even if it ran against our inclinations, but it is only when the contrary inclinations are present that we are really doing it out of respect for the law. From Kant it is a short step to saying that temptation is a necessary ingredient in morality and the major source of moral tension.

In the human context it is difficult to conceive of morality except in terms of struggle. There are, however, other tensions, for example, that created by what Reinhold Niebuhr calls the "impossible possibilities" of Christian morality, the acceptance on the one hand of an absolute ideal, of love or justice or equality, and the recognition on the other hand of the compromises imposed upon us by difficult, intractable situations which oblige us to relativize these absolutes. Once again, if this sort of tension does not exist for us in our moral practice, then it is either because we have set ourselves much too low a standard as our absolute, or because we are still operating with an absolute which is irrelevant to the eccentricities and moral ambiguities of the political, social, economic and personal problems which confront us. Another pressing tension is that between the universal and the particular, between the command to love all people and the necessity to choose between helping this or that one, or between the command to "love your enemy" and the knowledge that if you do so he may kill your whole family or platoon. There is, too, the tension for the Christian between what Bultmann calls the "indicative" and the "imperative," the assurance that we are already new creatures in Christ Jesus, and, on the

9. Ovid, *Metamorph.*, vii, 19f.

other hand, the imperative to enter into the authenticity of new existence by deciding for Christ. These tensions — and I have only dealt with them briefly — give the moral life one of its most characteristic features: the total absence of all complacency, of ever feeling that the struggle is over. In the case of the humanity of Christ once again, the genuine character of such humanity is evidenced by the presence in his moral life of some at least of these tensions, the temptations, the longing to gather the whole of Jerusalem under his wings, the sheer physical impossibility of bringing to everyone in person in Galilee and Judea the love which he had for each in his heart, the forward look to the resolution of all tension in the realized kingdom of God.

From the tensions of morality we turn to the *form of morality.* In other ethical systems, the form of morality may be the desire to bring the greatest happiness to the greatest number, to do duty for duty's sake, to seek the *summum bonum* of virtue and happiness. Christian morality has as its formal structure obedience to the will of God. Purposely I have used the term "form" in this connection because in most cases this form does not supply its own content. Very, very rarely — much less frequently than some would try to persuade — does God give to people such unmistakably clear orders that they can obey directly. His "imperative" is mediated to them through a whole variety of contingent circumstances — the application of a rule, some insight into a problem, the word of a friend, something read in a book; but when the Christian responds in the action which the situation requires, the intention is to obey God. Another way of describing the same circumstance is to say that "obedience" is a second-order concept when applied to morality; it covers a wide range of very different actions done for a whole range of moral motives, which are the forms obedience takes in different situations. Sometimes the second-order form of morality, the obedience coefficient, is present in a lively, even a dominating way, and it may seem almost to become primary in its motivating power. Even then, however, if we look closely enough we may well discover the primary structures which I have mentioned. Nevertheless, it is most important to retain the notion of obedience in our analysis, not only because it contains the God-ward reference and makes our morality religious-ethical, but also because it appears so frequently as an aspect of the moral life of our Lord. "My Father, if this [cup] cannot pass unless I drink it, your will be done" (Matthew 26:42), speaks for a dozen similar texts, declaring the obedience of the incarnate Son to the Father.

So finally, to what I would call the *condition of morality*, namely, forgiveness. It is only as the power of the past over the present is broken, through the assurance that it is not being held against us, that morality is possible. Without the assurance, we could not but find ourselves becoming more and more the victims of our own past. We ought, however, to put the case still more positively. It is because the past, with its condemnation of us, its bad memories and unhappy associations, has been destroyed by the forgiving grace of God that we receive the motivation to inspire us to new effort and purpose. The morality becomes, not a task to which we flog ourselves unwillingly and grudgingly, but rather the grateful expression of our response to what God has done for us. That response will cover the range of what we called the "structures of morality," giving them an inspiration which they would otherwise lack. It will save us from throwing in the towel whenever the tensions of morality begin to depress us. It will, too, personalize the obedience which is the form of morality, so that it is not simply the honoring of a code, or respect for a categorical imperative, but the way in which we give demonstration to the love which is in us for the one who has so forgiven us. Here, quite frankly, I cannot say that the humanity of Christ receives its motivation from the forgiveness of God. The motivation of love and obedience to God is still the source of all he does, but that love is his by right, whereas it is ours by grace, by forgiveness, by adoption. The form is still the same, but its source and inspiration come by a different way.

Our contention in this chapter has been that the morality of Christ's human life gives his humanity concrete content and links incarnation to atonement in indissoluble unity. To the person who raises the question of biography again, and who argues that we do not have a large canvas on which to draw the moral portrait of Christ any more than we have for his historical portrait, we must reply that the two cases are not the same. A moral portrait requires only representative situations, episodic occurrence, test cases, simple instances of which the Gospels provide plenty, and we need look no farther, nor need we complain about what we have. The moral picture is complete enough, it is challenging enough, and it is more than enough for any of us to live by.

CHAPTER 5

Theology of the Humanity of Christ

Humanity as Revelation

At first, it may seem rather as if we were stating the obvious in affirming that the humanity of Jesus Christ is the medium of divine revelation. The incarnation, the enfleshing of the Word of God, is the fact of the revelation. But not all recent studies in the theology of revelation bear out this simple assessment of the situation. It is quite some time now since Emil Brunner wrote the opening words of his classic, *The Mediator,* "Through God alone can God be known."[1] Brunner intended by this statement to substitute for the old distinction between revealed theology and natural theory a distinction between knowledge revealed by God and knowledge of God achieved by us through study of the natural world — a restatement of the old distinction between general revelation and special revelation. In order to initiate this distinction, Brunner had to establish a prior position, namely, that whenever there occurs knowledge of God, it is made possible because God has revealed himself. Such revelation may take place in a general way, as in other religions, or in nature to some extent, or in a special or particular way as when God reveals himself in the Hebrew-Christian tradition, promising a Messiah under the old covenant and fulfilling the promise by

1. Emil Brunner, *The Mediator* (ET London, 1934), p. 21.

sending him under the new covenant. What Brunner had to say about general revelation could, without too much difficulty, have been extended to include the old natural theology, on the grounds that what theologians were doing in such proofs as composed natural theology was to present in logical form the natural revelation of God which they observed in causal, cosmological or teleological settings. The generality that can be given to the word "revelation" — and I mention the fact only to show how diverse a term it is — can be illustrated in the view sometimes advanced that all knowledge involves some kind of revelation, in the sense that the object known or discovered "reveals" itself to me. To my mind, once the term "reveals" is made equivalent to "is discovered" in this way, it is robbed of its proper meaning. For the same reason, I would argue that Brunner's distinction between "general" revelation and "special" revelation confuses the issue. If God reveals himself, then surely he reveals himself specially, particularly, non-generally to this person, at this place, to this purpose. In fact, if it is general, it is not revelation. If it is revelation, it is not general. Brunner tends somewhat to cut the Gordian knot of the problem of the revelation contained in other religions by calling it general, hoping thereby to give it a second-class status. But the distinction will not work. God does not do things by halves, or quarters. Thus, at a time when the discipline of comparative religion has acquired new life, we shall require to revise our categories with the greatest care, not only not to cause offense but also to ensure that we do not, by our aprioristic assessments, eliminate all possibility of discussing the truth in other religions.

While Brunner's dictum was intended as an attempt to deal with the problem of revelation in a world which seems to know God in ways other than through Jesus Christ, nevertheless his dictum, "through God alone can God be known," became in the event a rallying point for a certain theory of how revelation takes place in the person of Jesus Christ. "Through God alone can God be known" is designed to emphasize the fact that of the two natures which coexist in the person of Jesus Christ, it is through the *divine* nature that God reveals himself, and through the divine nature that God is known. This theorem can be restated in the form, "God cannot be known through what is not God, or less than God," which contrasts sharply with the classical statements of St. Thomas, "God is only known through his effects *(per suos effectus)*," or "through the things he has made *(per ea quae facta sunt)*."[2] In Thomas we have the clear statement that God *is* known through what is less than God; the process of inference outlined in the famous "five ways" is how that knowledge is achieved, while we find there also his equally clear rejection of the suggestion that God is known in his pure essence, in himself separated from the created order. When this theme is taken up by Barth, it is carried farther than Brunner was prepared to take it with his acceptance of natural theology, even if in a reduced form. If God cannot be known through what is not God, or less than God, then he cannot be known through sunsets, flowers, poetry, music or art; he can only be known through what *is* God, namely, the divine nature of Jesus Christ. In a single thrust he removes natural theology entirely from the scene of respectable theology, and establishes the special revelation in Jesus Christ as the sole permissible claimant to the title.

When the emphasis is laid so heavily upon the divinity of Jesus Christ as the medium of revelation, certain consequences follow for the interpretation of the role of the humanity of Christ in the revelation situation. For example, the humanity of Christ tends to be regarded as a window through which we look at the divine nature (a view already commented on as occurring in John Robinson's *Honest to God*). The function of the human nature is to be self-effacing, to be transparent, to allow the observer without any delay to pass from the human nature to the divine nature as being the means of knowing God. I must confess that I find it difficult to sustain explanation of this view for very long. I am unsympathetic towards it, and though I try very hard, it seems eventually to break down altogether when I press it for an amplification of the idea of how the divine nature of Jesus Christ can be the medium of knowledge of God. After all, the divine nature of Jesus Christ *is* God, *essentialiter* as the Scholastics would have said, in which case to know the divine nature is to know God; that process does not require the title of "revelation." Alternatively, if the divine nature of Jesus Christ the Son is to be distinguished *modaliter* from God the Father, then we still have a little explaining to do to indicate how knowledge of the Son leads to knowledge of the Father — and again, whether it is properly called revelation.

Another consequence for the humanity of Jesus Christ which follows from this view that it is through the divine nature of Jesus Christ that God

2. Thomas Aquinas, *Summa Theologiae,* 1a. 2,2; *Summa Contra Gentiles,* I,12.

is known is that the humanity of Christ becomes little more than the locus of revelation or incarnation, the vanishing space-time point where it all occurs, the occasion of the event itself, without content and with very little form. On this view, it would seem, Christ's humanity is merely the jumping-off place for approach to the divine nature, and nothing of particular importance or interest in itself. It is not, therefore, surprising that there should be no great concern in such theories of revelation for the elaboration of the historical basis of the faith in the development of the presentation of the humanity of Jesus Christ; since the humanity is not loadbearing in the revelation situation thus conceived, it does not require extensive or detailed examination. Often theologians of this persuasion have been shown to have affinities with existentialism, which deals another blow to the question of Christ's humanity, for they are so affected by the existentialists' historical agnosticism that, from the beginning, they *cannot* attach great importance to the humanity of Christ, for it is seen as inaccessible by definition to historical criticism.

It is of great interest to me that Barth, who in spite of his known association with the view I have been examining, should nevertheless have expressed himself totally differently at times in his writings. Barth asserts:

> The power and authority of God are revealed by Jesus Christ and to him in his words and in his action. But while this is the case he does not cease to be a man as we are, our Brother. . . . What was and is and will be effective and revealed in this man and therefore in and through human essence is not a supreme form of human and creaturely power and authority. . . . It is nothing less than absolutely divine power and authority. . . . [In] the existence of this man we have to reckon with the identity of his action as a true man with the action of the true God. . . . What takes place in this event is that it acquires even in its pure creatureliness divine *exousia*, even in its human weakness divine power, even in its human meanness divine authority, even in its particularity (for individuality with all its limitations belongs to its humanity) divine universality — and all this in the occurrence of this event, or to put it more simply, as Jesus Christ lived and lives and will live.[3]

3. Barth, *Church Dogmatics*, IV/2 (ET Edinburgh, 1958), p. 99.

This is not a random remark for he repeats the point again: "The divine expresses and reveals itself wholly in the sphere of the human, and the human serves and attests the divine."[4] This account of the role of humanity in the revelation situation is entirely different from what we have so far seen it to be in Barth, and what is not perhaps so obvious at first sight is that the understanding of how revelation "works" has considerably changed from what it was on the previous accounts.

To take the latter difference first. Revelation does not take place through our being pointed beyond the revelation situation to something above and beyond it, something wholly transcending it. The revelation occurs in the area of the situation itself, so that to comprehend the revelation we have to examine further this situation, and not penetrate through it to something else or peer through it as through a window at a reality beyond. This consideration is of obvious importance in relation to the person of Jesus Christ. We dare never slip into the position of thinking that he is the occasion of our knowledge of a reality that somehow lies on the other side of him, so that when we have glimpsed the reality we can dispense with him, or that he is a window whose sole function is to be totally unobtrusive. He is the area to be explored, for revelation is given *in him* and does not lie *beyond him*. This is a fact concerning which we ought to be left in no doubt when we acknowledge that revelation takes place through the humanity of Jesus Christ.

The humanity of Christ has an opacity, furthermore, which does not lend itself readily to association with the idea of a transparent window giving clear vision to an ulterior reality. The opacity of the humanity as a medium of revelation has always been a subject of fascination for theologians, particularly in the Lutheran tradition, and in modern times in Barthian theology. "Veiled in flesh the Godhead see," the words of Charles Wesley's carol, anticipates a whole series of paradoxical statements of the order, "In his revelation, God conceals himself," or "In his unveiling, God remains veiled," or "*Deus revelatus est Deus absconditus.*" The intention of these statements is not to convey simply the idea that at times God is revealed and at other times he conceals himself; or that he reveals part of his nature and purpose, and conceals other parts; or that he reveals some things to some people, and some things to other people, and conceals different things from different

4. Barth, IV/2, p. 115.

people. A more subtle suggestion is being made, namely, that it is in the midst of his veiling of himself that he reveals himself, and that even in the process of revealing himself he conceals himself. Such enigmatical statements can be found in many theologians,[5] but they are all rather facile unless we relate them to the humanity of Christ and to the revelation which takes place through that humanity. God, whom the heaven and the heaven of heavens cannot contain, and who nevertheless dwells among us as a man called Jesus, in that very action conceals himself so effectively that all of his contemporaries in his lifetime were deceived, most of all the religious leaders, those who had been watching and waiting all their days for the coming of the Messiah. The familiarity of our hindsight has made us insensitive to the almost total concealment that took place at the incarnation, that the God of Abraham and Isaac and Jacob should appear as the carpenter whose brothers and sisters are known in the village. It was all unthinkable and impossible, yet it was true and it was there that the revelation took place, not beyond this man Jesus or above him but in him. This view, therefore, of the quite unique role which the humanity of Christ plays in revelation revolutionizes our presentation of the way revelation happens.

This is a view which also, however, inevitably compels us to give a fresh assessment of the importance of the constituent aspects of Christ's humanity. We can no longer refer allusively to the humanity of Christ in general, or treat it comprehensively as a *totum simul* which yields immediate awareness of the divine being. Two consequences follow. First, the revelation takes place in what might be called a distributive manner — across the board of Christ's earthly existence. Even if the Gospels themselves seem to show preference for a fuller treatment of the death of Jesus than of other parts of his life, nevertheless these other parts are important as filling out the account of who this man was whose death was to prove effectual for the salvation of the world. Secondly, therefore, the individual "parts" of the incarnation (for lack of a better term) have to be regarded in their own right as contributing to what happens when God is revealed through Jesus Christ, and they therefore deserve examination and consideration individually. The humanity which is the locus of revelation, in other words, is composed of a variety of elements of which the Gospels tell us a good deal. There

5. See John Dillinberger, *God Hidden and Revealed* (Philadelphia, 1953).

are, for example, the many sayings of Jesus which, despite being marshaled and re-marshaled according to the instructions of the form-critical and redaction-critical sergeant-majors, still retain something of the authenticity and authority of their original source. We have too, the many narratives of what Jesus did, and again, even once we allow the accretions of idealizing tendencies among the storytellers, we have to concede the element of veracity which ensures that we are not finally deceived as to the character of the man whose conduct is being recounted to us. There is too, the whole moral tone of such conduct, what must still be called the "religious" quality of his life and conduct, his sayings and his commands, which constitute an area of high revelatory intensity. Through the whole description of the events of the passion and the cross, we are made sharply aware of the fact that in the midst of all these events recorded for us there is a meaning, a reality, a God, who is known *in the midst of them,* not above them, or beyond them, or beneath them as their ground, but at their very heart — in the sweat which was as drops of blood, in the wounded side, in the cry of desolation and in the darkness that was from the sixth to the ninth hour while the sun's light failed. When, therefore, we come to this stage of our discussion we are affirming *all* that has gone before in our account of the humanity of Christ — its universality however we interpret it, its particularity as historicity, its moral character, its involvement with the specificity of daily existence and its entanglement with the affairs of life — and arguing that all of these together constitute the place where the revelation of God takes place.

Accordingly, there is no shortcut to revelation, least of all to the revelation of God, which can bypass the complexity which in our analysis constitutes the humanity of Christ. If we wish to know *who* God is, what religion is about, we have to be prepared to probe further into the life and actions, words and conduct of this man Jesus. At times that probing will lead us into all the difficulties of assessing historicity, separating out competing literary forms, of tackling problems of textual criticism, of making comparative judgments on exegesis of texts, of asking questions about why particular miracles or parables should ever have come to be included in a Gospel. When such probing leads us into difficulties, we may well be tempted to say that they have nothing to do with the question of revelation, and less still to do with the humanity of Christ. Such a conclusion, however, would be premature and inaccurate. The recognition of the humanity of Christ commits us to the investigation of the story of how that humanity expressed itself. *A fortiori,* the belief in the humanity of Christ as the medium of revelation enforces the closest scrutiny of the only evidence that we have for that humanity and of the only way by which we have access to it. What is unpardonable is the view that holds to the reality of revelation through Jesus Christ, but which for textual-critical or skeptical-historical reasons makes light of the humanity of Christ in its moral character, its historicity or its textual documentation. When such a cavalier approach is adopted, it is difficult to understand what then is the basis or medium of revelation, and how in fact the whole process escapes being a form of magic or at the best mysticism — magic, because of the apparently fortuitous connection between the sacred event (Jesus Christ) and the object of worship (God), or mysticism, because there is a disregard of the phenomenal existence and a concentration on the spiritual reality. The humanity of Christ alone is in the final analysis the guarantee of the authenticity of revelation.

Humanity as Redemption

Let me use Karl Barth once again as my point of departure. According to Barth, "The saving act of God takes place in the man Jesus of Nazareth. . . . This work concerns man and the world. It therefore demands a human soul and a human body, human reason and human will, human obedience and human humility, human seriousness and human anger, human anxiety and trust, human love for God and the neighbor. And it demands all this in an existence in our human created time. The speaking and acting, the suffering and striving, the praying and helping, the succumbing and conquering have all to be in human terms."[6] Shortly before this passage, Barth writes of "the grace addressed to human essence in Jesus Christ" as "His qualification to be the organ of the action or work of the Son as the Mediator between God and men, the Reconciler of the world with God."[7] While I do not particularly like the word "*Organ*" which Barth employs to describe the role of humanity in the salvation event because of its rather unconcealed

6. Barth, *Church Dogmatics,* I/2 (ET Edinburgh, 1956), pp. 98f.
7. Barth, I/2, p. 96.

Nestorian character — especially since, if he means the sentences I have quoted to be read in a Nestorian sense, then he is asking a lot — nevertheless, this account by Barth can be read, even if in a manner not intended by him, to draw attention to certain facts about the redemption which are fundamental. Most important of all, these remarks act as a corrective to associating the redemptive effectiveness of what the Savior does with one special part of his existence. There are three possibilities, and they have been adopted by different thinkers at different times.

First, the redemptive effectiveness of Christ has been associated more closely with the fact of the incarnation than with the rest of his earthly life or death. Popularly, this view is regarded as the Greek view of redemption, and it can be arrived at by the inversion of the saying, "What he did not take he did not redeem," which would then read, "What he took he redeemed." He took human nature, and his assumption of it was his redemption of it. This so-called Greek view has found its way into some popular forms of modern theology, which use it to highlight the relevance of Christ's redemptive work to aspects of contemporary life. Christ took on the responsibilities of family life and thereby redeemed and consecrated the family. He worked at a man's craft and so made toil sacred. He participated in the life of the society of his day, in its political forums, and thereby redeemed society and politics. In spite of the uses to which such theory can be put, it is substantially inadequate insofar as it neglects the part played in the redemptive economy by the death of Christ, and thereby fails to perceive the central atonement element which any adequate soteriology must incorporate.

Secondly, there are theories which have enjoyed considerable popularity which have observed in the exemplary character of the life of Christ, his love and forgivingness towards others, his self-sacrificial concern for them, and his total dependence upon God, the way in which we must live in order to overcome our sins and remove our guilt. One's redemption is in one's own hands. Apart from the optimistic assessment of human capacities involved in this view, such an account of the way in which atonement is effected offers no real account of the universal and compulsive character of human sin. It cannot be exorcised by incantations of good intent. It has an objective as well as a subjective status, and no theory which fails to recognize the former as well as the latter has come to terms with its full character.

So thirdly, those theories which have related the redemption effectiveness of Christ exclusively to his death, have gone farthest perhaps of all in their appreciation of the gravity, inevitability and universality of human sinning. St. Anselm spoke for this whole group when he wrote, "To this end was he made man that he might die."[8] There have been many theories of how Christ effected the atonement, as penal substitute, as satisfaction, as victor over the powers of darkness and death or as reconciler. In each case, there is a narrow concentration upon the death of Christ, which was stated quite openly by Kierkegaard, who was prepared to see in the death of Christ all the knowledge that faith required for salvation. Evangelical hymns have reinforced the same contention, beginning out of gratitude with an emphasis on the death of Christ, rather than on other events in his life, and ending in an almost exclusive concentration upon the death. Such exclusiveness, however, no matter how pious the reasons for it may be, are distortive of the true role of the humanity of Christ in redemption.

In short, when we reflect theologically on the redemptive work of Christ, we should be very careful not to assume that it is opposed in some way to his person, as if incarnation and atonement were two separate parts of Christ's existence upon earth, or to give the impression that redemption is not a feature of the whole event which is the birth, life, death and resurrection of Jesus Christ. As I see it, when we associate the redemptive purposes of God with the humanity of Christ, we are thereby securing the redemptive purpose in *all* aspects of Christ's earthly existence. His incarnation certainly did involve the assumption of the human nature, with all the human situations which entailed, of fear and hope, friendship and enmity, trust and doubt, hope and disappointment, anxiety and assurance; that assumption, however, was not in itself the fulfillment of atonement, for it was only the beginning, the inauguration of it, which had to wait for other things to happen. It is right, too, to fill in the earthly life of Jesus as bearing its share in the redemptive purpose of the incarnation. The man who was to be crucified had in his earthly life shown himself to be no ordinary person. The obedience which he displayed finally when asked to drink the cup which he would dearly have allowed to pass was the same obedience which governed all of his relations to God and to his neighbor throughout his life previously.

8. St. Anselm, *Cur Deus Homo,* II,16.

In fact, the quality of that earlier life heightened the value and intensified the drama of its final episodes in Gethsemane and on Calvary. Perhaps the greatest single argument against accepting the life of Jesus Christ as the atonement-effective element in the incarnation is that he *himself* did not so understand the situation. It is difficult to assign originality to biblical texts, but if any can be allowed a primary quality, Jesus' own word at Mark 10:45 must come very close to it: "For the Son of Man came not to be served but to serve, and to give his life a ransom for many." In what must be one of the earliest passages in the New Testament, the rehearsal of the institution of the Lord's Supper in 1 Corinthians 11:24ff., Paul ascribes to Jesus the same interpretation of his death, linking it in a redemptive way to the partaking of the Lord's Supper. But equally, we cannot lay all the emphasis upon his death, because without the life, that life of obedience, love, understanding, identification and involvement, his death could not have the significance or the value which Christian faith has found in them. In a word, the whole of Christ's birth, life, death and resurrection was redemptive through and through, and each part shares in that single purpose. When we look at the situation in this way, we have a hermeneutical principle to interpret not just the last days of his earthly life, but also his teachings, his parables, his miracles, his relations to his fellow men and women and to God — and indeed the resurrection, through which, displaying God's powers over sin and death, he now lives to make effective in us what was first initiated at Bethlehem.

It is for this reason, quite apart from the associations with Nestorius, who is believed to have said, "Mary bore a man who was the organ of Godhead," that I cannot accept readily Barth's view that "the human essence" (as his translator rather ineptly calls it) is the organ of the action or work of the Son as Mediator.[9] The notion of the human nature as an organ which the divine nature or the *hypostasis* of the Logos "uses" for purposes of redemption fails miserably to do justice to the rich and varied content of the humanity, and more importantly, the tremendously *active* part which the humanity plays in the whole redemptive process. The use of the word "organ" is a betrayal of the relationship of the two natures to one another, and of the identity of Christ's human nature with our own. This dehumanization of the human nature which

9. Barth, IV/2, pp. 96ff.

allows it to become an organ is perhaps one of the unexpected consequences of that logical process called *anhypostasia* which removes the *hypostasis* from the human nature and finds a *hypostasis* in that of the divine nature *(enhypostasia)*. The danger of such a view is the depersonalization of the humanity of Christ — a danger which H. R. Mackintosh detected over eighty years ago in the Chalcedonian Symbol. As against the view that the humanity of Christ is the organ used by the divine nature or the divine person of Jesus Christ to effect the redemption, we have to ensure for the whole range of human experiences of "speaking and acting, suffering and striving, praying and helping, succumbing and conquering" a sufficient degree of independence to be themselves participants in, and executives of, the redemptive process. It is in and through the whole range of the humanity that the redemption takes place. The humanity is not a means, neutral and utilitarian, to some extraneous end beyond itself, as a tool or an organ which is external to and discontinuous with the purpose it serves. The purpose, the redemptive aim of God, is embraced within the humanity of Christ.

Humanity as Contemporaneity

I originally had in mind to entitle this section of our study "humanity as existence or *Existenz*," but I abandoned the idea because of my reluctance to divert the discussion towards technical existentialist analysis of what humanity is — considering its thrown-ness, its fallen-ness, its inauthenticity, its anxieties and the like. Such an analysis would have been valuable, but should perhaps have been the starting point of our whole investigation of Christ's humanity. Not even Bultmann described the humanity of Christ in these terms, largely because of his skepticism towards history. It might have been interesting to write a two-nature theory embodying an existentialist analysis of the humanity of Christ. Nor am I drawn to use the existentialist terms for a second reason. I have no intention of demythologizing the humanity of Christ, even those aspects of it which have proved to be a *skandalon* to the modern intellect. If anything, my method has been the reverse — to endeavor to discover new meanings for old terminologies without sacrifice of ultimate positions.

Having dissociated myself from these two possible existentialist lines, I should, however, like to employ one part of the approach to theology which is characteristic of such existentialism, namely, its concern to establish the validity of theological doctrines by giving them contemporary relevance and interpretation. We could go farther and add that whenever such contemporaneity cannot be established, then the doctrine is not so much false or invalid as meaningless. Another way of making the same case is to say that we do not properly understand any theological doctrine unless and until we are religiously engaged with the subject-matter which it affirms. A simple example can be given. In the Apostle's Creed, I confess "the forgiveness of sins," but such a confession is not a flat statement like "I see it is raining." It is a shorthand way of saying that I have sinned, have confessed my sins and come to know the forgiveness of sins offered to me through the redeeming death of Jesus Christ. Fuller examination of the situation yields farther entailments, such as, that I shall endeavor hereafter not to repeat sins which I have previously committed, and that my earnest endeavor not to do so is evidence of the measure of my appropriation of the forgiveness which God offers me. Even such a statement of a *credo* as "I believe in God . . . Maker of heaven and earth" implies as part of its meaning that I acknowledge God as my Creator and myself to be his creature, that I shall give to him the honor which this relationship requires, that I shall obey his will for me and seek to implement it, that I live in a world which has also been created by him and which I cannot use as I wish to my own ends, polluting it and ruining it for future generations. This view of the nature of theological truth, while it is not advanced explicitly by existentialists, owes a great deal to their way of approaching theology, and it is a very proper reaction to those theologies which lay so much stress on a much-vaunted objectivity or ontology, which in a sense leaves you cold, and however true makes no contact with the realities of living faith. It is from such an approach that I intend finally to look at the humanity of Christ, and shall do so under the title of the "contemporaneity" of his humanity.

The immediate fact to confront us when we think of the humanity of Christ in relation to ourselves is the way in which it acts as a bond between him and us. We have considered earlier how the humanity can be regarded as a totally unexpected mode of divine self-revelation. So different are God and humankind, separated as Kierkegaard said by an infinite qualitative difference, that the self-revelation has become a self-veiling. But once that humanity is recognized for what it is, the way in which the "infinite qualitatively different" God comes alongside us and sets himself in the very middle of our human situation, then that humanity which may to others have been foolishness or a stone of stumbling becomes a bond uniting us to God through Christ, a completely new way of looking at God and of understanding what he is like. We have often spoken of Christ through his humanity making himself one with us; by doing so, however, he also makes the reverse true — he makes us one with himself and one with God. That bond which he has created is the first element in the contemporaneity which he has with ourselves, or more precisely, that bond is the basis of the contemporaneity, the condition of its possibility. We have acknowledged in the earlier discussion that we can make too much of the notion that human nature is unaffected by cultural, civilizational, economic and political change, for there is a case for the idea that human nature varies to some extent from age to age and culture to culture. In spite of that acknowledgment, we have not denied that in many ways men and women are much what they have always been. The glory for us of much of Greek tragedy, for example, lies in the fact that we see something of ourselves in the jealousies, the hatreds, the ambitions of their characters. It was affinity of this sort that Collingwood extended into the whole sphere of historical study, making some degree of empathetic involvement in the period studied a qualification for historiography and for the criticism of historigraphy.[10] Croce had something similar in mind when he proposed that we need to discern in the period of history we are studying some need of which we are ourselves aware in our own existence, before we can properly write the history of that period. The relation between Christ and ourselves based upon his humanity, which endures the afflictions, pains, sorrows and trials, and expresses the joys, the happiness and the friendship known to our own humanity, is ultimately the ground of our knowledge of him and through him of God. It is the identity of that humanity of his with ours which lifts it out of the past and relates it absolutely to the present. From that starting point proceeds a whole range of implications concerning this contemporaneity.

10. R. G. Collingwood, *The Idea of History* (Oxford, 1946); cf. also my *Faith Theology and Imagination*, pp. 109ff.

First, I should like to go back to what I had to say about the universality of Christ's humanity earlier to indicate that the contemporaneity of Christ's humanity shares in this universal quality. When we discover through faith and through the humanity of Christ our oneness with him, there is a temptation to interpret the situation in an elective, exclusivist way, as if this humanity were for me, or for believers, or for the Church only. This humanity of Christ, however, which is contemporary with us is shared in by the whole of humankind, no matter who they are or what they believe or even what they do. Perhaps we have now passed the point where we genuinely believe that humankind will be united through faith in the one God, who may go under several names in different religions. When you contemplate the hunger and distress of so any of our fellow men and women, you begin to wonder whether it is not almost a mockery to speak to them of faith, even of the Gospel, when the one thing they really need is food to eat, in order to continue living. At such a time, when faith is failing to unite and when hope is fading hourly, it is possible that humanity, the humanity of Christ, may prove to be the rallying point. It is interesting to notice how many groups, Christian but many of them non-Christian, are actively and sacrificially expressing their concern for undernourishment, homelessness, and underprivilege of many sorts all over the world, solely in the name of humanity. Christians have almost ceased to use the religious sanctions for enforcing love towards the distressed, partly because they recognize that sanctions are motivationally unproductive, partly also because of the suspicion of a possible charge of self-righteousness. The common ground is now humanity, the very humanity which Christ assumed and which now unites him with all people everywhere, so that he hungers where they hunger, thirsts where they thirst, and dies where they die. It is out of that unity with him that, in the Christian's judgment, the unity of all people everywhere springs. Of themselves, they are black and white, brown and yellow; of themselves, they are Muslim, Jewish, Bah'ai, Christian; of themselves, they are upper upper, upper middle, lower middle, or plain lowest class. But in him, through him, because of him and his humanity, there is no difference of color or class or creed. He is the universal man-for-others in this sense, at least.

Secondly, and paradoxically, this contemporaneity has also a very particular character, for this man who is one with all with whom he universally shares his humanity, is also one particularly with *me* in *my* particular situation. The curious aspect of this humanity of his is that it relates very precisely to where I am and what I am doing, to the kind of person I am at this very moment. When I hold my life, my humanity against his, then it reveals to me things about myself of which I had never previously been aware. This revelation of myself is not something I deduce from some general theorems which I find in the Bible about all people loving one another, or forgiving their enemies, or having a Father in heaven. It comes with precision and definiteness in one single action from the humanity of Christ to my particular person and character with all the intensity of immediacy and the conviction of authenticity. The relation between his humanity and my own is a matter of direct reference, and not of syllogistic deduction or circumstantial inference.

Thirdly, another aspect of this directness of reference between the humanity of Christ and our own, or my own, which gives it its contemporaneity is the situational character of the two related terms in the reference. Much has often been made by New Testament scholars, who reject all possibility of the Gospels being biography, of their episodic character. I would prefer to name it their *situational* character, for that is another key to the contemporaneity of Christ. The accounts we have of his existence as a man, and these we must not forget are all we have to go on in describing his humanity, narrate to us the many situations in which Jesus found himself on different occasions. They were situations in which he healed the sick, ate with his friends, had altercations with his enemies, taught the crowds or explained difficult sayings to his own disciples. Most, if not all, of his sayings, whether epigrammatic, didactic or hortatory, occurred in the context of some situation. It is not for nothing then that Joseph Fletcher seized upon this single fact to formulate what he called a "situation ethic," not in any wildcat attempt to torpedo all formal ethics with a round of antinomianism or libertinism, but rather to acknowledge both the particularity of every moral situation in which *we* find *ourselves* and the consequent necessity to relate what we have to do to the circumstances of our precise responsibility, and the highly contextual quality of all *Jesus'* moral teaching and activity. At one time the ethical problem was thought capable of being put in simplicist terms, such as, "What would Jesus do if he were in this situation?" Few people would do so today. But the spirit which inspired the question was sensible enough; it erred in thinking that there could be any quick answer to the question, or that it was necessary only to put the ethical question in that way to get an answer.

But to develop this theme we have to move to our fourth feature of the contemporaneity of Christ's humanity, its *ethical* character. While it is naive to think that we can readily solve ethical problems by the attempt to discover what Jesus would have done in a given situation, nevertheless on many occasions we do tackle our moral problems by some kind of analogical thinking which connects our situation here and now to some situation of which we read in the Scriptures. The very particularity of many of the biblical situations, a fact which might seem to disqualify them from all kinds of universalization or transference, seems to provide the insight to direct us to some kind of decision. Very often, too, it may happen the reverse way. Some circumstance in our own lives, to the reality of which we have been blinding ourselves because of emotional entanglement or sheer moral obtuseness, may suddenly acquire its true proportions from a reading of an account of a situation in which Christ said this or that to someone with a not dissimilar problem. In fact, Christian ethics has, I believe, been too often wrongly presented as if it were an attempt either to discover in some immediately direct way what the will of God is — "*senkrecht von oben*" — for a particular situation, or to subsume some situation under some such universal principle as "Love your neighbor," "Forgive your enemies," or "Seek first the kingdom of God." Our present emphasis upon the contemporaneity of Christ's humanity, with its situational and ethical features, however, suggests a third way of interpreting the working of Christian ethics: We discover some sort of situational relationship between our problem and the human situations in which Christ acted and expressed himself, either directly or parabolically, and derive our projected action from that relationship. It is a form of analogical thinking, but then all ethical thinking must contain some element of analogy, for in the words of a truism, "no two situations and no two persons are ever the same." There is nothing particularly novel or original about such a suggestion. It is the implicit procedure for a very large number of sermons, which begin with an elaboration of the original situation in which the text has occurred, and follows up usually in a three-headed way, with directives towards similar circumstances in contemporary life. Had the phrase not been used already and in a different connection, we would have called it "lateral thinking," opposing it to the vertical thinking which searches for the divine imperative or endeavors to derive an ethical conclusion from universal major premise and a particular minor premise in an ethical syllogism, and maintaining that we think ethically across the board, from similar situation to similar situation. But in terms of our main thesis, such lateral thinking rests upon the contemporaneity of the humanity of Christ and our own, the association of the two here-and-now in a single act of thought and decision.

Fifthly, since the humanity of Christ is contained within God's purpose for the redemption of humankind, it is not surprising that we should also observe that the contemporaneity of Christ's humanity has a *redemptive* role. The great problem which exercised Bultmann, and for which he has not always been given the credit he deserves, was a very real one: how an event which happened two thousand years ago can also be the contemporary event which effects my salvation. "How can *Historie* be *Geschichte?*" to put it in his own terms. Bultmann's answer to that question was that it is in the preaching of Jesus Christ, crucified and risen, that this contemporaneity happens. This answer, so far as it goes, is true, for preaching is the occasion *par excellence* on which this takes place. But I have often wondered whether Bultmann did not stop too soon in his answer by simply giving us the occasion on which the contemporaneity occurs, for he did not go on to probe into what happens once the occasion has made the contemporaneity possible. That farther examination would have yielded the conclusion that it is through the humanity of Christ that such contemporaneity is effected, through the humanity of Christ, moreover, that the contemporaneity is not just intellectual, or academic, or merely interesting, but also redemptive. Much of the discussion of the humanity of Christ in the history of theology has been concerned with showing how we can become so related to the humanity, and that humanity be so related to us — by incorporation, by penal substitution, by vicarious penitence or by identification — that we are made sharers in the redemption it effected. The humanity of Christ, therefore, is the vehicle by which that event which happened so long ago is made so contemporary with us now that we are redeemed by it. What happened then becomes effectual now because of the present relationship into which we enter with the humanity of Christ.

Sixthly, for similar reasons, we should add that the contemporaneity of Christ's humanity has a *revelational* function. It is of the very character and definition of revelation that it must be completed in the mind or will or heart of the person to whom it is being made. There is no such thing as a revelation which no one perceives or appropriates. Revelation is of something (or someone) by something (or someone) to someone, as I have said elsewhere.[11] The whole point of the process is that it should be consummated contemporaneously with the person receiving it. If it is revelation *to me,* then it happens to me in my time and in my existence — not two thousand years ago. So the humanity of Christ, because of its centrality in God's purpose of self-revealing, of making his mind and purpose and character known to men and women, acquires because of its contemporaneity a revelational role, so much so that, without it and without its contemporaneity, revelation would not take place. But when we say so, if we are not once again to resort to time-honored theological Indian rope tricks, we have to hold closely to what the humanity of Christ means, and not merely to some vagueness that he may probably have lived then, or said or done this or that, taught in this manner or that, though perhaps with a slightly greater precision over the details of his passion for soteriological rather than revelational reasons. We must be prepared to look for and to find that revelation in the humanity of his earthly existence as it relates to ours here and now, an existence with its fears and hopes, sufferings and joys, expectations and disappointments, its robust vigor and its painful death. If it is the humanity of Christ that we regard as revelational and contemporary, then it must be life and blood humanity, not the attenuated probabilities of a historical calculus or the remains of form-critical surgery.

So finally, seventhly, if we are to give any credibility to what has gone before about the contemporaneity of the humanity of Christ, we must reaffirm an item of belief which has often appeared rather doctrinaire and whimsical, namely the *continuing humanity* of Christ. This item of belief has occupied a somewhat marginal field, partly because of the ambiguity which has attached to the resurrection appearances of Christ and therefore to the character of the resurrection body of Christ, partly also because of the assumption that the humanity of Christ was as-

11. McIntyre, *The Shape of Christology* (London and Philadelphia, 1966), pp. 146ff.

sociated exclusively with the incarnate work of Christ, which somehow came to an end when he said, "It is finished," or perhaps when he rose from the dead. It may well be, however, that one of the implications of all that has gone before is that the idea that the risen and glorified Christ retained his humanity must be defended and developed as one of the key claims of Christian theology. Barth writes of "the humanity of God," though when we examine what he means and take account of his view that it is in Jesus Christ that God is known, we must conclude that he is in fact speaking really of the humanity of Christ. More importantly, however, one of the points he is stressing is that the humanity which the Word assumed at the incarnation is not surrendered after the resurrection as if it were a passing phase of God's action or purpose, for the humanity of Christ is at the center of God's action and purpose in the world. This is so much the case that it is retained by God in the second person of the Trinity, to become eternally our assurance that God as he was in Jesus Christ is God as he shall be for ever. In short, the contemporary humanity of Christ is the ultimate guarantee both of God's reality for us and of our salvation in him.

Theology of Prayer

CHAPTER 1

The Problem of Prayer

Prayer in the Modern World

It is now many years since Fernand Ménégoz wrote his classic, *Le Problème de la Prière,*[1] and yet, it is curious to discover how contemporary a document it is — with its recognition of the impact of neopositivism, subjectivism and nihilism upon prayer, with its consideration of the contribution to be made to the solution of the problem by Heim and Barth and Scheler, and supremely by its contention that the problem of prayer takes us to the heart of the questions of theological method, of the reality of God and of our relation to him. For it has become clear that the crisis of prayer is substantially the crisis of faith, and that though people may cease to *pray* before they cease to believe, nevertheless the discontinuance of prayer must be taken as the early warning signal that the end of faith is at hand. Too much has happened in these years for us to take Ménégoz as normative in definition either of the problem or of its solution. These we must discover for ourselves. Ménégoz teaches us, however, that whoever is concerned with prayer is moving close to the realities that religion is about, and is likely in dealing with the one to stumble upon truth which will be a guide in thinking about the other. It would be almost a truism, were not contemporary practice beginning to gainsay it, that there can be no religion without prayer. Paradoxically, we are being forced to face the fact, too, that there may be prayer where

1. Fernand Ménégoz, *Le Problème de la Prière* (Strasbourg, 1925).

there is no religion, certainly none which the traditionalists will acknowledge, where pop stars take to Indian mysticism or some corruption of it. To sharpen the contrast almost to the point of inaccuracy, it might be said that within the Church, prayer is a problem, that it has reached such a crisis that it is losing its significance, whereas outside of the Church, people are often longing to pray, or are at least fumblingly praying. Somewhere in this situation there is a lesson to be learned — and quickly. At present, however, our concern is mainly with the problematical situation in which prayer now exists, and with the analysis of the circumstances contributing to the situation.

It would be wrong to pretend that none of the causes of the crisis of prayer which Ménégoz discerned are present in our world. Positivism, or as he called it, neopositivism, is still with us; in fact, if anything, it has been strongly reinforced by the movement from science to technology which has taken place in the past fifty years. As the philosopher Norman Kemp Smith pointed out, of the three competing systems of thought — naturalism or positivism, idealism (which for our purposes will include Christian theism) and skepticism — none finally succeeds in driving the other two from the field of intellectual credibility.[2] At any one period of philosophy or culture, the evidence for any one may seem to be more compelling than for the others, but even so the others remain in existence as providing alternative modes of thought for minority groups. In spite of the massive revival of dogmatic theology which we have witnessed in the past seventy-five years in the Protestant and Catholic camps, none of these systems has succeeded in refuting the case for a naturalistic or positivistic interpretation of the world, of humanity, of society and of history. Indeed, a strong argument could be made that there has taken place a vast complexification and intensification of the naturalistic case, that new evidence is constantly coming to hand for the self-explanatory character of areas of the universe which had previously been thought to require mind or God. Nor is it difficult for the skeptic to demonstrate with a considerable degree of conviction that the tragedies of the present century and its appalling inhumanities pose seemingly insoluble problems of

2. Norman Kemp Smith, "How Far Is Agreement Possible in Philosophy?" in *The Credibility of Divine Existence: The Collected Papers of Norman Kemp Smith,* ed. A. D. J. Porteous et al. (London and New York, 1967), pp. 189ff.

the character of the universe, of its ultimate or immediate purpose, and of its possible value.

The dimension of the sorrow of the human situation as portrayed by the skeptic, together with the success of the naturalist in extrapolating ordinary causal explanations to cover so much that was thought to be mind-dependent or mind-conditioned, has made it almost impossible for the serious-minded Christian to relate God to the world around in terms of any of the direct simplicities of older forms of prayer. Intercession becomes difficult if the person praying is strongly convinced that the phenomena that take place in the natural world are conditioned by natural laws, or fixed causal uniformities — a conviction instilled by years of education in a secular context. Prayer for the starving multitudes in another continent, which in another age might have been based upon an assumption that God, if faith were sufficient, could intervene to feed not five thousand, but five million, suddenly becomes meaningless. A world of miracles, a world in which nature miracles were an open possibility, was for centuries the accepted context for intercessory prayer. But in our world, where it is commonly accepted that hunger and poverty among the world's population can only be ameliorated by better control of the economy of supply and demand, by better training and by the redistribution of property, rather than by any expectation of a literally miraculous divine intervention, it is clear that the nerve of much of our intercessory prayer has been cut. The seeds of doubt have been sown, and have yielded their harvest of questions concerning the foundations — metaphysical, scientific, or more accurately prescientific — upon which some intercessory prayer depends.

Similar doubts on occasion beset the person who embarks upon a prayer of thanksgiving: the crops gathered in the autumn which our ancestors would have attributed directly and without mediation to God, the modern sophisticate sees all too clearly as the consequence of climatic conditions, wise use of insecticide and good labor relations. It would be absurd to suggest that theology, and particularly apologetics, has not for a hundred years or more been attempting to provide a rationalization of these situations which allowed thanksgiving and intercession to remain in business. What has happened in the last half-century or so, however, has been a wider acceptance than ever before by professing Christians of the naturalism and materialism of contemporary culture. An example that springs immediately to mind is that provided by Bultmann's programmatic essay in *Kerygma and Myth* entitled, "Demythologizing and the New Testament," where the almost unquestioned acceptance by the author of an outmoded determinism is even more difficult to comprehend than his total adherence to existentialism, which he certainly comes close to validating and for which he has been so often criticized.[3] In fact it is one of the ironies of the history of that controversy that the critics strained at the gnat and swallowed the camel as they did — thereby indicating, however tacitly, the degree of their complicity in mechanistic determinism.

Mention of that particular essay takes us inevitably to the influence of a changing cosmology upon prayer, in theory and in practice. We are at the moment concerned, not with the capital made by new theologies out of this change, but with the evacuated frame of reference that remains for prayers of adoration and glorification, and for many prayers of approach, once the old three-decker cosmology is replaced by infinite space or space returning upon itself or some other inconceivable model. Even the Lord's Prayer, with its opening address, "Our Father, which art in Heaven," carries with it a high factor of improbability or imposes burdens grievous to be borne of reinterpretation, or retranslation, or internalization, in a society in which the family is losing a good deal of its integrity and even validity, and where the father is not automatically perceived as the provider or as kindly and well-intentioned. Certainly a great many fathers of a great many children nowadays are not always there to call upon.

When we come to the *language* of prayer itself, from the consideration of its forms and structures determined by human needs, and consider the personal concepts it uses and the personal consequences it hopes to attain, we are embarked upon areas where the influence of naturalism as an explanation which requires no transcendent causes or power becomes most serious. We now pass from the external and naturalistic to the psychological circumstances which are helping to accentuate the problem of prayer. This father-language to which we have just referred meets difficulties from sociological quarters, as we have seen — for the role of the father in the family and its economy, or of marriage in society, is now

3. Rudolf Bultmann, "Demythologizing and the New Testament," in Hans-Werner Bartsch, ed., *Kerygma and Myth*, 2nd ed. (ET London, 1964), I, pp. 1-44.

so insecure that it has difficulty in providing us with a uniformly normative concept for universal prayer. The questioning of the usefulness of the concept may range from the completely destructive implications of the Oedipus Complex with its model of the hostility of son to father and the incestuous fantasy relations between son and mother, to the psychologically unhealthy father-figure notions which suggest that the attribution of fatherhood to God may not create the right impression of the dependence implicit in the creature-Creator relationship. The difficulty attaching to the notion of Father as used in prayer is not greatly dispelled by the commonplace remark that when Jesus taught us to say "Abba" he was really saying "Daddy," even if that were a correct interpretation of the term (which is no longer by any means assured), for while it may help children whose fathers are genuinely kind to them to understand who God is, it can scarcely be easily employed by grown men and women without a certain feeling of foolishness or embarrassment. This difficulty is so obvious that I do not wish to press it.

An allied problem, one which has not been greatly discussed and which arises out of the present or at least the not so recently past mood of theology, is the excessive emphasis on the notion of obedience, used greatly in prayers to Christ. Of course, there is again a great deal of biblical evidence for regarding obedience as the dominant response of the believing heart to what God has done for humankind in Jesus Christ, or of the disciple to the command of his Lord. At 2 Thessalonians 1:8, we read of the dire consequences which will befall those who do not obey the gospel, while Romans 10:16 speaks in similar terms; further, there are countless references in the Old Testament to obeying the commandments, and even more frequently the voice of God. That concept of obedience has been given dominance in modern theology through two themes, the first of which deals with the Word of God, and expects the responses of listening and then of obedience, and the second of which speaks explicitly about the divine *imperative*, or the command of God, which requires obedience *instanter.* To put any question mark against the concept of obedience is, for my generation at least, the language of revolution and irreligion. Yet two points ought to be made. The first is that very rarely do we "obey" what we think to be the will of God without our being aware that there is some inherent morality, rationality, and integrity about what we are commanded to do. Undue regard has been paid, with all apologies to Kierkegaard, to the apparent immorality, even unthinkableness, of God's command to Abraham. The "teleological suspense of the ethical" was not intended by Kierkegaard to be taken for the abandonment of the ethical for the subethical, but for a *higher* ethic.[4] What we are invited to obey commands our respect because of its intrinsic "obeyableness," and that most particularly when it surpasses what we thought we knew for ourselves about our duty. This analysis of the concept of obedience has obvious cross-reference to ethics and to the dominance of the Kantian-Brunnerian imperative, but we cannot now pursue them apart from their relation to praying. Secondly, obedience is a word which already carries for us associations of the wrong kind of superiority and of alienation, of domination and inconsiderateness, on the part of the person issuing the commands, all in all a feudal separation which does not find a ready place in the modern psychology of prayer. Obedience is no longer a concept which is part of the pattern of interpersonal relationships of the ordinary sort. It may be appropriate to life in the army, the police, or even the Scouts, but in the realm of ordinary, day-to-day relationships, an "I" would not so impose his or her will upon a "Thou," to use Buberian language, as to expect him or her to obey it. In an atmosphere of prayer, where the I-Thou relationship is paradigmatic, obedience therefore seems somehow to be culturally incongruous; if obedience is regarded as an essential of valid prayer, then those who are unsympathetic to the whole notion of obedience are likely also to reject prayer.

We have noted the effect upon prayer habits of the questioning of a theology of the Fatherhood of God and of obedience to the Gospel. To complete, though not on any basis of strict correlation, the trinitarian reference, we have to acknowledge the ill effects upon the whole psychology of prayer of inadequate analysis of how the Holy Spirit is related to moral endeavor. Admittedly, the part which the Holy Spirit is expected to play in the renewal of the human spirit, or soul, or mind, is extremely difficult and perhaps impossible to define with any psychological accuracy. But two circumstances have prevented any clarity even for which one might have hoped. First, in certain biblical passages the Holy Spirit is associated with what can only be called psychological abnormality. For example, in the Pentecost Story of Acts 2, we read of speaking with tongues and strange physical happenings in the rushing

4. Søren Kierkegaard, *Fear and Trembling* (ET Princeton, 1954).

mighty wind; in Acts 8:39, we read of the physical removal of Philip after he had baptized the eunuch, which is in its turn reminiscent of 1 Kings 18:12, where Obadiah expresses the fear that the Spirit of the Lord will have carried Elijah away before Obadiah can tell King Ahab where Elijah is. If Pentecost is in any way part of the gift of the Spirit for which much earnest prayer is made, then either many people must develop a high degree of guilt over their total failure to receive that gift, or they cease to ask for that part, at least, of the gift. At this point, one ought to remember the rationalizations which constitute much of New Testament commentary upon Acts 2. Secondly, the naturalism which is such a widely accepted feature of contemporary analysis of social movement, economic trends and historical happenings has acquired a wide though not always recognized vogue in the sphere of psychological explanation; processes of spiritual or mental healing, which might in biblical times have been related immediately and exclusively to the Holy Spirit and in more liberal times to the *help* of the Holy Spirit, are now interpreted even by Christians at times in purely naturalistic terms. Consequently, where a previous generation would have prayed for the gift of the Spirit in order to curb intemperance, or the biblical generation would have invoked the Holy Spirit direct, our generation more readily takes off to the psychiatrist or calls upon Alcoholics Anonymous, though the latter is not necessarily thought of as committed to naturalistic or even group-naturalistic explanations of the remedial work which it effects. Once again, Christian apologetics has made efforts to relate the Holy Spirit to natural processes of the mind, but the frequently unconvincing character of the arguments, combined with the persuasive influence of continuing cures from naturalistic sources, has led to a diminishing faith in the value of prayer.

When we have embarked thus far upon discussion of the impact registered on prayer habits and assessments by psychological theory, we have to add further that certain psychological theories of the self cannot be readily reconciled with many of the presuppositions for Christian prayer. The unwillingness, even the refusal of psychiatrists to attach moral coefficients to many attitudes, reactions and affections which would come under the severest Christian condemnation and would form the basis for deep repentance, puts a question mark against many prayers for forgiveness with their assumed implication of guilt. In some patients, it is this assumed guilt which for the psychiatrist is actually the greatest *obstacle* to securing the patient's health. An insistence upon forgiveness, or any sustained prayer for forgiveness, particularly where there is not properly sin, only serves to complicate the patient's condition and to retard a return to stability. Admittedly such circumstances seem to obtain only for the psychologically disturbed, but the appearance is illusory; there is a sufficiently great injection of this understanding of mental ill health and of how it is to be cured into all our ordinary thinking about how we recover from anxiety upsets and slight mental disorders, depressions, infatuations and so on, to lessen the seriousness with which many ordinary people pray for the gift of the Spirit to enable them to possess virtues, win victories, and think holy thoughts. The world of the mind and the spirit can no longer be regarded simply as the abode of God's Spirit, or as amenable only to God's curing. There is a medicine of the mind as of the body, and we often seem to be as competent to practice the one as much as the other.

Probably too, in a less exalted and less technical way, the old attempts to discredit prayer have lingered on to sap the effort of many of our contemporaries to submit to the discipline of prayer. I am thinking of the idea that prayer is a form of auto-suggestion, that if we persuade ourselves sufficiently, that which we had hoped to achieve by prayer comes to pass. The results would be the same whether we prayed to a God beyond ourselves or simply repeated a few formulae to ourselves. Not very many people are likely to take such a view seriously as in itself a refutation of prayer and of the validity of prayer. It *is* worth mentioning, however, for two reasons: first, because it is an example of the way in which a criticism repeated often became partly accepted; and secondly, because in honesty it is a true account of what a certain amount of prayer actually is — a form of auto-suggestion. By a process of guilt by association, however, the efficacy and validity of the rest of our prayers begin to be called in question. The questioning does not require to be explicit; it may not yet have reached the threshold of consciousness, but its influence tips the balance when we are in too much of a hurry, or too lazy, or too lacking in enthusiasm to make the extra effort to pray.

So far in our analysis of the elements which contribute to the present crisis in prayer, we have been drawing upon material which might have been valid generally at almost any point in the twentieth century. In a sense we have been moving closely within range of

Ménégoz and his kind of difficulty. But to turn the discussion from the general to the particular, we have to go to two other areas, closely allied with one another yet distinguishable — the religious and the theological. Let us take them in turn.

Religious Difficulties

Let me begin by pursuing the implications of a point made earlier, when reference was made to the way in which the evil in the world makes it difficult for anyone who prays to believe that he or she can thereby affect the course of nature as it is determined by natural laws. Quite apart from the deterrent effect of such evil upon the practice of intercession, it also, if it is dwelt upon to any great extent, poses for the believer a problem of such intolerable proportions as to make the practice of prayer, any kind of prayer, an act of consummate faith. It is almost as if the believer has first to make peace with the problem of evil and only then make an act of prayer. In fact, there are many who are unable to solve the problem, and who for that reason cannot pray. It would be wrong, then, to minimize the enormity of the problem of evil as it faces us in the contemporary world. In addition to the five to six million Jews slaughtered in concentration camps, and the many more millions of Russians lost in two world wars, or who survived only to be killed by Stalin, there is the daily mounting toll of men, women and children who die of hunger.

Less dramatically, though also in a sinister way, the sciences of psychology and psychiatry have been employed to blind the minds of many of our contemporaries to state-controlled ideological patterns, while the advertising industry exists through the suggestibility of the human mind and its malleability in any direction. We have come a long way from the Platonism which locates evil in matter and virtue in the mind. The Scriptures were nearer the truth, even as stated in the Authorized Version: "The imagination of man's heart is evil" (Genesis 8:21). It is as if evil has acquired spiritual dimensions of such enormity as to constitute a major threat to the power of good. The trouble with evil — both in its physical and spiritual character — is that under the mass media it comes home universally to men and women as it never did before and becomes a challenge to faith as it never was in previous times — except, of course, to those directly involved in its occurrence. Faced with this threat and this challenge, it might appear necessary for faith first to answer the challenge, or dissolve the threat before we begin to pray. The logic of such an order seems convincing: how can we pray if the existence of evil brings the reality, power and character of God into open question? Must we not be sure of God and his being before we pray to him? *Credo ut orem,* one might say: "I believe in order that I may pray." In fact, whatever else we have to say of prayer, we must expect that it will be a medium of the strengthening of faith. It must therefore be embarked upon in some degree of uncertainty about its subject. If that uncertainty is great, baffling and even almost nihilistic, it can still be prayer, as an attempt to reach out to God, "out of the depths." If such a view may entail too paradoxical a relation of prayer to faith for us at the moment to contemplate, I hope that we will not simply dismiss it, chiefly because it corresponds so much to the position of so many of our contemporaries.

Let us now turn to the practice of prayer itself. In the private sphere, for many Protestant Christians the pattern of three hundred years, the pattern of Bible passage followed by meditation and prayer, has not been replaced by any similar structure which would sustain a like devotion. In fact, Protestantism has been singularly infertile in the production of devotional liturgies of any sort. All too often such devotional liturgies as we have had have been simply scaled down versions of public worship, similar not only in shape and outline but even in the language employed. There is perhaps some virtue in retaining a kind of spiritual contact in private devotion with what happens in public liturgy. When we pray, whenever we pray, we are members of the whole worshipping body of the Church of Christ, and we are united with that body. We may even be offering prayers for the other members of the body and do so appropriately perhaps in the public liturgy. In a genuine sense, *all* prayer is public, being said in the company and communion of the saints. But when such allowances have been made, the vacuum remains which was created by the disappearance of the discipline of Bible reading and prayer. Maybe it was biblical criticism which began to destroy the simple faith that the Bible was given into our hand to be an immediate Word of God for every situation that life can offer. Perhaps it was that the gap between many biblical situations and the contemporary world became too great to be bridged readily by a direct application of the text to the crises of society or industry, or even of family life. But for many people it is no solution to the problem to insist on a return to the old ways, to the Bible-reading and direct relating of it to our kind of world. Yet there appears to be no genuine alternative, and in its absence prayer too disappears by default.

In addition to devotional practice, what might be called the philosophy that underlies Protestant prayer is not without problems. There has long been a good deal of controversy over what the phrase *ex opere operato* means in Roman Catholic theology and Church life, but in one of its senses it means that the actions done by the priest effect results immediately in the world of objective reality. The *opus* includes, of course, the whole sacramental action, of words and deeds in the Mass, obviously, but also of penance and absolution, so that the Catholic view of prayer itself can be said at one level to emphasize the same element of realism. Protestantism has, on the popular reading, insisted on the opposed view that the *opus* of the sacrament is only effective where the faith of the believer is appropriately present to receive the sacrament. Nor is the effect of the sacrament to turn bread into body or wine into blood, but to renew the faith, to recreate the life of the believer and of the community to which he or she belongs. In Protestantism, then, the action of the liturgy "really," as we say, takes place in the domain of the spiritual, rather than in the material, physical world. The illustration which I have often used is the comparison of what is done by a Roman Catholic priest and by a Protestant minister by the bedside of an unconscious and dying man surrounded by his sorrowing relatives. The burden of the prayers and actions of the priest are on behalf of the dying man, that the passage of his soul from this world to the next may be eased, so that he makes the passage with all the spiritual aids and comforts entrusted by God to the Church. The Protestant minister, while he will take account of the condition of the patient, will devote the major part of his prayer to the comfort of the relatives and to their subjective, emotional state. It would be wrong to absolutize such distinctions, but there is enough truth in them to show where the Protestant philosophy of prayer when under pressure can begin to crack. Let me elaborate.

First, if the psychologically tangible preconditions or consequences of prayer are not present, then faith in the efficacy of prayer begins to waver. This situation is aggravated particularly when no clear criteria are offered for judging when a prayer is or is not achieving its result. Many first communicants are bitterly disappointed when, having been initiated into what they rightly consider a profound mystery, they find that "nothing happens." It is usual to lay the responsibility for such an emphasis at the door of Schleiermacher, or in a general way to attribute blame to the liberals in theology; the problem, however, is actually endemic to Protestantism and is an implicate of our emphasis upon the role of faith in knowledge of God, in receiving the sacraments, in prayer and so on. It is, if we can say it without vainglory, the vice of our virtue. Secondly, even when Protestantism has moved to the other extreme, as it did in the heyday of scholastic Calvinism, and has removed the emotional, palpably empirical element from prayer and prayer's results, from faith and all its concomitant attitudes, and has thrown all the weight "out there" onto Christ as the objective ground of faith, the case is no better, for the area of the palpably empirical becomes now almost inaccessible. I am thinking of the way in which great arguments were held about whether one's election was recognized as such by oneself, or whether one remained tantalizingly in ignorance to the end. The certainty of election in Christ was securely affirmed in the Gospel, but precisely who the elect were was supremely uncertain. In these terms, an emotional vacuum is created for the believer, or the would-be believer, which must be filled alternately with hope and despair, without effect upon one's ultimate destiny or upon the success of one's prayer. Thus prayer is made discontinuous with what actually happens in or through the person praying, and then it is a short step to doubting not just the efficacy of prayer, but its validity as a spiritual exercise.

Theological Difficulties

We have already noted that the external pressures upon prayer as a continuing Christian responsibility, and the psychological reinterpretations of its main concepts and structures, would scarcely account by themselves for the crisis in prayer which we face today; they have been around for most of the twentieth century. While the religious pressures have been growing in recent decades, it is doubtful whether they can by themselves be totally responsible for what has eventually resulted. It is rather because the religious pressures have received an access of force from the theological changes of the last decades, that they have become so influential. In a sense, they have channeled theological movements, revolutions if you like, right into the heart of the religious life and into the center of prayer itself. The new theology, had it remained within the schools, would have been another passing fashion. It was because it received such varied religious expressions, and had such consequences not only for but in religious life, and particularly prayer, that it achieved its widespread notoriety. It is aspects of the new theology — I use the phrase in the loosest sense to cover most forms of recent theology — which has brought the whole prayer situation to the crisis point we now face and which I have now to examine.

Most obviously, perhaps, we had some thirty years ago the immediate consequences for prayer of such a theology as T. J. J. Altizer's, who argued that, "Once the Christian has been liberated from all attachment to a celestial and transcendental Lord, and has died in Christ to the primordial reality of God, then he can say triumphantly: God is dead! . . . True, every man today who is open to experience knows that God is absent, but only the Christian knows that God is dead, that the death of God is a final and irrevocable event."[5] In Altizer's theology this was a sophisticated way of emphasizing the kenotic theory of the person of Christ, only extended to God; this was combined, too, with passionate affirmations about "the presence of the living Christ." Altizer's was no passing trend in the world of theology; we can see it alive and well still in a variety of themes in continental theological scholarship. Even those who cannot quite follow the logic which presses even Nietzsche into the service of the Church without exorcism or decontamination, nevertheless take away the main theme and write their own variations upon it and draw from it their own conclusions. The immediate consequence for prayer is the advice given to those about to marry: "Don't."

There is no point in dwelling long on this aspect of recent theology, because while it ascribes far more religion to religionless Christianity than its quoted statements seem to imply, it clearly has not evolved a method of communication with its object, or subject, which eliminates all the references to the God of the old Christianity, or does not simply use the old structures with new counters for the old. Paul van Buren gave us a

5. T. J. J. Altizer, *The Gospel of Christian Atheism* (London, 1967), p. 111.

good example of how such theology tries to handle the problem of prayer.[6] In his well-known book, *The Secular Meaning of the Gospel,* he examined "the secular meaning of prayer," recognizing that traditionally "the language of prayer is the language of address, of speaking to someone," and that a dilemma must exist for someone who wants to pray but is puzzled if in order to do so one has to posit "someone" out there. According to van Buren, the way out of the dilemma is to show what exactly modern secular society does in what we might describe as a typical prayer situation. In an ancient society, when a farmer wanted to help his neighbor whose crops were suffering from a drought, he would pray for rain. In modern secular culture, if the farmer in question were also a Christian, there might be a reflection upon the plight of the neighbor in the context of the Christian gospel, after which he would free himself from self-concern in order to be more open to his neighbor's troubles. He would then go to see his neighbor, to study his problems on the spot, or to discuss the possibilities of irrigation. If possible, he might give him personal help in his troubles. The ancient man and the modern are both, van Buren says, doing what they think most effective to secure relief for the neighbor's distress. The meaning of the prayer of the ancient farmer is its use, which is to seek to help the neighbor — and this, of course, is also what the modern farmer does directly, in taking active steps to help. Though in this way van Buren seeks to retain a place for prayer in his rewriting of "the meaning of theology," as he calls it, the reasoning is unconvincing, for he fails to recognize the simple fact that the typical modern Christian, unlike himself, never reaches the point of confusing prayer and helping one's neighbor. Faced with the situation which van Buren describes, we would be most likely to do both; and if we only help our neighbor, we know full well that we are doing something different from praying.

To sum up, the whole popular movement in theology which has taken inspiration from such sources as Dietrich Bonhoeffer's statement that, "Honesty demands that we recognize that we must live in the world as if there were no God," and that, "We stand continually in the presence of the God who makes us live in the world without the God-hypothesis"[7] — that whole movement by *appearing* to take away

6. Paul van Buren, *The Secular Meaning of the Gospel* (London, 1963), pp. 188-90.

7. Dietrich Bonhoeffer, *Letters and Papers from Prison* (ET London, 1953), pp. 163f.

the hearer of prayer, God, removed prayer itself from the realm of the possible. With no God to talk to there can be no prayer.

But it was not just the extremists who have spread alarm and despondency; there was also Tillich's often repeated view that God is not a person.[8] Tillich intended to provide the basis for a new way of looking at God, but its net result has, to say the least, created difficulties for the ordinary interpretation and practice of prayer. Tillich has to take considerable responsibility for this, and for the subsequent history of his dictum, for he speaks of the impossibility of calling God a "self," and yet makes the odd statement that God is nevertheless "personal" (how "personal" if not a person?), by which he means that God is the ground of everything personal — which is not a proper equivalence at all. He does, however, try to show that God is not less than person, but his followers missed the point, and have made so much of the view that God is not a person and so emphasized his notion of God as the Ground of being that the question of *what* God is becomes more and more obscure. The trouble is that once you deny that God is a person, it is hard to see what positive statement can be put in its place, for personality is the highest thing we know. It is hard to think of a Ground, any kind of Ground, as higher than a person. At the popular level, the idea that God is not a person caught on because it was thought to be a denial of the "old man in the sky" notion, the Israelite deity with the characteristics of jealousy, vindictiveness, and arbitrary favoritism, an anthropomorphism of a less attractive kind. So interpreted, the theme was understandably acceptable. Difficulty arises, however, when on the one hand it becomes necessary to describe what God is if not person, and on the other, to show how, if a Ground of being is to be the substitute for it, believers can possibly relate to this Ground. The difficulty for prayer in this latter concept is immense: One depends upon the Ground of being in some metaphysical or ontological sense, but the wider range of interpersonal relations which seem to be so much a part of the religious life and which condition prayer and give it its content becomes almost impossible. Therefore, though Tillich himself went on to say many positive things about prayer — which incidentally drew upon other parts of his theology — those who took away only his "God is not a person" theme have had great difficulty in explaining what prayer is, and in giving it an integral place in their theology.

8. Paul Tillich, *Systematic Theology*, I (Chicago, 1951), p. 245.

Closer to the central stream of orthodoxy, a tradition also grew up which led equally to difficulties over prayer, a tradition concerning the nature of revelation. In the seventeenth and eighteenth centuries, the accepted view of revelation was that it involved the transference of propositions from the divine mind to that of the human recorder who gave us the Bible, the communication of a body of truth by God to the world. The great change in the conception of revelation which we have in the twentieth century is the idea that what is offered in revelation is not some truth concerning God but the living God himself. John Baillie referred to revelation in this connection as "the divine self-disclosure."[9] The consequences for prayer of this revision of what revelation is about are complex, and significant, and yet scarcely ever have they been noted and properly examined. Some we shall discuss at length, but for the present we can note that whereas under the old conception of revelation as propositional, people operated with the notion that prayer consisted of our talking to God and listening to what he has to say, one side at least of this process is lost. He discloses himself to us, communicates his self to us rather than information about himself, but the character of our response remains inevitably in obscurity. If propositions do not travel in our direction, then should we expect them to travel in the opposite direction? The dilemma is increased when revelation and response are couched in the language of communion — God with us in revelation and ourselves with God in prayer and response to his gracious dwelling with us. The question to be raised is that of the medium of our traffic with God, and its basis in and reflection of his traffic with us. If we move away from propositional revelation, and if we construe the responsive moment in revelation on its human side in terms of obedience, acknowledgment and even "faith," then the role of old-fashioned, articulate speech in our relation to God has to be reexamined. I would go so far as to suggest that here, in the heart of so much contemporary orthodoxy, is actually to be found one of the sources of one of the odd phenomena noted in our introduction — that some religious people believe in God and in revelation but are desisting from the practice of any traditional kind of prayer.

A final circumstance which has precipitated the crisis of prayer is also of a formal theological sort — the recognition that we should expect

9. John Baillie, *The Idea of Revelation in Recent Thought* (Oxford, 1956), p. 19.

to meet God not simply in the privacy and quiet of withdrawal from the world, but over the entire spectrum of human activity. An older form of this had rested on the saying *laborare est orare*, but the modern form springs from a revulsion against a process which seemed to be forcing God to the periphery of human existence, and which had allowed science and technology to take over increasingly numerous areas where God had previously been thought to be in sole control. The answer to that God-of-the-gaps notion is to say that the whole earth, the whole universe, is God's, and that his writ is universal, so that to engage at any point in the world's problems is to engage with him. This type of activism replaces talk to God, to request his blessing, his guidance and inspiration, with talk together about how the job is to be done. Thus, the simple expression of human concern for the hungry, the underprivileged and the dispossessed — especially when coupled with such problems as that of the language of prayer, the gulf set between what we hope for in it and what we face in reality, and the more obviously theological questions and confusions which have arisen concerning God and revelation — has itself led to the diminution of the part played by prayer in the life of the Christian.

These, then, are the components of the problem of prayer: the continuing pressures from a naturalistic and secular culture to interpret all occurrences and all possibilities in terms of causal uniformities; the psychological reductions of the structures and concepts adopted in prayer; the pessimism induced in Christians themselves by the apparently ever-growing dimensions of the problem of evil; and finally, the link between these and the equivocal assessment of prayer, of its possibility and validity, which arise from several aspects of modern theology. Taken together, however, they constitute a *single* problem: Is prayer still an essential part of the Christian's relation to God, and if so, then what form should it take?

CHAPTER 2

Theological Dimensions of Prayer

What Is Prayer?

Having stated at length the problem of prayer, we shall find it helpful before addressing ourselves to the details of the problem to have before us some conception of what prayer is, in theological terms. It may be possible then to observe that a major part of the problem which we have to face, and which has not emerged in our previous analysis, is that changes are perhaps taking place in the theology of prayer itself. I propose therefore to state the components of a rather traditional conception of prayer, so that the points of deviation therefrom can be fairly firmly fixed.

To begin with the basic simplicities, we must say that *prayer is talking to God.* This description covers the whole range of prayer from the spontaneous utterance to the sustained address of the recluse performing a lengthy office as he goes through the several stages of a carefully constructed approach to God. On examination, this talking to God involves a number of presuppositions and implies a number of consequences which serve to amplify the theology of prayer. First, prayer is elicited as a *response* to a situation, which may be one of danger, of necessity, or of loneliness, and which in more developed forms of prayer may be an acknowledgment of God's being, or action. It implies some degree of sensitivity to the total environment, of appreciation of the relation of the person praying to the environment and of its impact upon the self; prayer, therefore, is what one *does* about that circumstance. While there may be idyllic accounts of the prayer which wells up within the heart, some kind of unprompted spiritual effervescence, its most obvious characteristic is that of response.

Taking the description one stage farther, we can add that, in the main, it is *articulate* response. It is reactive. Once again we do not rule out altogether the possibility, in the traditional forms of prayer, of some nonarticulate lifting of the soul to God, some immersing of our spirit in the Spirit of God, because clearly mysticism of this kind is a part of the Christian conception of prayer. Nevertheless, for the majority of the time for most people, prayer is something articulated. In other words, what we do about the circumstance to which the prayer is reactive is to say something so that the prayer itself becomes a kind of doing. Here J. L. Austin's and D. D. Evans' concept of "performative" comes to mind, for in saying we are *doing* certain things (and not just uttering statements).[1] It is proper also to notice carefully that the response involves articulation, a fact which implies that a degree of effort is required to bring the reaction to the point of speech. Such articulation brings the prayer to the point, not just of fulfillment, but of very existence. On the other hand, articulation of the prayer may equally prove to be its catharsis; if, when it comes to expression, it is seen to be merely the objectification of selfish desires or the projection of small-mindedness or hatred or frustration, it has to be rejected. It may, on achieving articulate self-consciousness, reveal itself as a prayer to have the cup of bitterness pass from its lips, and to prompt the further prayer of, "Not my will but thine be done." In a less exalted sphere it may appear as our prayer for an easier life, for the pleasures without the responsibilities — all the self-deceptions which we practice on ourselves and which when brought into the light of day we cannot but disown. Accordingly, the fact that prayer becomes articulate imposes upon it the requirement of exhibiting growth and maturation. There are childish prayers which are improper in an adult, and which, once spoken, must be rejected. Prayer may be abandoned, therefore, for none of the reasons mentioned in our opening analysis, but solely because the person praying has not cultivated prayer proportionally to his or her developing intellectual life.

Just as prayer in the main is response, so in many forms it is

1. J. L. Austin, *How to Do Things With Words* (Oxford, 1962); D. D. Evans, *The Logic of Self-Involvement* (London, 1963).

expectant, anticipating response. We have to admit the immediate exceptions of prayers of adoration and thanksgiving — though even here there is the anticipation that these forms of prayer will maintain and further the right relation between the person praying and the God of the prayer; to fail to pray in this way would break the relation. But otherwise, prayer has a positive, forward-looking character, expecting that certain results will ensue upon the prayer. Even when the results are almost impossible of achievement, the expectation remains as part of the prayer, and without it, the prayer would not be what it is. The results anticipated need not always be selfish; prayers are often thoroughly altruistic, expecting happiness and success for others, hoping for good even for enemies. The results when desired even for the person praying need not be happy, pleasurable or material; they may be self-sacrifice, a spirit of self-denial, or some exceptionally difficult responsibility. But the person praying sees the way to these results, either for himself or for some other person, whether happy or hazardous, as being by way of prayer. Prayer is the span between now and then, between hope and its fulfillment, and without the prayer the span remains unbridged. The futurist, anticipatory element in all prayer received its classic expression in Revelation 22:20 in the words, "Come, Lord Jesus."

One very important aspect of the articulate response of prayer is the fact that it is cast in a personal form. It is address of the kind which is directed to a person. In discussing the problem of prayer, we noticed that difficulty has arisen in practice when God was conceived of in other than personal terms, as the Ground of being, or simply as not a person; it is not clear what language is to be used in addressing such a God. That whole practice was called in question because of the ubiquity throughout prayer of the language presupposing what Buber immortalized as the I-Thou relationship. To take away the language of persons seems to invalidate the whole concept, for prayer and personal response seem to be inextricably bound up with one another. Account might be taken in this context also of the now almost universal practice of using "you" instead of "thou" in prayers. The immediate intention seems clear enough: namely, to secure for the prayer-relationship something more closely akin to the language normally used in ordinary person-to-person relationships. There is supporting evidence for this in the fact that when the word "thou" and its other cases were originally used, it was a word used in the context of intimate personal relationships. But the intimacy disappeared with the centuries, and came to be replaced by formality, distance, and even coldness.

Though the intention is clear enough and even laudable, the means are perhaps less sure. In fact, I wonder whether they have ever been clearly worked out. For example, it may be that although "thou" language has lost contemporary relevance as no longer connoting intimacy, it might have served another function — to do justice to the fact that God, if a person, is different from other persons. We have noted the embarrassment which Tillich feels over calling God a person, and his preference for concepts such as "Ground of being"; it is not inconceivable that a thinker who shares that embarrassment might find it useful to use "thou" language, precisely because it is *not* used by us in our relations with ordinary persons. Theologians of another persuasion from Tillich's have seen in "you" language a retrogression to the approach of an earlier Liberalism; they favor "thou" language because it helps to express and preserve the sense of the transcendence of God. In short, the choice between "thou" and "you" language is sometimes not simply a language choice, or even a choice of two ways of approaching God. It can just as easily be a concealed way of choosing between two totally different concepts of God.

Karl Barth on Prayer

Karl Barth has certain things to say characterizing prayer, which will serve to take our discussion somewhat farther.[2] First, prayer has its basis in the *order and command of God.* In a quite simple way, it is God's explicit will that we should come to him with our prayers — a view which Barth has no difficulty in illustrating from the Scriptures, both Old and New Testament. Statements such as, "Call on me in the day of trouble; I will deliver you, and you shall glorify me" (Psalm 50:15); or, "Seek the LORD while he may be found, call upon him while he is near" (Isaiah 55:6), are representative of the Old Testament, while the injunction, "Ask, and it will be given you; search, and you will find; knock, and the door will be opened for you" (Matthew 7:7), is central

2. Karl Barth, *Church Dogmatics,* III/4 (ET Edinburgh, 1961), pp. 87ff. Further references are given after quotations in parentheses.

to the New. The command of God to pray is relevant not only to situations of dire need, but to the total range of human existence; at all times we receive of God's goodness. While from whatever source help may appear to come when we need it, it comes ultimately from God. Barth, therefore, brushes aside unceremoniously those "pious and impious arguments" against the permissibility and possibility of all asking in prayer. The all-knowing and the all-wise God has taken into account both the degree to which our wrong asking may militate against his purposes, and the fact that our contrary wills are taken up into the covenant of his salvation. If God by his command to pray has bridged the gulf of the infinite qualitative difference between himself and us, then it is improper for us from our side to attempt to open the gulf again. According to Barth, therefore, the person who says, "I cannot pray," is really lying; what that person really means is, "I will not pray" — the point being to try to evade the commandment and grace of God (p. 96). There is a certain direct simplicity about Barth's emphasis which does justice to the nature of prayer as the Bible describes it, while his discussion of the question raises serious questions about the possibility of dispensing with prayer as an element in the religious life.

The next aspect of prayer to which Barth draws attention is its character as *petition* addressed to God. The fact that prayer is petition is an indication of the willingness of human beings to acknowledge their unworthiness before God; they come with empty hands which God in his goodness will fill. To the question whether true prayer should not also include thanksgiving, penitence and worship, Barth has an answer to make in each particular case. On thanksgiving he points out that no one can ask aright without being grateful to God for his goodness in all the great and small things that happen in the world, and without responding to this same God's command that we should come to him with our needs. On penitence, he remarks that we cannot come to God with our requests without being aware of the deep abyss that separates us from him and without therefore confessing that we are unworthy of the bounty of his blessings; so moved by penitence, we go on to ask how this penitence may be saved from concentration upon itself and turned in an effectual direction. The Penitential Psalms, according to Barth, illustrate the way in which true repentance reaches its climax in petition: "Only when [penitence] results in the corresponding request is it prayer" (p. 99). On the relation of worship to petition the case is perhaps more difficult to carry, for worship, in the sense of turning to God, being quiet in his presence, and contemplating his majesty and depth has come to be recognized as emphatically in the center of prayer today. Barth is, however, afraid that this sort of emphasis can produce ambiguity. It may become obsession with the *Deus absconditus, tremendum et fascinans,* a kind of solemn stupor. If it is to be true worship of the *Deus revelatus,* then it must issue in petition to him, as he has commanded us and within the limiting and at the same time the immensely free conditions of his own being. Although, for Barth, true prayer also involves thanksgiving, repentance and worship, the fact remains that it is essentially petition, and that only as such is it also thanksgiving, repentance, and worship. The others are all elements of petitionary prayer (p. 100).

Certain comments might be made in passing on Barth's attempt to make petition the determinative principle of prayer. It is characterized by a certain biblical primacy and immediacy, together with a certain honesty about the character of prayer and about the measure of our dependence upon God, a dependence of which prayer is both the evidence and the medium. Our prayers so often begin spontaneously in some request to God and proceed reflectively and almost self-critically and self-apologetically to some of the other moods which Barth mentions; or they begin reflectively, one might say sometimes even self-righteously in a mood of adoration, but very soon proceed to petition of some kind or other. Barth is right in this respect that there is almost invariably a component of petition in all human prayer. Where he does not quite succeed is in his reductionism — i.e., his attempt almost to *reduce* all prayer to forms of petition. Other forms of prayer originate from or lead to petition, but equally petition presupposes these other forms of prayer, both for its motivation and its very meaning.

Barth argues further that true prayer is prayer which is sure of a hearing; that is, it is assured of its incorporation by God in his plan and will for humankind and for the person praying (p. 106). Almost in anticipation of objections that might be brought against such a categorical statement — for example, that prayer then seems to impose limitations upon the sovereignty of God, or that it sets an extremely high premium upon assurance — Barth immediately sets up his defense works. First of all, he affirms that such assurance as we have in praying is determined by hope; it is hope which gives it its unquestioning certainty. He cites in this connection Luther's *Greater Catechism,* according to which we are not only commanded to pray, but are told that our asking is well-pleasing to God, and that he grants what we ask (p. 107). Secondly, however, why should hope in this way be the basis of assurance? Barth gives an involved Christological answer to this question. The person who prays belongs to the body of Christ, and in praying is in Christ through the fellowship of the Spirit. Thus, "the praying man is not separated from God nor God from him" (p. 108); through our being in Christ, rather, we pray "with and after Christ," making the great requests which he has made, so that to pray to God is to be assured that we have him on our side from the very start. Barth's view is thus that in the incarnation, God has taken his stand on our side and by our side. When Christ asks, we ask, and *vice versa;* the Father cannot fail to hear the Son, and therefore, our requests will be heard. It is not arrogance but the humility of faith which confidently assumes that God will grant what it asks (p. 109). To hope, therefore, which has already been mentioned, Barth now adds faith as a prerequisite of the assurance implicit in all true prayer.

I must confess to even greater uneasiness over what Barth has to say about true prayer being sure of a hearing than I had over his view about petition. For example, his presentation involves a shift of ground — with a consequent move from security to insecurity. His position would seem to be secure if he were taken to be saying only that true prayer can be certain that God is going to listen to it. True prayer will be conscious of the proper motives of prayer — a sense of dependence upon and gratitude to God for all the mercies of life, an acknowledgment of God's command to make needs known to him, a genuine desire to exclude from the prayer anything that might spring from unwarrantably selfish desires or ambitions. In the light of these precautions, and with a proper attitude to God, it will *hope* that God will answer its requests. Barth, it seems, moves from that fully defensible position to one which is much more questionable — namely, that God *grants* what is asked in prayer. It is true that Barth, even when stating this rather unwarranted view, still continues to speak of God "hearing our requests," but there are sufficient occasions when he goes much farther to justify talk of a shift of position (e.g., pp. 108ff.). The shift is matched, in fact, by a change from talk of hope, to talk of faith — faith of which is expected a very much higher degree of absolute conviction than had been previously attributed to hope, which, after all, allows for the possibility of non-fulfillment of the request made.

Three comments may be made. First, the record has to be put straight at the start: There can be allowed no shift of position from the view that true prayer is sure of a hearing from God to the view that true prayer is sure that God will grant the prayer. Unless the latter view is refined to the point of saying that it is only when God grants the prayer that it is prayer, and I am sure that that is not Barth's intention, then it exposes prayer to the widest refutation, and raises an almost impossible host of difficulties for prayer. We know of too many genuine prayers which have gone unanswered to be happy for long with an attribution of success to all real prayer. In a sense, this view makes prayer too easy and too difficult: too easy, because it leaves the impression that you get what you want; too difficult, because it carries such a load of contrary evidence in the area of ordinary requests for many worthwhile ends that it has to be applied only to prayers of a highly formal and spiritualized kind — for example, for spiritual growth or a deeper knowledge of God or for the coming of God's kingdom.

Secondly, it may prove profitable to enquire concerning *why* Barth makes the shift of ground mentioned above. The answer lies in the Christological section which, in a way, separates the two views (pp. 107ff.). The essence of the incarnation is that Christ takes to himself our human nature, so that we are in him and he is in us. Accordingly whatever we do — say, in prayer — we do as incorporated in Christ, or alternatively he does it, as it were, through us. This incorporation — and it amounts almost to identification — entails that God receives us, and our requests, as the Father would receive those of the Son. Again, there is a slight equivocation in Barth, as he appears now to say that we are in Christ and Christ in us, that we are even bound up with God, and that we pray with and after Christ; and again to say that we pray with Christ "at our side" as our Brother, from whom we are distinguished even as we are conjoined with him. Perhaps the equivocation makes very little difference, for either way Barth so closely relates Christ to the person praying that the margin of error is inevitably reduced or even eliminated. A more realistic and acceptable view would be that believers and Christ are not identified, in which case there is a margin of permissible error, whether entailed by human sin, creatureliness, or ignorance; because of this margin, however, our attitude in prayer, while it may be one of hope, and faith, even of assurance, can never be one of conviction that what we pray for will be granted.

Thirdly, in the treatment normally given to the problem which Barth here not so much fails to solve as totally ignores, that of whether unanswered prayer is real prayer, recourse is had to the phrase "in Jesus' name" (p. 108). The suggestion is that when this qualification is added to a prayer, the person praying recognizes the possibility of error or sin in making the request; the petition is therefore made "in the name of Jesus," since through him the dross of the prayer can be refined and its "permissible" clauses granted. The phrase is also, of course, and I hasten to note the point, intended to acknowledge *the* person through whose life, death, resurrection and continuing advocacy at God's right hand, all prayer can be heard, validated and answered. The phrase is a summary of the relevance of the totality of the gospel to the immediate needs of the person praying, but it is not a guarantee of the fulfillment of any of our petitions. Barth oddly enough takes note of the phrase but gives the following exegesis: "In his name" means under Christ's leadership and responsibility, in the unity of our asking with his, and in obedience to his summons, with the support of his power as the Son, and in the strength of his unity with the Father (p. 108). Where traditionally there has been the recognition of the possible diversity between what we say and what may be God's will — and the hope that through the name of Christ the diversity will be reconciled — Barth seems to press a higher degree of identity than the phrase itself can possibly sustain.

There is, however, another, more important point which Barth makes simply in passing, which has great relevance to the developing picture of the theology of prayer which I have been describing. He says that we are obliged to approach God completely as we are. We have to drop the *persona,* the mask, which we adopt in the very varied situations in which in ordinary life we play so many varied roles. The person who prays and petitions God is in this act stripped of all facades and pretenses, and stands before God simply as a man or a woman who needs something. One fact of which we are becoming very conscious in the modern world is the way in which we are never truly ourselves, cast as we are in different roles in the different contexts in which we find ourselves throughout the day. It was some time ago that my eyes were first opened to the variety artists that we all are, unconsciously changing from act to act, not only dressing differently but behaving differently and speaking differently. We did not use the word *persona* in those days, but it is ideally suited to the purpose. There are two implications to the concept. On the one hand, if the actor adopts and identifies with too many *personae* the possibility of loss of identity of personality becomes real; actors who play a part over a long period find that after they give up the part they continue not only the mannerisms they have acquired but also the outlook, the typical reactions and so on. In this sense the *persona* is an inescapable factor in modern existence: we have to behave as different people in different situations throughout any day — as parents, teachers, club members, car drivers, conveners of committees or committee members, as Scots, or Irish, or Britons, or Europeans. It only becomes a dangerous character of modern existence when we vary the constant too much from role to role, one of the most obvious examples being the change which takes place in certain God-fearing citizens when they take to the road at the wheel of a car.

One of the functions of prayer, then, is to lead through the dropping of these *personae* to the strengthening and integrating of the person behind or within the *personae.* If he or she has a strong identity, there is nothing to fear. On the other hand, the *persona* may be not simply a consequence of the complex existence that we all have to live in varied textures of relationship, but rather an attempt on someone's part to conceal the reality that lies behind, and to project some totally different concept, to create an illusion for the benefit of the observer — or perhaps for his or her own benefit. The *persona* is then a medium of deception, and in its more pathological forms even of self-deception. It is this *persona* that we have to learn to drop in prayer, not only so that we may be ourselves, but also in order that the healing grace of God may reach us in reality and not in the illusoriness of the *persona* adopted. In such terms, prayer is generally a means of grace, as has been said so often in the Protestant tradition, but it is also clearly a medium of self-knowledge.

Prayer and the Human Relation to God

Leaving Barth, I should like to change direction somewhat and examine the proposition that prayer covers the *entire spectrum* of the human relation to God. There are several aspects to this characterization of prayer. First, by it we are saying that it is wrong to treat prayer as if it were one aspect of the religious life to be added to all of the others — to faith, hope, trust, obedience, devotion and so on — as if these could all be carried on by themselves independently of prayer, which either comes before them as preparation for them or after, as a consequence of them. It is, in fact, a necessary concomitant of them all, so that there is no situation which does not have what might be called its prayer-reference. In an extreme sense this fact is of immense devotional importance for any person *in extremis* of one kind or another. The fact that our Lord prayed in Gethsemane and on the cross is the classic demonstration of the ubiquity of prayer. But in less exceptional settings, the fact is no less compulsive that prayer covers the spectrum of religious existence. It can be illustrated from the sacraments and all the major ordinances of the Church. In baptism, it is through the prayer of the minister that the water as well as the hearts of the parents and congregation are made ready for the receiving of the child into the membership of the catholic Church in the action of baptism. The sacrament of Holy Communion turns on the massive movements of the great eucharistic prayer — the prayers of the veil, the bidding to thanksgiving, the thanksgiving, the Gloria, the offering of the elements, the *epiklesis,* and the self-offering of the people to God. The whole occasion is unthinkable without prayer both spoken outwardly and inwardly said in the heart. In Confirmation we have the petition that God may confirm in the young adult the vows taken on his or her behalf by parents years before, and this prayer is again the axis on which the service turns. We could add the service of ordination — by prayer and the laying on of hands, the prayer being the point in the service (if any single point is to be selected — and I feel we must or we may end with none) where, in the Reformed tradition, the presbyters, "to whom it doth belong," pray and act for the inclusion of the ordinand in the apostolic succession. There is too the service of marriage, which as an act of the Church is distinguished from the civil ceremony by the setting of prayer in which the civil elements, here present too, are placed; it is here that the Church's significant seal is placed on the union. In the funeral service, it is the prayers of the people which bear the weight of Christian meaning which the occasion has, and which turn into that circumstance of hope which is the core of resurrection faith. But the full story is not told until we relate prayer, not only to the major events on the religious spectrum, but to all the infinity of lesser points between — to grace before meals, to daily prayer morning and evening, to the emergency prayer uttered in an instant of sudden impulse and spoken even before we are aware of it. The whole spectrum of the religious life is covered by prayer.

Perhaps we ought to take this view to its logical conclusion and affirm that prayer is the medium of articulation of our relationship to God — and as such both maintains and is the expression of the *nonarticulate* aspects of that relationship. It would be wrong to deny that all of our relations to God can be put into words or, more precisely, are verbal in character; love, faith, hope and obedience may be, as occasion demands, verbalized, but in the first instance they are attitudes, mental sets, commitments, even emotions, and never, never words. Indeed, were we to suggest that they were words, we would be opening them to the accusation of hypocrisy. Nevertheless, only as they *issue* in words, the spoken words of love, thanksgiving, adoration, expectation and devotion, can they properly express themselves; it is only as overt actions whose character can be described in words and so communicated to others that they can ever hope to be explicit and understood. Such expression serves the further purpose of maintaining them in existence and indeed furthering their growth and development. It is for that reason peculiarly difficult to understand how faith, love and the others can mature in a religious experience which rejects prayer altogether, except on the assumption that their character has been in some way altered, or perhaps that the religious experience has learned to do without them. When this close nexus is established both between prayer and the great occasions of the Christian's life, and between prayer and the peculiar concepts of the Christian religion, it becomes clear that prayer is the medium and expression of religious existence, growth and maturation.

Any discussion of the validity of prayer thus becomes automatically a discussion of the validity of religion itself. The method of prayer is the method of religion, because prayer is religion. Discussions about religious epistemology are discussions about the epistemology of prayer, for prayer is how you know God, how you talk to God, yet it is remarkable that so many treatments of religious epistemology totally ignore the question of prayer, and regard the knowledge of God as some kind of inarticulate knowledge. The comparison with knowledge of other selves and the epistemological problems involved is very interesting. In this latter field the knowledge and the means of communication have been studied together, so that communication and the part that it plays in how we come to know one another are studied as part of the same problem. Religious epistemology typically moves between the two poles of some sort of semi-mystical knowledge on our part and revelation on God's part, whereas the part which the articulate knowledge involved in prayer plays has been almost entirely disregarded in this whole field. The epistemology of prayer, however, is a perfectly valid field of philosophical study, and one which, because of its articulateness, might well yield to methods of analysis which are applicable to other forms of articulate communication. It is odd, too, that the propositional approach has been applied to God's side of the God-humanity relationship, that is, to revelation as far as it is contained in the Scriptures — though even here the flight from propositions has brought its own little crop of epistemological headaches — and not with comparable thoroughness to the human side of this relationship.

Prayer in Theory and Practice

When we ask for the *theology* of prayer, we are, I believe, not simply asking for accounts of what prayer is, definitions of prayer in other words. There is an implicit desire to know what theological circumstances ultimately condition and validate prayer. We ask questions, then, about the ultimate context of prayer, its determining grounds, as well as the implications which it carries for the rest of our theology. It is necessary for us to turn now to these more conceptual formulations.

To begin with, I should like to draw out the sense and the intention of Jesus' prayer in John 17, and reaffirm that the prayer (or prayers) of Jesus are the ground of the *possibility* of all Christian praying to God. Clearly, there is much evidence throughout the New Testament for the necessity of prayer for the disciple, imposed both by the oft-repeated command of Christ and by the force of his example. But what I have in mind goes much farther, for the command may fail because of our weakness or neglect. The example, by its very grandeur, may discourage. The prayer of the incarnate Son to the Father, standing as he does in such a peculiar relation to the Father that he can both pray to the Father (a symbol of his humiliated state), and at the same time be assured of the acceptance by the Father of his prayers (the point which Barth made so forcefully), is the condition of the very possibility of all prayer which the brothers and sisters of Christ may therefore make. I am thinking not so much of the content of that prayer of Christ's, which was in the beginning a request that the Father should recognize him as he was recognizing the Father, each glorifying the other, but rather of the very *fact* of the prayer itself. There are many metaphors that can be used to describe how this prayer of Christ's effects the possibility of all Christian praying. We can, as Barth does, use the metaphor of our incorporation in Christ, so that we think of ourselves, being human, as comprehended within the human nature of Christ which is the historical circumstance of his praying. Christ includes our prayer in his. We can think, as the writer of the Hebrews does, of the whole life, death and resurrection of Christ as opening a way into the holiest of holies and as thus guaranteeing a hearing for human prayers. We can picture Christ, as the First Epistle of John does, as an advocate who pleads the cause of those for whose sins he was made propitiation. The idea is not, therefore, confined to John's Gospel and to the prayer recorded in chapter seventeen; rather, it is essential to the whole conception of prayer as the New Testament understands it that our prayer is somehow made possible through the prayer of Christ.

We have to go one stage farther and affirm that Christ's prayer *validates* the prayer of the Christian. There is no need to go again over the ground we traversed in discussing Barth's concern to establish the Christian's expectation that his requests would be granted. The same strictures apply at this point. The prayer of any Christian will contain requests and petitions which even from a human point of view can be seen to be inadequate; in Christ's eyes *a fortiori* they will not be susceptible to validation. But because Christ has prayed, we pray validly — not expecting that our prayer will be without flaw, but earnestly hoping that what God cannot accept he will forgive and where possible change. Whereas in other areas invalidity entails rejection, in prayer invalidity is the converse of conversion and redemption. Nothing is lost.

The prayer of Christ in John 17 imparts form, content, quality and ultimate purpose to our prayer. The form is clearly structured: glory given to the Father, the request to share in the glory so that the prayer may be effective; concern for the disciples, for their needs, their loneliness, their mission; the intercession for them as they take up their discipleship in the world, and for the others who will come after them in the heritage of faith; and the recognition of God's ultimate purpose of love for humankind. The content is the relating of the nature of God — as glory, goodness, savior, love — to the demands to be made of the disciples and to the reality of their responsibilities in a world which would be largely antagonistic to them. It is rather interesting to note how, in this prayer, "the content" includes what we might call "narrative" material interlaced with petition and intercession: "Now they know that everything you have given me is from you," in verse 7, leads on to, "I pray for them," in verse 9. Again, in verse 11, narrative is followed by petition: "And I am no longer in the world, but they are in the world, and I am coming to you. Holy Father, protect them. . . ." The quality which Christ's prayer imparts to human prayer is the quality of joy. Joylessness is the crime perpetrated upon prayer by a thankless and unforgiving generation. Jesus prays (v. 12) that his joy may be fulfilled in his disciples. Joy is the last thing we expect to find in our prayer or through our prayers, and the very suggestion appears almost to be in poor taste. Yet Jesus, knowing the tribulations that lay ahead of his disciples, particularly in the immediate future now filled for him with the shadow of the cross, and for them with the foreboding of disaster, nevertheless prays for joy, and the fulfillment of joy. The ultimate purpose of the prayer is that through the unity of the disciples the world may come to know that the Son was sent into the world by the Father. This is not the place to pursue the fortunes of this prayer in ecumenical discussions where it has, I believe, wrongly been employed as an argument for the conception of Church unity as organic rather than, say, federal. But the point is inescapable that the purpose of the unity for which Christ prays is not the resolution of interdenominational conflict, or even the creation of some ecclesiastical higher harmony, but rather the spread of knowledge of who Christ was and is. In other words, the end of unity is evangelism, and the scandal of disunity lies not in some new crucifixion of the body of Christ, but in the frustration and stultification of the Church's mission.

Two final points may be made in the area of the theology of prayer. First, prayer, while it can be regarded as coterminous and coincident with the whole spectrum of Christian existence, is not to be equated with the detail of that spectrum. It may be true to say that *laborare est orare,* to work is to pray, so long as we do not take work as a constant substitute for prayer and finally as a replacement for it. But it would be false to attempt the converse — *orare est laborare* — as if we expected thereby to escape the implications of our own prayers. Prayer is a transient, however frequently recurrent, phase of Christian existence. Some religious orders have tried to change this transiency into some kind of sustained spiritual permanency, but even when they succeeded in some measure, they were the first to publish the selective character of the call to such a life. If petition is the central component in prayer as Barth proposed; if the will of Christ for his disciples is that they should go into the world to demonstrate what God's purpose was in Christ; if prayers for all humankind are going to be, not the inhibitors, but rather the inspirers of service — then prayer has to stop, in order to give way to the action which implements it. In holding such a view, I am well aware of the fact that there is a body of support for the alternative claim that ideally we should be in constant communion with God, and that prayer is the medium by which such communion is sustained. While respecting the piety of such a view, I wonder whether it is not more angelic than realistic. It is only in heaven that they gaze eternally and without interruption upon the face of God. Here we have to break off the prayer in order to do what we asked for the power to do in the prayer, or to do that which, if we neglected it, would be a denial of the spirit and instruction of the prayer.

The final comment I have to make upon prayer is directed to its eschatological character, for it is so in a number of ways. For example, the hope and expectation that we have so often noted as distinctive marks of prayer have as their ultimate objective the coming of the kingdom of God. Whatever is validly prayed for is comprehended within that objective. It is not for nothing then that we say daily the Lord's Prayer, which has at its center the petition, "Thy Kingdom come," and link it so closely with the petition, "Give us this day our daily bread," for the immediacy of present hunger is heightened by the prayer for the kingdom, which is the condemnation of all systems which produce hunger and the fulfillment of all the attempts we make to deal with hunger. Prayer also would see the eschatological event, the coming of the Lord Jesus, as the fulfillment of all that it validly embodied: adoration brought to perfection face to face with its subject, thanksgiving raised to the pitch of highest gratitude, hope finding itself in the presence of all it had hoped for and infinitely more, penitence knowing in its dejection the source of its forgiveness, and intercession now assured that all the sorrow and bitterness in the world had finally been gathered into the heart of God. Prayer in its eschatological reference, therefore, paradoxically wills itself into nonexistence in its very fulfillment, in the achievement of all for which it prays; but if you take away that reference, it ceases to be prayer and becomes a form of self-communion, or at most moral uplift. There is therefore a microcosmic form of that eschatological tension in every prayer: It is poised between now and then, between what we do now and what we hope to be, between what we are and what we pray God will make of us. That tension exists when either our eyes are turned backwards upon our sins and shame of them possesses us, or when we remember God's mercies to us in the past; for penitence becomes an anxiety state or a guilt state if we do not look forward to the renewal of God's forgiveness, while remembrance of God's goodness is the basis of our anticipation of his continuing presence with us in days ahead. Prayer invests the present with the urgency, the hope and the assurance of the eschatological ultimate, while through prayer the ultimate, the *eschaton,* is kept in organic relation with the continuing life of the Church.

CHAPTER 3

Prayer and the Mode of Response

God's "Answer" to Prayer

The question which I propose to discuss under this title is both one of the most difficult to answer and one which, because of this difficulty, is an increasing cause of the failure of belief in prayer, or in the credibility of prayer. The question concerns the manner in which God is expected to answer prayer. It is not the question of *whether* he answers prayer but *how,* though obviously to some extent any answer indicating how can be also an answer to the question of whether. Some people may have been missing God's answers because they did not appreciate the variety of answer that he might give. Obviously the question must therefore be narrowed down, and I should like to say that I am concerned with the way in which God is to be expected to communicate his answer to prayer, or even to keep up his side of the I-Thou relationship of prayer.

Emphasis has already been placed on the idea that prayer is articulate address to God, or if we feel that some room must be left for sheer contemplation, we say that prayer is dependent upon and related to explicit address to God, when it is not actually taking such a form. But how exactly the situation is to be described in the God-ward reference becomes a problem for us when we consider four contemporary quotations on the subject, which by their very diversity of source create no small impact. Karl Barth writes, "The distinctive feature of the specific, conscious and express prayer required by divine commandment is that like confession it takes the form of speech. To be sure, it is speaking with God (not from God)."[1] Hans Urs von Balthasar says something similar: People at times feel "a pressing need to converse with God otherwise than in stereotyped formulae, but how many know how to do so? It is as if they had to speak in a language whose rules they had never learned; instead of fluent conversation, all they can manage are the disjointed disconnected phrases of a foreigner unacquainted with the language of the country; they find themselves as helpless as a stuttering child who wants to say something and cannot."[2] Very significantly, von Balthasar continues, "This image could be misleading, for we cannot hold conversation with God." He immediately goes on to explain that prayer is an exchange between God and the person praying, even a dialogue, though what he means by an exchange which is not a conversation but a dialogue we shall later investigate. It is his denial of prayer as a conversation that is of immediate interest to us. The terminology is echoed by D. Z. Phillips, who argues that, since prayer does not involve actual "conversation" or use of personal pronouns of the sort employed in everyday speech, prayer cannot be construed as such.[3] The point appears again in Tillich, according to whom prayer, if "brought down to the level of a conversation between two beings . . . is blasphemous and ridiculous."[4]

Here is a very substantial body of opinion drawn from a wide variety of sources, and it bears a close relation to what has happened in recent times in the world of general theology. Let us take, step by step, the different points that are implicit in these remarks. First of all, each of the writers is aware that prayer, on the human side, involves at least on some occasions talking to God — even von Balthasar, who equates prayer at times with contemplation, would agree to that statement. There is no intention on their part to substitute any other form of approach to God for explicit speech. Secondly, then, what they deny is that God uses the same form of speech to answer us. The reasons for this denial forms the subject which we must explore for a time. One reason was noted earlier, namely, that we seem to have moved away from the idea of revelation as the communication of propositions from

1. Barth, *Church Dogmatics*, III/4 (ET Edinburgh, 1961), p. 89.
2. Hans Urs von Balthasar, *Prayer* (ET London, 1961), pp. 11f.
3. D. Z. Phillips, *The Concept of Prayer* (London, 1965), p. 50.
4. Paul Tillich, *Systematic Theology*, I (Chicago, 1951), p. 127.

God to ourselves, so that even if we still think of ourselves as talking to God, we still cannot expect him to talk to us in similar terms. Some people, as we have noted, find that sufficient reason for breaking altogether with the conception of prayer as talking to God. Propositions for them are out — in either direction. So much we can add to what was previously said: that there has been an unfortunate failure to correlate the theology of prayer with the theology of revelation.

Another reason for doubting the idea that God answers in the forms of words we use for our prayer to him is the longstanding suspicion of statements that claim to come from God. The suspicious may have had political rather than religious grounds for doubt when Joan of Arc heard her voices, but the suspicion has been reinforced in modern times by psychological reinterpretations of the phenomenon described as "hearing God speak." The skepticism thus bred has inhibited the possibility of any genuine "hearing" that there might have been, and as a result the situation which now confronts us is one where both the fact and the possibility of God's speaking to us in articulate terms are denied. A further reason may be found in a preconceived notion of what conversation may mean. In other words, it may have so close an affiliation with what goes on in human affairs as to be inapplicable to our relation to God in prayer and his relation to us. Phillips uses a form of this argument in order to substantiate his case.[5]

"Conversation," it might be pointed out, implies a common context shared by its two partners. The sharing will consist in their having similar needs, similar weaknesses and wants, ambitions, hopes, or fears. They will have a common social context — even when they find themselves widely separated from one another by standing or rank, as were "Good King Wenceslas" and the poor man who came in sight. They will be bound by the same limitations of life and death, limited by similar loyalties to friends, and subjected to the same pressures and controls of body and mind and conscience. They will share the common condition of sinners, who do not have in their own hands the power finally to alter that condition. The sharing too will extend to the language they employ, which even if they do not have the same verbal language can equally well be the language of signs. If, however, the signs are not intelligible to either party, there is then no conversation. It is a problem,

5. Phillips, *The Concept of Prayer.*

therefore, not simply of God's not speaking audibly in our human language, but also of agreement as to what are the valid signs of God's answering. "Voices," "noises in the head" in the form of spoken sentences — these at least, if they were acknowledged as happening, would be evidence upon which different parties could agree, because they have by definition their own meaning. But there can be no such agreement upon "signs," which will recur as phenomena in the world of space-time and be liable to confusion with events of material origin.

Conversation in the human context implies the possibility of one's answering back, of refusing to accept what the other person has to say, of refusing to be dictated to, and of rebelling against anything that seems in the least like command, of seeking to carry conviction for one's own point-of-view by argument, inference and illustration. Many of these features of human conversation would be obviously out of place in the context of prayer, and would imply an attitude of irreligiousness. Nor *a fortiori* would we ever expect God to adopt such reactions to our own approach to him in prayer. In other fields of theology, considerations of this sort are not regarded as settling the matter on the spot. Recourse is had to the doctrine of analogy with its recognition, as it would be in this case, that admittedly there are many features of human conversation which are not likely to be present in the conversation which takes place between God and us in prayer, but there are also sufficient positive features remaining to justify retaining the term. Such a solution seems to be invalid, it is argued, because the distinctive features of approach and response in articulated speech or in an agreed form of sign-making appear to be entirely absent in the case of prayer. Here, then, is the thesis that we have to examine, the view that God does not speak to men and women today in articulate speech.

Does God "Speak"?

To begin with, though we may acknowledge the fact that people generally do not nowadays speak of hearing the voice of God speaking to them, this situation is not to be accepted without further reflection as normal or proper to Christianity. People may, for example, fail to hear God speaking for a number of reasons. They may have lost the habit of quiet meditation and preparation for prayer, and being involved in the busyness of modern life do not take the time required to become rightly attuned to God's address. There is certainly a good deal of evidence for this, because the kind of talking which has in the past been expected of God in response to human prayer has taken place in the context of a prepared situation. The preparation may have been the classical devotional exercises of an office or a liturgy, where the practitioner by his or her exercises gradually grew in receptivity. In Protestant circles, the preparation has generally taken the form of Bible-reading and reflection upon the passages read, so that a degree of *rapport* has begun to be set up between the person praying and God. Without some such preparation, it is not surprising that those who rush into God's presence are not favored with articulate response. Religion has never pretended that God was on the end of a telephone line and could be reached on seven digits, or eleven for inter-city. Orthodox theories of prayer, moreover, have not been slow to admit that even after preparation for prayer, often over a sustained period, God may still not appear to give any kind of articulate answer to prayer or even any indication that he has heard it. Those medieval mystics who were more expert than any in the art of approaching God were the first to confess to long periods of "black unknowing," when there was no response whatsoever from the subject of their adoration. We are not producing any new facts about prayer when we draw attention to its frequent apparent failure to stimulate reaction from God's side, for that fact is as old as prayer itself. More mature theories of prayer have also always been aware that the fact exists even when great care is taken to prepare the human soul to receive what God has to say in answer to the prayer, but they have never agreed that the fact in any way invalidates the process of praying.

Those who are not prepared to acquiesce in the view that people do not often now "hear" God speak to them in answer to their prayer as proof that he never does speak, add that there may be a farther explanation of their incapacity, namely, that such people bring to prayer far too many preconceptions, not simply about the kind of answer that they expect from God and that they therefore to some extent try to impose upon him, but also about the whole credibility of prayer, about whether God does answer prayer, about how he works, and in fact about his whole nature, his goodness, his love, his power. There is in contemporary religion and theology a far greater admixture of skepticism and of agnosticism which have somehow contrived to remain within these disciplines than has ever been the case in the past history of the Church. Such skepticism and agnosticism impose great strain upon their supporters at the points of public worship and private prayer: in worship because traditional forms of belief are firmly structured into a series of liturgical acts, expressions and postures which do not respond readily to radical revision; and in the field of private prayer because here agnosticism and skepticism have an immediate outlet, and constitute a formidable barrier to prayer as normally practiced. There is not the same strain in the field of theological reflection and discussion, where the dialectic creates a milieu of such flexibility as to accommodate a wide range of opinion.

Traditionalists in the theory of prayer might well insist, therefore, that so long as people introduce into their devotional exercises those preconceptions about God's being, power, reality, and goodness which in their theological study issue in a high measure of skepticism, they cannot expect to hear God's articulate answer to them. We must try in some way to silence every doubt, to quiet our own feverish questioning, before we shall succeed in hearing God speak. The reply to the view that God appears no longer to use articulate speech for his approach to humankind is that he certainly still does but that we no longer have ears attuned to his speech. People have lost the art of listening.

Two comments might be made at this point. On the one hand, it would be quite wrong to preclude *a priori* the possibility of God's speaking to us were the "art of listening" to be revived. If we allow Barth the right to say, as we must, that God may speak through anything from communism through to a flute concerto or a dead dog, then we dare not deny *a priori* that he can speak direct to believing, praying people in answer to their petitions. Every Christian has the right to expect that God will so speak. On the other hand, what one must also be prepared to do is to introduce into such listening, such claims that God has said so-and-so, some degree of questioning which insists upon criteria of one sort or another to check what, it is claimed, God has said. Since any such claimant is human and sinful, there must be an openness to a degree of error in order for there to be a balanced approach to the whole question. Not to allow for this would amount to inordinate self-righteousness, or perhaps even insanity. Sometimes these checks will be easily come by in the biblical record, through a Gospel, a prophecy, or an Epistle; alternatively, the tradition of the Church, the conscience of the community or even the much more vague criterion of the like-mindedness of all sympathetic believers might serve this function. On other occasions, however, it has to be admitted that the word which it is claimed God speaks in answer to prayer may cut across all these criteria, for God's word has often challenged every one of them — Scriptural interpretation, tradition, community-conscience and so on. In that moment, there is no alternative to Luther's, "Here I stand; I can no other," but it is necessary to be very, very sure, and it does not happen very often.

Perhaps the most convincing argument that can be employed to support the view that God *speaks* in answer to prayer is the wide prevalence throughout the whole of the Bible of that very event. At Exodus 5:22 we read, "Then Moses turned again to the LORD and said, 'O LORD, why have you mistreated this people? Why did you ever send me? Since I first came to Pharaoh to speak in your name, he has mistreated this people, and you have done nothing at all to deliver your people.'" But the answer comes in Exodus 6:1: "Then the LORD said to Moses, 'Now you shall see what I will do to Pharaoh; indeed, by a mighty hand he will let them go; by a mighty hand he will drive them out of his land.'" In the book of Job, we have extended speech by God, prayer by Job and answering speech again by God; though the whole book is in the nature of a drama, its themes being the relations between success and virtue, and between faith and suffering, it is clear that it rests on the assumption that God articulates himself in speech. Again in Isaiah 37, for example, the words of the prophet report what God has to say, and it is the apparent intention of the prophet here, as so often elsewhere, to convey the impression, or more accurately his own assured conviction, that what he says has in the first instance been spoken to him by God. The general theorem could be illustrated from many Old Testament passages.

In the Gospels, understandably, there are very few instances of God's speaking directly; the baptism of Jesus and the transfiguration are the most notable instances, but neither occurs in response to prayer. In the Gospels, the focus is upon Christ, and upon his words. Nevertheless, it would not be difficult to maintain that throughout the Gospels, there is no escaping the idea that through Jesus, God makes his mind and will, his purpose and nature known in words as well as in actions — a point to remember when theological emphasis is so heavily placed on "the mighty acts of God," while the interpretative role of the words of Jesus in relation to these "mighty acts" is neglected or even denied. In the Acts of the Apostles, we find references to the ascended Jesus speaking again, for example, in the account of the conversion of Saul (Acts 9:4ff.), and later in the address which the Lord makes to Ananias, instructing him to go and find Saul; he even answers Ananias' protestations. In the events in Acts 12, the occasion being the release of Peter from prison, after "earnest prayer for him was made to God by the Church," it is the angel of the Lord who appears, but he speaks in the most comprehensible, forthright language: "Fasten your belt and put on your sandals" (v. 8). Notice is even taken of the fact that though Peter "thought he was seeing a vision," "what was happening with the angel's help was real" (v. 9). There is therefore implicit in this story the assumption that in answer to prayer, God expresses himself in direct speech, though in this case through an angelic being. At Acts 22:17ff., Paul reports in the course of his defense in Jerusalem how, when he was praying in the Temple, he fell into a trance and heard the words, "Hurry and get out of Jerusalem quickly," he identified them as coming from the Lord. Again at Acts 23:11, God speaks to Paul: "Keep your courage! For as you have testified for me in Jerusalem, so you must bear witness also in Rome." The Book of Revelation is from the viewpoint of our present investigation perhaps rather different, in that it is cast very much in the forms of the visionary apocalyptic genre, where there is an established pattern of unusual occurrence and of a voice speaking; nevertheless, throughout it we have numerous examples of God expressing himself in definite language.

Let us pause to draw together certain considerations that emerge from this all too brief review of the biblical references to God's speaking. The first noteworthy point is that whereas in the Old Testament there are many references to the fact that God speaks to his people, often in answer to prayer but not infrequently on his own initiative, there are comparatively and proportionately very few similar references in the New Testament, scarcely any in the Gospels, a few in the book of Acts, none as one might expect in the Epistles, but quite a large number in the book of Revelation, though because of the peculiar literary and apocalyptic style of the book it may have to be discounted in our present comparative study. The problem that immediately engages us is that of why there should be such a marked difference between the two Testaments. The quick answer is that there is a maturing conception of how God responds to human prayer and of how he makes his purposes known to men and women. In the Old Testament, he is pictured as a superperson who can talk, in addition to expressing many emotions which appear to have a human quality, and who can directly "interfere" with events that take place in the world of human affairs. Something of that conception of God, as talking and as "interfering" in human affairs, reappears in the book of Acts, but not to any great extent. It is entirely absent from the Gospels, where Jesus' presentation of God's character and of how God is related to human affairs is different altogether. Jesus does not hear a voice and then report what he has heard; rather, his communion with God seems to be more like what we would call spiritual communion. The account that John gives of the relation of Christ to the Father is certainly most aptly described in such terms.

The situation demands, however, that we probe the matter farther than the single assertion that we have in the New Testament a more mature conception of God and of how he communicates than we have in the Old. One reading of the situation is to say that, whereas in the Old Testament God speaks from without the human situation in a verbalized mode, he speaks from within the human situation in the New Testament in an incarnate mode. This view has been thought to be classically stated in the opening verses of the Epistle to the Hebrews: "Long ago God spoke to our ancestors in many and various ways by the prophets, but in these last days he has spoken to us by a Son, whom he appointed heir of all things, through whom also he created the worlds." It is possible to present this view stated in Hebrews as if it were a very sophisticated reflection upon the Gospels, as if in short it were a fully developed doctrine of the Word of God, almost as if the writer to the Hebrews anticipated Barth's doctrine of the threefold form of the Word of God. The elaboration of this view includes the notion that in Christ, God has altered his mode of address from verbalized language to a human life. There is, however, no justification for that sophistication in the actual words of these opening verses of Hebrews, which refer to God having spoken previously by prophets and now again *speaking* by his Son, for no doubt the writer could have said that in both cases there were *words,* even if there were in addition things which God had to "say" through the actions or person of Jesus.

It is difficult now, if not impossible, to recapture the mind of the New Testament writers, and through them the perceptions of the first disciples, but it is surely more than pure conjecture to suggest that, for them, Christ spoke for God in some immediate way, a way which implied a greater closeness between himself and God than existed between the prophets and God. That is at least part of the intention of the remark that "he taught them as one having authority, and not as their scribes" (Matthew 7:2). That "authority," however, while it must admittedly have derived from what later theology was to call his person, nevertheless attached to the *words* which he spoke and what he had to say. Because of this closeness, as I have chosen to call it, between Christ and God, no great case can be made at that point for any theory about a departure from verbalization in God's address. For the writers of the New Testament, Christ speaks for God with a degree of intimacy and authenticity impossible for a prophet; in his speaking, God himself speaks in a sense more direct than he spoke through the prophets.

In the book of Acts, there are obviously occasions on which God is thought of as speaking to individuals very much as he had done in the Old Testament, but there has also developed a new mode of address — the sermon. There is here no longer the "thus says the Lord" of prophecy, nor the recorded actual speech of God himself. A new form of divine communication, it might be said, has evolved — at least as a literary form if not as a medium of public communication, a disjunction that cannot completely be resolved now, either for the book of Acts or earlier for Christ's Sermon on the Mount. Whether it is a literary or a spoken mode of communication — a problem that in a way homiletics has not yet solved even after two thousand years — it is certainly an essential part of the conception of the writer of the book of Acts as to how God addressed himself to the world in the situations he has described.

The conclusion, therefore, to which I have been moving is that throughout the Bible the notion that God speaks to people obtains, though *how* the speaking takes place varies — from direct speech, in the Old Testament and in the book of Revelation, through prophecy, where a prophet tells people what God has first told him (for it is not automatic talking), to Christ himself speaking with all the authority of God, to the sermon in which God speaks in and through the words of the preacher. I cannot find any substitution for verbalization of any other form of communication; not even in the New Testament is there the notion that God now "speaks" in a person and not in words. If, therefore, our self-imposed task has been to examine the thesis that God does not speak to men and women in the language of articulate speech, we have now to note that if that situation is the case, then it is a substantial departure from the biblical understanding of such matters.

In the light of that strong body of evidence for the prevalence in the Bible of the notion that God addresses people in a literal fashion, ought we not now to have a fresh look at what we perhaps rather too hastily assumed at the beginning of this Chapter — that it is no longer credible that God addresses us in this way, because his revelation is a process of self-communication, or even of personal manifestation, but not in any sense verbally or propositionally structured. Examined more closely, the arguments of Barth, Balthasar, Phillips and Tillich perhaps intended chiefly to disavow the view that prayer consisted of an *exchange* of speech, a bandying of words backwards and forwards. But if we allow that the rejection of prayer as a conversational process does not imply that there may not be some kind of verbal, propositional communication from God, how in fact would such communication take place, and how credible is the suggestion anyway? What has not been fully appreciated by those who claim that revelation is self-communication is the immensely important role which words and sentences play in the structuring and in the appropriation of that self-communication. There is a danger that we may forget or fail to understand the absolutely necessary function the Bible fulfills in mediating revelation, even in the form of personal manifestation to us, and that we should uncritically antithesize propositional revelation with self-communication or self-manifestation. These two "modes," as they are sometimes called, are in fact not antithetic but complementary to one another. For this reason, I been never been convinced by anyone who wished to speak of God's self-manifestation as if it were a process which could take place in even dialectical separation from the Bible. The Bible is the means by which we apprehend God, and conversely, it is the means by which God still addresses us. All the problems about the authority or infallibility of the Bible are, I agree, raised by this view that I have outlined, and on the other side there are also problems about the extension of the range of revelation beyond the *words* of Scripture to take account of the fact that the center of revelation is a *person.* But none of these problems must be allowed to divert us from the main central affirmation that the revelation of God in Jesus, what God communicates to us through him, comes in the first instance through the medium of the written, and we have to add the spoken, word.

Speech and Divine Communication

Prayer, it might be said, is one of the contexts in which God makes himself known to us. We have in the Protestant tradition made a good deal of the role of faith in knowing God, and that claim is not to be gainsaid; nor would it be sensible to suggest that prayer is a mode of knowing God additional to faith, for faith is involved in prayer even when the prayer reflects weak faith. But prayer and faith are different, and perhaps we have not done full justice to the place of prayer in the knowledge of God. Our subject in this chapter has been the mode of God's response to prayer. Our previous discussion, based on biblical material, encourages us to expect to find some kind of articulate address in that response of God. Is it fair then to say that such a mode of answer to prayer need not now occur? I am not so prepared now to allow the possibility as readily as I might once have been on first reading von Balthasar and other writers on prayer.

Let us take the simplest context in which prayer for many of us takes place, the context of Bible-reading. We have in the Bible a vast corpus of articulate language about God, and of God's address to us. We become steeped in this language, so that we think in it and talk in it. It becomes the medium of our approach to God, for from that point we move into prayer, often taking the biblical situation with us, often placing the insights of biblical narrative, prophecy or sermon at the center of some problem we are trying to solve, some difficulty we hope to overcome. It is a caricature of this practice to liken it to the old device of a text box from which a tiny scroll printed with a sentence of Scripture could be extracted and applied directly to the problem or the difficulty at hand. When a biblical situation is laid alongside a problem or an opportunity, the two seem to become interfused with one another, and out of the interfusion which takes place on the other side of prayer, the response comes and the prayer is answered. The mode of the answer is not infrequently — and I would be wrong to claim any universality for the event — some articulate proposition which the person praying could formulate were he or she asked to do so. Even if the "response" takes the form of the person's finding himself or herself doing something which he or she had never anticipated doing or hoped to do, the activity itself could readily be described in articulate form as the way the prayer had been answered.

Two comments may be made on this occurrence which I claim does still take place, and in doing so acts as the contrary instance to invalidate the universal negative — namely, that God does no longer answer prayer in articulate speech. The first comment is that it is not necessary to believe in the literal infallibility of the Bible in order to expect this articulate response to take place. It may be possible to take a quite critical approach to the biblical literature, and still use it in a devotional context. It might even be possible to regard large sections of it as no more than human searching after God, and not as divinely dictated literature, and still be prepared to reflect upon it as part of one's own approach to God. What I have said of the Bible could be said equally of many of the prayers in the liturgies and books of prayers; stated in words, human words, they are adopted as the medium of our self-expression, but they may easily and do become the medium of God's response as well. The second comment is that it would be possible to suggest that this articulated speech which came into the mind of the person praying had its origins solely in his or her own mind and nowhere else. Even an observer with Christian sympathies might have to admit that in certain cases the answer God gives in the particular ideas or formed judgments in question bear a very close relation to what the person has been thinking on other occasions, and that they can be seen more or less as the logical working out of those previous thoughts and ideas — as something, in short, which in many cases could have been done without praying. At this point, we begin to move into the question of how God works in the world anyway, and of how he relates to human behavior and historical events, but this is the subject of our next chapter. For the present, we may note the validity of the comment, namely, that there is some degree of continuity between God's answer to prayer and the prayer itself, which is not surprising, and that situations in which God has been claimed by Christians to be involved have always been open to non-theological interpretation. The incarnation itself is the abiding memorial to that fact.

I should like in the final stages of this chapter first to draw attention to certain implications which our discussion has for our understanding of God's self-expression in answer to prayer, and secondly, to examine the relation of the verbal or propositional elements in God's mode of response to certain other matters. On the first topic, let me begin by saying that it may be necessary to clarify the impression that I must have begun to create by my lengthy emphasis upon the role of articulate speech as God's mode of response to prayer in the biblical literature and in modern religious life. The impression I may have been giving is that I am pressing for the view that God actually and literally speaks to people, and that the simple role of the human being is to listen; if a person "gets it wrong," then it is because he or she has not listened carefully enough, or has allowed some human predisposition to distort the quality or character of what has been heard. In fact, the real point that I wish to make is simply that words, concepts and propositions, as the media of human comprehension, must also be used by God if he is to communicate with us at all, in the sense that what is communicated must be *received* by us in these media. What is thus communicated does not necessarily — and may well not possibly — issue from God in words, concepts and propositions, but what does so issue on entering the human world has to be converted into such terms.

It is perhaps somewhat risky to use the world of ordinary epistemology to prove or even to illustrate anything in the field of religious knowledge, but in the present connection it may not be unhelpful to do so. The world around us is known to us in terms of sense-data; it conveys itself to us as a world which is colored, tasteful, cold or hot, resistant or not resistant to pressure, sweet-smelling or foul-smelling, and so on. Common sense, in the form of "naive realism," may imagine that the "real" world bears all of these qualities in itself, but philosophers, however much they have disagreed on other aspects of this situation, have agreed that the source from which these sense-data emanate is not in reality as the evidence seems to suggest, and that the qualities which the external world has are due in considerable measure to the nature of the sensory organism. There is a well-known medieval phrase which could in fact be used as a text for the history of modern epistemology, and which is relevant to my present purpose. It is that all knowledge is *ad modum recipientis,* that is, all knowledge is in accordance with the capacity of the knower. Our perception of the external world is determined by the capacity of our five senses, and what we know of it is conditioned by the limits of these senses operating separately and in concert. The external world may have many other qualities which we could perceive if we were gifted with six, seven or eight senses. But we have only five, and what we perceive of the world is what can be seen, tasted, smelled, heard and touched. One of the marvels of this perceptual situation is that what often exists externally to ourselves as energy waves of one sort or another should on contacting nerve endings be converted into electro-chemical processes and finally into visual or other images. I have called this situation a "marvel" because we seem to be no nearer, with all the research into, for example, the physiology of visual perception, to understanding how the conversion takes place. It would be wrong to press the analogy any farther than my present intention, namely, to see in the way in which the ultimate form of perception of the situation external to ourselves is different from the form in which the original stimuli existed a kind of clue to the fact that though we understand God's answer to prayer to be verbal, conceptual or propositional, we are not obliged to say that the communication issued from him in so much actual speech. Nevertheless, if God is to *communicate* with us, then his communication must eventually be convertible into verbal, conceptual, propositional form. But we are not thereby affirming that the source of the communication is verbal, or even that God's response can be atomized into discrete thoughts. On such matters we have to remain agnostic. It is, though, at this point of agnosticism that the danger of the analogy appears. So far in philosophical epistemology, even when it has been aided by the resource of submolecular physics, it has proved impossible to establish any correlation among the sense-data in terms of which we perceive the external world, and the ultimate physical structure of that world. If there were thought to be a similar failure in correlation in the religious situation between what we apprehend and the "real" nature of God's will for us, then the life of that situation would be destroyed. So we must not press the analogy, perhaps remembering from it that there may be, and there is oftener than we have the honesty to admit, failure in correlation between what we think to be God's answer and what that answer genuinely is.

The view which I thus advance is of significance in two directions. On the one hand, it ought to deter those who believe without self-criticism that they have heard God speak thus and thus to them, and remind them that if God communicates to us, he does so through a human medium which is known to be highly fallible. Distortion of the signal is difficult always to avoid, and our creatureliness, if not also our sinfulness, is a constant factor likely to entail misapprehension of what God is trying to "say" to us. On the other hand, some people have departed entirely from the notion that God communicates to us, because they wrongly assume that because we "receive" God's communication in verbal or propositional form, it must have come all the way from God in that form. They have, quite rightly, refused to believe that God univocally speaks to us, pointing out that speech is a function of a brain, vocal cords, tongue, lips, teeth and so on; quite rightly, they have rejected the implicit anthropomorphism in the whole idea. They have equally refused to apply the notion of speech in an analogical sense to God, because when the dissimilarities are stripped, there is nothing of possible value remaining to give any substance to the notion. It was, I believe, partly reaction both to the anthropomorphism involved in such a view, and to the *hybris* which attached to so many confident and patently false claims to hear God's voice, that led to the idea of revelation as self-disclosure and self-manifestation. But the reaction, while it may have been justified on other grounds, was not substantiated on this particular ground. The fact that we apprehend God's answer to our prayer in terms of human speech does not entail that the answer issued from God in that form.

It should be observed that my analogy illustrates what it does not prove. It does not prove or even try to prove from the fact that people think that God has answered their prayer in the form of an articulate response which they can themselves express, either that God has done so, or that there is a God who might be capable of doing so. The analogy illustrates this point most competently because epistemological analysis of the problem of perception, even when assisted by modern physics, has not succeeded in "proving" the existence of an external world. The question of the existence of the external world has to be argued on independent grounds. There is certainly no doubt but that the person who takes the sense-data as serious pointers to the character of his or her environment is going to be more often right than someone who lives in an atmosphere of perpetual Cartesian doubt. We cannot say the same of the person who accepts what God has to communicate, not because that person may not be more often right than the person who does not, but because an acceptance of what one feels God has to say is a matter of faith and not of sight, even when one is convinced of the absolute accuracy of one's reception of the divine communication.

Having emphasized the propositional and verbalized form of our apprehension of what God has to convey to us in answer to prayer, I must not be understood to mean that God gives himself to us in no other way. Two considerations are relevant here. First, it is so obvious as scarcely to need statement that God's answer to prayer may take the form of some sort of action, whether forgiveness, redemption, renewal of heart, "regeneration" as the Catechism would say, or the removal of prejudices, suspicions, ill-feelings, or any number of other consequences that we could add. These are the circumstances which persuaded the supporters of the view that revelation is not "propositional" and that revelation is "self-communication" to adopt their clearly defined position. God *does* all of these things without saying anything, and these often enough *are* the modes in which God makes himself known to us, whereas propositions can be merely intellectual, theoretical, academic and dead.

Secondly, however, there is another view of propositions; it is that they constitute both the self-conscious human commentary on much that happens, and the content of that which they signify. Let us take these components of the theory of propositions in turn. The person who receives the forgiveness of God, or his redemption in Christ, or renewal of heart, or who comes through God's grace to a new sense of forgiveness towards his or her enemies, is not likely to go far without explicitly acknowledging this fact. The verbalization, the proposition, accompanies or succeeds the event as the person's awareness of its happening. In fact, it is the verbal acknowledgment of it that nails it to reality, so that there is now no going back. One is committed, in short, from this point on. Further, while we have had the application of the Austinian notion of performatives to the words and assertions of human persons ("I take thee to be my lawfully wedded wife"), it might with equal validity be applied to the verbalization which is the mode of God's answer to our prayers. "Your sins are forgiven," when first spoken by Christ, was both statement and act, and the appearance of that proposition within our consciousness has the same continuing performative efficacy. "Go your way; sin no more," as the sequel to forgiveness, is both the statement and the imposition upon us of the purpose of God for our lives. In such a context, there is no such thing as a "mere" proposition; rather, the proposition conveys the reality of which it speaks — forgiveness, redemption, sanctification. When that end is achieved, then the response to the prayer and the mode of the response have both been validated.

CHAPTER 4

Prayer and the World

The Efficacy of Prayer

The question of the efficacy of prayer has always been one of the main problems to be discussed in any examination of the nature and validity of prayer, the question, that is, of whether God does respond to our petitions to him to act in the world for the good of the person praying or prayed for, or maybe even for the ill-being of his or her enemies. There has always been thought to be in the Christian faith a very considerable predisposition, based on biblical evidence, towards expecting prayer to be effectual. Many texts flash to mind in justification of the predisposition. "Ask, and it will be given you" (Matthew 7:7), a word coming from Jesus, seems to settle on the spot the question of the efficacy of prayer. Or, "if two of you agree on earth about anything you ask, it will be done for you by my Father in heaven" (Matthew 18:19). Here is conclusive assurance, it would seem, for counting on God not only to hear the prayer, but to take the necessary action. If we add Christ's other word, "if you have faith the size of a mustard seed, you will say to this mountain, 'Move from here to there,' and it will move" (Matthew 17:20), then the presence of such faith as part of the attitude of prayer leads to the understandable expectation that God will respond.

Such confidence seems to ring through all Paul's references to prayer. In his letter to the Philippians, we read: "Yes and I will continue to rejoice, for I know that through your prayer and the help of the Spirit of Jesus Christ this will turn out for my deliverance, as it is my eager expectation and hope that I will not be put to shame . . ." (1:18ff.); and similarly, in Philemon: "One thing more — prepare a guest room for me, for I am hoping through your prayers to be restored to you" (v. 22). Likewise, but in another tradition, James writes, "Therefore confess your sins to one another, and pray for one another, so that you may be healed. The prayer of the righteous is powerful and effective" (2:15ff.). The selection is random, and it could be supplemented from the Book of Acts and from most of the other parts of the New Testament, but the general contention is unambiguous — prayer is efficacious; it does result in the occurrence of what is hoped for and earnestly intended. Nevertheless, as indicated in the introductory analysis of the problem of prayer, it is precisely here, in the area of the relation of prayer to the world, of the fact as well as the possibility of its efficacy, that the question of the credibility of prayer most acutely arises.

The question has been examined in many different contexts, and across many centuries, and I hope to look at a number of such contextual frameworks for the problem, but perhaps we may begin with a very simply stated question. It is the theological difficulty that if God, either in terms of general or special providence or on the basis of some form of predestination, wills in eternity that which comes to pass in time, then is not a prayer that so-and-so should come to pass in effect a request to God to change his mind? Such a question has a certain pious quality which cannot be denied, for it springs from a deep awareness of the facts of God's omnipotence and of his transcendence over the vicissitudes of human day-to-day existence. At another level, it poses sharply a genuine theological problem of how the omnipotence of God and the predestination which he effects are to be reconciled with both the freedom of individuals and the very temporary character of so many of their prayers. In the event, however, it is a question to which a variety of different answers have been given.

First, a simple apologetic answer has been devised, namely, that God being also omniscient foreknows what the prayer of the individual person is going to be at the given time in history, and, as it were, adjusts accordingly what he eternally wills to do. In this way, he is never taken by surprise, while, on the other hand, our prayer is not reduced to an empty mouthing of words. It has had an effect upon the event to which it related, and it has been efficacious. Theologians such as St. Augustine who have considered this solution of the problem have not been slow to recognize that it raises yet another problem, that of whether the fact of God's foreknowledge of what we will pray in some way curbs or indeed eliminates our freedom in praying. That problem cannot, however, be solved except in the context of God's relation to and involvement in the whole natural order and its so-called laws or uniformities; to these subjects we shall later return. For the moment we note that to say that God foreknows the content of the prayer and accommodates to it in his providential and predestinating will is an inconclusive answer to the problem.

Secondly, we may follow a hint given by Herbert Butterfield that God is like "a composer . . . who composes the music as we go along, and, when we slip into aberration, switches his course in order to make the best of things."[1] Butterfield was there thinking particularly of wrong actions spontaneously done, which disrupt the harmony of God's will for our lives and for history, and of the way God modifies his score to take account of such variations. It is no great refinement of Butterfield's theory to suggest that God makes similar modifications in favor of our prayers, for he would himself set high value on the extent to which what he comes close to describing as *divine* organization is interwoven with the unpredictability of human freedom. Even on such terms, however, we cannot be sure that we have solved the problem of the point at which, if it appears that the harmony is going to be destroyed and the organization stultified, such freedom must be curtailed, and the prayer which expresses it rendered inefficacious.

Thirdly, a further way round the problem that prayer must on occasion be regarded as ineffectual in spite of the strong biblical affirmations apparently to the contrary, or alternatively regarded as an attempt to change God's will, is to suggest that in view of our ignorance and of God's omniscience and omnipotence, on occasion no answer or indeed some answer totally different from that requested is God's answer. We know not what we ask, but we know that God is good. Therefore whatever comes to pass is what God has willed and it is for the best. It is certainly proper to praise the piety of such an attitude, though it is difficult to resist a conclusion concerning its insensitivity to the reality of evil as well as its evasion of the problem of unanswered prayer. If we say that whatever happens after we pray is by virtue of its very occurrence identifiable with the will of God, then we are saying too much

1. Herbert Butterfield, *Christianity and History* (London, 1950), p. 19.

and too little. We are going too far in the direction of a predestinarianism which historically has had little to distinguish it from necessitarianism. We are on the other hand not going far enough, for we still leave untouched the question of how our prayer, as a request for a specific occurrence, relates to what comes after it. In fact, this view suggests almost that what was to happen would have happened anyway without the prayer. Moreover, it is a bold step to take to say that whatever comes to pass is of God's will, in face of the enormity of the evil which is and has been in the world. It is perhaps simple-minded, but nonetheless irresistible, to claim that if certain circumstances in the world around us are anathema to us, an offense even to our somewhat dulled senses, then they are *a fortiori* an abomination to God with his profound love for all his creatures and his opposition to all evil. It is a blasphemy to proclaim, as do some forms of predestinarianism, that all that comes to be is willed of God, comprehending as it does the destinies of both the elect and the damned. No matter what problems remain in the area of unanswered or ineffectual prayer, it is too high a price to pay for a solution to suggest that whatever happens consequent upon the prayer is to be interpreted and accepted as God's answer to the prayer. The single extenuating consideration in favor of not rejecting the notion outright is that on *occasion* God will answer a prayer in a way which seems at the time to be no answer whatsoever. This consideration is usually, however, held to be operative only where the connection between the prayer and the very special and different answer given to it by God is retrospectively seen to be a much *better* answer than that hoped for by the person praying.

Fourthly, a slight modification of the previous *apologia* is offered in the view that the "real" answer to the prayer lies not in the external occurrence, even when what is prayed for occurs, but in the mental adjustment of the person praying to what comes to pass in the circumstances around which the prayer has been constructed. By entering into relation to God in prayer, the person effectively requests God to make him or her into the sort of person who will accept whatever God regards as best. In an extreme form this view would be expressed by saying that prayer is its *own* answer, and that its efficacy is entirely internal. Its efficacy and answer, in other words, would thus be contained within itself, so as to be unmeasurable by anything that happens outside of prayer as such. This view is different from what I would call Christian necessitarianism. For the latter, whatever happens is construed as the answer to the prayer, whereas for the view presently under discussion, what happens subsequent to the prayer *may* be what was requested but it may not be: The answer to the prayer lies in the mental or spiritual motivation of the person praying, which enables him or her to accept whatever happens (even though what happens may be contrary to God's will), without a breaking of spirit or purpose.

The "Augustinian" and "Thomistic" Views

The question of the efficacy of prayer is traditionally discussed in the context of the problem of the *possibility* of God's actual intervening in the natural processes of world occurrences, human history and natural events. The view which we have now to examine is in its way fundamental both to classical and modern understandings of the relation of prayer to the world; it can be found, as we shall see, in Augustine, but it can also be seen in the theology of miracles set out for us very forcefully by John Macquarrie. According to Macquarrie, the traditional conception of the miraculous as a divine intervention in the natural order must be abandoned as irreconcilable with the modern understanding of both science and history. In our thinking, we proceed on the assumption that events occurring in the world can all be accounted for in terms of other similar events within the world; "if on some occasions we are unable to give a complete account of some happening . . . the scientific conviction is that further research will bring to light further factors in the situation, but factors that will turn out to be just as immanent and this-worldly as those already known."[2] Macquarrie's position is thus that the way of understanding miracle "which appeals to breaks in the natural order and to supernatural interventions," or which suggests that "the so-called 'laws' or regular procedures of nature are on some occasions suspended" is a view which "belongs to the mythological outlook and cannot commend itself in a post-mythological climate of thought."[3]

It might be tempting patronizingly to write off such views as if they came from a nineteenth century modernist, but it is worth remembering,

2. John Macquarrie, *Principles of Christian Theology* (London, 1966), pp. 226f.
3. Macquarrie, pp. 226f.

as I have already indicated, that Augustine argued something very like it sixteen hundred years ago. According to Augustine, although God sometimes acts in a way which is contrary to what we know of nature, he never acts against the supreme law of nature which is beyond our knowledge, any more than he acts against himself.[4] At first glance, there may seem to be a contradiction between St. Augustine and Canon Macquarrie, the former allowing that miracles may be contrary to the common course of nature, and the latter flatly denying that it is other than objectionable to suggest that the so-called laws or regular procedures of nature can on some occasions be suspended. In fact, the disagreement between the two is to a great extent illusory, because they both agree that on some occasions there may be a *prima facie* case for saying that normal events or uniformities have been violated, and further, that these violations will ultimately be resolved, either through success in relating the unexplained events to other similar this-worldly events (Macquarrie) or through a demonstration that God has in fact all along been following some higher law of nature (Augustine). It is possible to follow the parallelism between Augustine and Macquarrie one stage farther. Augustine wrote, "Our Lord Jesus Christ desired that what he did physically should be understood spiritually, for he did not perform miracles as an end in themselves but in order that what he did should be marvelous for those that saw and true for those that understood."[5] In Macquarrie, similarly, we read, "Every event, insofar as it is embraced within the divine providence, can be understood as potentially an event manifesting God's action yet some particular concrete events stand out in a special way in the experiences of individuals or communities as vehicles of the divine action, and such events are miracles."[6] The two agree that the significance of the occurrence (which they have both agreed is reducible to natural law, or at least to some supreme law) lies not in any superficial spectacularity, but in its revelatory quality as directing the believer to God.

While the discussion in this immediate context has related to miracles, it has in fact been no diversion from our main task, for two

4. St. Augustine, *Contra Faustum Manichaeum,* 26.3.

5. St. Augustine, *Contra Faustum Manichaeum,* ET in Augustine, *Works* (Edinburgh, 1871-76), V, p. 509.

6. Macquarrie, p. 230.

reasons. First, God's answer to prayer, when it is thought to involve active intervention in natural events, is very often construed as a miraculous event. Secondly, the general theology of miracle normally has a good deal to say about the possibility of such intervention, and the one discussion very often serves the double purpose of apologetic for, or explaining away of, both miracles and the efficacy of prayer. With such a strict view of the inviolability of nature, and given his interpretation of miracles, it is interesting to see how Macquarrie goes on much later in his *Principles of Christian Theology* to discuss prayer.[7] He dissociates himself at once from any suggestion that prayers of this sort amount to an attempt to manipulate the world by occult or magical means. After affirming an interest in the sort of topic we have earlier discussed, namely, whether prayer is some kind of conversation between us and God, and having reached conclusions not dissimilar to our own, namely, that the absence of a background of ideas shared with God makes the idea of prayer as mutual discourse problematic, he comes to the problems of petitionary and intercessory forms of prayer. Macquarrie argues that many of these prayers are silenced once they are exposed to the judgment of a holy God, and that the egocentric motives in some intercessory prayers are also eliminated. Some prayers may involve a high degree of renewed commitment to God in our praying them. But the question remains whether such prayers have only a psychological value, so that their answer consists purely in the recreation of our faith. It is rightly pointed out that few Christians would accept such an answer, while the alternative offered is as follows: ". . . may we not also believe that the sincere prayer of faith is a strengthening of the movement of Being itself in its threefold action of creation-reconciliation-consummation" involving "an 'objective' strengthening of the kingdom beyond the lives of the actual persons concerned"?[8]

It would perhaps be unfair to press Macquarrie too hard on this answer. He would seem to mean that by our praying in the right spirit we lay our hearts and lives (individually and as a community) so open to God's indwelling, that we can cooperate with him in the accomplishment of the ends of his kingdom. But there are two difficulties attaching to such a view. First, it does not include in its explanation those areas

7. Macquarrie, pp. 437ff.
8. Macquarrie, p. 440.

of intercessory prayer which deal with subjects in which our cooperation is impossible, and would seem to imply that perhaps these areas should be excluded from intercessory prayer. In other words, these would be, for Macquarrie, areas in which something like occult and magic means are being invoked to "deal with" a position which has gone beyond control or alleviation. Secondly, the answer seems to ignore the fact that the concept of our prayer as strengthening "the movement of Being itself" involves something not unlike occult means of action as much as any process that operates in the opposite direction. Transfer of energy, in the psychological sphere as much as in the physical sphere, constitutes "interference." Again, however, it would be wrong to press Macquarrie too far on this point, because the discussion of prayer appears in the section entitled "Applied Theology," where he is not necessarily committed to fully examining the theological or apologetic problems attaching to his views.

What I have offered so far is what I should like to designate the Augustinian account of the relation of prayer to the world, Macquarrie being selected as a modern exponent of the view. Before we depart from it, I should like to summarize some of its main features. First, it seems to accept the inviolability of the natural causal order, Macquarrie referring to "so-called "laws" or "procedures of nature" and St. Augustine to "the supreme law of nature," acknowledging that there might be from time to time apparent violations of such "laws" but insisting that in due course they can be subsumed under the causal rubric. Secondly, there takes place an interiorizing of the answer to prayer: It purifies the soul of the person praying, in the very moment of his or her praying. Thirdly, this interiorizing tendency is the converse of the unwillingness to look for anything that would pass as extraordinary or miraculous in the ordinary course of nature. There is a skepticism, even denial, of the possibility of God's interfering with what might normally happen in nature. Fourthly, there cannot be a total ignoring of the fact that ordinary intercessory prayer expects something to happen in the world. This expectation is validated by results, which may be variously described in non-miraculous terms, whether as by Macquarrie when he suggests that the praying person is enabled to cooperate with Being itself in the strengthening of the kingdom, or as by Augustine, who adopted in regard to the most extraordinary situations such as the wedding at Cana of Galilee what was later to be called the theory of "accelerated natural process,"[9] and regarded the "miraculous" answer to prayer as homogeneous with what God does at other times, though reduced greatly in timescale. Fifthly, there is a firm recognition that the miracle, while it is not part of an occult or magical process set up by prayer, is nevertheless revelatory of God. The revelatory component in the situation is linked to an external occurrence explicable in natural terms, and is the subject of faith and wonder, or still more precisely, of thanksgiving.

For purposes of broad, if rather imprecise categorization, I should now like to turn to what could be called the Thomistic view. Again what can be said of prayer in the Thomistic context is conditioned by what St. Thomas Aquinas himself has to say about *how* God acts in the created order. Two fundamental points are of importance. First, drawing a basic distinction between first cause and secondary causes, Thomas acknowledges that God cannot work against, or intervene in, the order of things as far as they depend upon the first cause; he can and does act, however, outside of the order of things as they depend upon secondary causes.[10] Here recognition is given to the facts that God, as it were, initiates action from outside of the order of secondary causes, and that he can intervene in the natural process. What precisely Thomas is saying in all of this is an extremely complex problem, and I have no desire to be drawn too deeply into the detail of Thomistic interpretation. But if we may be allowed to take what he has to say at its face value, we can note one or two points which proved to be regulative of the discussion for close on seven hundred years. First, he is acknowledging the closeness of the nexus which holds together the system of secondary causes: he notes the obligation on God should he elect to act within the order of secondary causes, to break into this nexus in some specified way, which amounts to disruption of it. When this intervention takes place, it is not possible to explain the effect in terms of its antecedents within the line of secondary causes. The problems to which I have briefly alluded in introducing this short commentary on Thomas' view are that it is not clear how the nexus of causes is to be broken without some manifestation of this first cause which operates so immanently in the process; nor whether the first cause has somehow to become a secondary

9. Ernst Keller and Marie-Louise Keller, *Miracles in Dispute* (ET London, 1969), p. 25, with reference to Augustine, *De genesi ad litteram,* 6.13.

10. St. Thomas Aquinas, *Summa Theologiae,* 1a, 105.6.

cause to produce the secondary effect; nor yet how a first cause can produce other than a first-order effect. The subsequent discussion of the problem of how God acts in the world is the working out of these points. Secondly, it would be wrong to leave the statement of the Thomistic position without reference to another point which he makes on a rather different tack. He writes, ". . . the same effect is not attributed to a natural cause and to divine power in such a way that it is partly done by God, and partly by the natural agent; rather, it is wholly done by both, according to a different way."[11] Whereas in the case of what Thomas had to say on miracles, the argument relates to God's anticipated miraculous intervention in natural processes (or secondary causes) as a result of prayer, the present quotation from the *Contra Gentes* is concerned with God's less spectacular action in nature, although this may nonetheless be part of the response to prayer. The account Thomas gives, then, is of God's activity in the world being indissolubly interwoven with secondary causation, so as to be best described, perhaps, as "in, with and under" it; God is not to be regarded as cooperating with secondary causes in a synergistic sense in a process of part-causation. This view is an interesting modification of the earlier account of miraculous intervention, for it does allow God to act in the secondary causal series without intervening in it or disrupting it. The issues with which we shall concern ourselves in more recent accounts of the way in which God relates to the world in what follows center around the questions of the inviolability or otherwise of the causal series, the ways in which God might be thought, if not to intervene, at least to become involved in, or to make his will effective in, the process of world events. The range of answers is quite interesting.

Divine Action and Modern Physical Science

The problem of God's action in the world came to be highlighted theologically at an earlier point in this century when it was felt that the Heisenberg Principle of Uncertainty provides a new basis for allowing God's direct action in the world of causally connected events. Clearly,

11. St. Thomas Aquinas, *Summa Contra Gentes*, III, 70.8 (ET Notre Dame and London, 1975).

if it had been firmly maintained that the law of causality was of universal application throughout nature, then the possibility of God's acting in nature could only arise through some invalidation of the causal principle. It was at first thought that the principle of indeterminacy entailed such invalidation. Heisenberg wrote in 1927: "Quantum mechanics has definitively established the invalidity of the principle of causality,"[12] while Nils Bohr in the same year wrote that in the case of atomic phenomena, "there can be no question of causality in the ordinary sense of the word."[13] With the breaking of the causal nexus, it was felt by many theologians that God was now free to invade his world, and to act at will within it. It was thought that the weighty evidence of scientific investigation and experimentation could at last be invoked to support the possibility of miracles, God's extraordinary intervention into natural forces, a possibility which had for many centuries been disputed by theologians and scientists. Unfortunately, the excitement and success, if so it may be called, was exceedingly short-lived, for it was soon pointed out by, for example, Max Planck, that the view of some indeterminists that the law of causality in physics had been decisively refuted by the Uncertainty Principle was simply a rash assumption.[14] The fact that the law of causality could not be applied in quantum mechanics or microphysics is in itself a refutation of the universal applicability of the law of causality. But it is necessary to observe how little that admission affects the main support for the law of causality; first, because the law of causality holds for the relation between the manipulation and reading which constitute the experimentation and the characteristics of the observed object; and secondly because the law seems to remain applicable within the macrocosm. Since God's intervention in natural process in miracle, or in response to prayer, takes place on the level of sensible objects in the macrocosm, we seem not to have made any great advance after all.

The matter did not rest there, however, but became more complex through the attempt now made to use the notion of statistical laws. It may

12. Werner Heisenberg, *Zeitschrift für Physik,* 43 (1927), p. 197, quoted by Keller and Keller, p. 162.

13. Nils Bohr, *Atomic Theory and the Description of Nature* (ET Cambridge, 1934), p. 54, quoted by Keller and Keller.

14. Max Planck, *Scientific Autobiography and Other Papers* (New York, 1949), p. 134.

be the case that individual particles individually behave in what can be called an arbitrary and indecisive fashion, but when sufficiently large numbers of them are considered, they begin to appear to behave with statistical regularity. The extrapolation of this concept from the sphere of molecular behavior to the macrocosm was once again analogical rather than strictly logical-deductive. If molecules behave in a noncausal way which produces statistical-average patterns, then it might be possible to think of macrocosmic entities behaving in the same way — and so once again to breach the law of causality. If so, then what were once thought of as causal laws could be described as statistical averages. An opportunity was thus created for God to intervene in the non-average case, or more precisely, the non-average case could be regarded as an instance of God's intervention. On this view, the miracle performed by God in the event which supersedes the forces of nature does not destroy the patterns of the universe. Rather, it might be argued, it would be through miracles that God's activity becomes visible, as a series of "improbabilities" combine together to produce a meaningful event, by virtue of the sovereign power of God.[15] This view, however, though superficially attractive, is not without considerable difficulties.

To begin with, the analogical extrapolation from molecular to macrocosmic entities is not justified by any sort of evidence or argument. The question is simply begged. Secondly, it might well be asked how frequently the non-average event in the macrocosmic world is likely to occur. If we are thinking of many of the nature-miracles, or of some prayer which requests of God some fantastically improbable interference with the natural order, then the improbability of the event contemplated will be so extremely high that it will verge on impossibility. Thirdly, then, either God has to wait on such extreme improbabilities to happen in order to intervene in the natural order, which in effect destroys the whole case, or else God himself creates these improbabilities which are the occasion of miraculous events, in which case this theory reduces itself automatically to the old "interfering with the laws of nature" theory, even though the laws so-called are now conceived as statistical averages. In other words, God has to be regarded as a further force in nature, or in Thomistic terms, as producing the effects of secondary causes without the causes themselves.

15. Keller and Keller, p. 169.

I should like now to turn to three other attempts to deal with this same problem of how God can be conceived of as acting in the world — that is, in a world which we and so many of our contemporaries regard as governed by the principle of causality — without resorting simply to the theorem that he suspends these laws in answer to our prayer, or spontaneously in some miracle. I have chosen to begin, perhaps for sentiment's sake, with a little-known name of my own acquaintance, that of Daniel Lamont, who was himself a physicist who had been greatly affected by the theories we have just been discussing, but who evolved a theory peculiar to himself. He sets out his views in a book called, *Christ and the World of Thought.*[16] Lamont holds that the framework of our earthly existence is constituted by three forms of existents: "(1) the subject-form in the Present; (2) the corridor-form, which is on the way from the present to the Object-Moment and is neither subject-form nor object-form; (3) the object-form in the Object-Moment."[17] This structure needs a little explanation. The Present is the vantage-point from which the subject looks out upon the world; it is the sphere of self-consciousness and of willing, so that whatever exists in the Present exists in a nonobjective or spiritual realm. God, as the Subject of all subjects, exists wholly in the Present, the eternal Present. Objects, however, exist in the past because the process of objectification takes time. Lamont takes the simple example of the visual perceptual situation. A clock is in front of me and I can see it; the seeing, however, in the sense of the objectification of the clock in consciousness, so that the clock is an object to me, comes as the final term in a complex process which is partly physical (light rays from an external locus radiate towards me), partly physiological (physical stimuli set up reactions in the retina, the optical nerve and the appropriate cortical area), and partly psychological (I classify the object conceptually as "a clock"). The object therefore which I "see" is not the object as it exists at present but as it was a short time in the past. The same point has been made many times over concerning the stars, some of which we now see as they were when Abraham lived. The idea is here uniquely employed, when it is extended to the will. My actual willing, as subjective act, is in the present, whereas the thing willed, the resolution or action, is in

16. Daniel Lamont, *Christ and the World of Thought* (Edinburgh, 1934).
17. Lamont, p. 109.

the past. If we designate the time in which the object exists as the Object-Moment, then we can see that there is an interval between what Lamont calls the Present and that Object-Moment. The time-interval between the two, Lamont calls the Corridor; in it he locates atoms, electrons, and those quanta which are not objects, for as he properly points out, they are existents on the way to becoming objects, or elements on the way to building up physical phenomena.[18] Returning to the analysis of the Present, Lamont claims that the will-form of nature is a creation of God's will, and that the Present is the medium of concurrence of the human with the divine will.[19]

I cannot even now pretend that I have fully understood what Lamont was saying. There is much that is fanciful, and much even that is obscure — for example, his statement that no direct creation by the Absolute can retreat into the past (we might add "to become Nature as the object we know"), for whatever the Absolute wills is a will, or a will-form. There seems to be little room for the traditional notions of creation, and a good deal of room, despite his protests, for a series of demiurges and emanations. But what he says is, if extremely elaborate, one man's attempt to show how God relates to the world as understood by modern physics, and to suggest how prayer can be efficacious in such a world. The Present is the arena for the conscience of wills. Because our wills are so often morally inadequate, the world which emerges from the compounding of the morally perfect absolute will and our sinful human wills is miserable, imperfect and distorted. What so greatly surprises me with Lamont's account of these matters is that he does not link what he has to say on prayer to this earlier discussion.[20] Disappointingly, he presents a very psychologically oriented account of how prayer works. He calls it a "concentrated faith-attitude," and says that it is "the chief of the requisites for a healthy soul"; it consists in "passivity of soul." It is constituted of "resistance to the solicitations of objects," "surrender of self-will" and "trust in God" — in other words, in expectancy and inspiration by the thought of God. Nowhere in the whole account does he show any sign of being aware of the problem of whether God answers prayer. It is, as I say, disappointing, for his earlier concept

18. Lamont, p. 87.
19. Lamont, pp. 112f.
20. Lamont, pp. 181ff.

of the Present as the arena of the concurrence of wills supplies a possible answer, in so far as we could imagine that the praying person by his or her will has contact with the divine will, and that from this concurrence emerges something in the Object-Moment which is closer to what that person wished to happen than would otherwise have been the case. If what was prayed for does not come to pass, the failure is due to the presence, in the Present-Moment, of other wills influencing the universal will in other directions. Lamont's view would then amount to a total inversion of the Thomistic view, insofar as it virtually affirms that we may be also first causes, disrupting the fixed order of secondary causes.

It is quite remarkable how close our second example of a modern attempt to deal with the problem of God's relation to the world and to describe prayer in that context comes to the first. I have chosen H. H. Farmer's, *The World and God,*[21] and though Farmer takes no cognizance of Lamont's work, and seems not even to have heard of it, what he says follows directly upon our final account of Lamont's views. He affirms that in "the ultimate order of things there stand human personalities, as created creators set in a dimension of personal relationship with the Eternal Personal."[22] There is a wide range of such independent creative realities below humankind, all of a fundamentally mental kind existing in relation to God. Their activities and their interrelations take place in what Farmer calls the "creative present," so that, according to Farmer, "Nature as it presents itself to us is a sort of *depositum* of this activity as it passes from the creative present into the past and so becomes on the one hand, phenomenal to our senses, and on the other a fairly settled routine which is never completely determined,"[23] though it is amenable to scientific examination and categorization. Here we have something very similar to Lamont's Present and Object-Moment, with the Corridor between; Lamont's Nature, or World, is Farmer's *depositum* in the past, while his "dimension of personal relationships" is extremely close to Lamont's "commerce of wills." Farmer continues, however, as Lamont failed to do, to show how God works in such a context and how prayer is effectual. The creative will of God is in rapport with the created wills, though in the case of human will God waits and hopes

21. H. H. Farmer, *The World and God* (London, 1935).
22. Farmer, pp. 175ff.
23. Farmer, p. 175.

for active cooperation. In prayer we seek not simply to accept God's will but also to cooperate with that will in its self-fulfillment, a process of identification which takes place in the present. What happens in the phenomenal world, then, is the result, in part, of prayer. In its examination of the phenomenal world, however, science will never be competent to say whether prayer or God, the human creative will or the divine Creator, or neither of the two, has been at work in the situation. So Farmer would conclude by coming down solidly for the efficacy of prayer: "Just as man brings about effects in nature which would not otherwise happen by redirecting its routines in relation with one another, so does God, except that God works from the inside, so to say by inner rapport and not by external manipulation in the gross."[24]

It should be noted before we leave Farmer and Lamont that there is a fundamental problem which neither of them seems to have solved. On the one hand, they both seem to cling to what could be called the traditional view of God's action in the world, namely, that God does in fact exert influence upon what happens in the physical order. Lamont writes, for example, of the will-form of nature as an effluence of the Absolute will, and Farmer, of God as achieving results in the physical world through being in inner rapport with human or other creaturely wills. They retain, in other words, a residuum of belief in God's power to bring about physical effects in the world about us. On the other hand, they are both highly ambiguous as to how these effects are achieved. They both seem to recognize that whereas human beings express their wills in the physical world through their bodies, God has no such physical body, Lamont carefully saying that it is the will-form of Nature which is an effluence of the Absolute will, and Farmer holding that the rapport which God has is, first, with human wills, and secondly, an inner rapport. They seem almost to imply that God's influence in the physical world works by a process of remote control, through intermediary human wills. This fact comes out clearly in Lamont's avoidance of discussion of the possibility that God's answer to prayer may take the form of some physical intervention, and in Farmer's seeming at times to allow, as in the case of the children of Israel crossing the Red Sea, that God redirects routine physical events or activities, and so physically intervenes, and at other times retracting to maintain that God works in some inexpli-

24. Farmer, p. 178.

cable way from the inside of events. So the basic issue remains, namely, that of how necessary it is to affirm that miraculous intervention by God in the processes of the world is part of the normal expectation of intercessory prayer, and of the extent to which belief in the possibility of such intervention is *de fide,* and still tenable.

Before turning to this question, however, I should like also to mention one other writer who has reflected upon the problem of God's relation to the physical order and to human volition, namely, E. L. Mascall.[25] Mascall makes the point that the supersession of classical physics by quantum physics has not been without important consequences for our notions of causality in the physical world, contrary to the opinion of those who wish to claim that the variable behavior of quantum phenomena is imperceptible in the macrocosmic events which are still governed by statistically arranged laws. He cites two cases. The one is from biology, where an individual quantum phenomenon occurring in a single gene may entirely transform some characteristic hereditary feature of a group and consequently the entire succeeding history of the group. The other is from nuclear physics, where if a device were set up to link the detonation of a nuclear bomb to the click registered unpredictably on a Geiger counter and amplified on a loudspeaker when an alpha-particle arrived in it from a disintegrating atom, we would then have a macrocosmic event whose occurrence could not be predicted by any established uniformities. Mascall, turning to our problem, adopts the Thomistic distinction between primary and secondary causality, emphasizing that in traditional Christian theology the reality of both is affirmed. If classical determinism is adopted and combined with such a Christian doctrine of the two causalities, then God is pictured as sustaining secondary causes in this causality. Mascall prefers, however, to combine the classical primary/secondary causality distinction with quantum physics, and he does so in this way. God allows a sufficient certain degree of autonomy to finite agents to enable their behavior to acquire a specifiable frequency, whose probability can be noted. Whether they act or not at one certain point in their frequency modulation rather than in another is a decision which God makes. "To the secondary cause it

25. E. L. Mascall, *Christian Theology and Natural Science* (London, 1956), pp. 195ff.

belongs merely to determine that there is a certain probability of the event occurring. . . . To the primary cause alone it belongs to determine whether the event shall occur, and when and where."[26]

Mascall is an extremely cautious writer and he does not attempt to build Christian theism upon nondeterministic physics. Nor is he tied to saying that alpha-particles and the like are "things" and not "models," for what he ascribes indeterminacy to in the example cited above is a macrocosmic event, a click heard over a loudspeaker. But he could be taken to have maintained certain points: first, the indeterminacy previously associated with quantum physics can be linked to what we might call large-scale physical occurrence; secondly, the universality of causal determinism in the latter sphere is open to question; thirdly a connection has been established between the primary/secondary causality distinction and that between quantum and traditional physical theory; and fourthly, though Mascall does not add this point, the creature could make its requests known to God in prayer, and since God is free to decide *when* the event expected to occur within a certain probability range will occur, he could take account of that prayer in his decision. On the side of assessment the question could be raised whether Mascall completely succeeds in his correlation of the distinction between primary and secondary causality with the parts played by God and by a finite agent as interpreted in modern physical terms. On the primary/secondary causality theory, the activities of primary causality and secondary causality were coextensive; by contrast, on Mascall's view God and the finite agent are both related to the whole of the event, but in different ways, so much so that he can affirm that the secondary cause has "no part or lot" in the occurrence of the event. The departure from the view that the two causalities are coextensive is therefore considerable and amounts almost to its rejection; certainly it is doubtful whether the term "cause" can be used where the so-called "secondary cause" has no part or lot in the occurrence of the event. But certainly if Mascall intends no more by the term "primary cause" than God, and no more by "secondary cause" than human agents or finite entities which enter into what are commonly regarded as causal occurrences, then it has to be agreed that he has opened up a basis upon which to affirm the possibility of God's effectually answering prayer in the physical order.

26. Mascall, p. 201.

But such optimism is by no means general. Let me set out in summary the views of those who seek a less direct view of how God acts in response to prayer in relation to the world and human beings. First, there are not a few theological objectors to the view that God is to be expected automatically to answer prayer, whether for some natural occurrence or for spiritual renewal. It may be a prayer for something that is not good for ourselves or for others, for something quite contrary to God's will. It may as a prayer be little short of superstition, a kind of magical incantation to persuade God in our direction. The more acquainted we become with the physical structure of the world, the economics of international relationships, the politics of world affairs, the less confidence do we come to have in the *Deus ex machina.* These good purposes of a physical or material nature which we hope will result from our prayers ought now more properly to follow from new agricultural methods, revised economic policies, hard bargaining in the council chamber and so on. With honesty on these points will come a fresh awakening of the spiritual consequences of praying, as uniting spirit with Spirit, ourselves with God and with other people. From that communion may well follow a new mood in the conference room, in the agricultural board, in the decisions made by economic groups. Prayer we shall expect, then, to be efficacious not necessarily in some miraculous way but often through human will. When there appears to be no answer to the request for some material result, therefore, there is nevertheless, by virtue of the communion which is heightened by the prayer, a greater readiness to adjust to what is to happen.

Secondly, there is a major problem for any account of the efficacy of prayer at any time created by the development of physical science. Apologists in this field have tended to take one or other of two views. On the one hand, they say that physics is a well-developed, well thought-out theory of the nature of the universe around us, that it must be allowed its autonomy like any science and that it cannot be altered to accommodate the interests of any specialized group, such as the religious. These people may add that certain physical theories were held in biblical times and that certain biblical views on other subjects were formed at that time with these theories in mind. But once we depart from the physics contemporary with the Bible we can no longer cling to biblical views associated with such science. At this point much demythologizing appears. On the other hand, some theologians take the hard line: We must decide, for example, on *a priori* religious grounds whether and how God answers prayer, and search around in contemporary physical theory for views with which that aprioristic theorem is congruous. If we totally fail, then we have to revert to the physics of another generation. Some religionists have done so, rejecting contemporary physics as part of contemporary secular culture, and canonizing the physical theory of Biblical times. This, however, is not a legitimate possibility. Our theology, including our theology of prayer, does not develop in a cultural vacuum. It grows though its contact with other disciplines, as indeed, we hope, they grow in contact with it. The answers we give to the problem of the efficacy of prayer are answers that we can give only in the context of contemporary life and thought. Contemporary theory may be thought of as restricting the kind of answer we can give to the problem, but it might just as well prevent us from giving a wrong answer by inviting to greater maturity, by drawing us away from the prayer of magic, the superstitious prayer, the penny-in-the-slot view of prayer which expects instant answers.

Thirdly, when we speak of answer to prayer, and the sorrow involved in accepting an answer which involves bitterness and not the sweetness of immediate deliverance, we dare not think other than of the prayer of Christ concerning his own death: "My Father, if it is possible, let this cup pass from me." The proper preface is there certainly, but the spirit of the prayer is for release. God's answer was to reaffirm his will, and Christ accepted. In that answer, which was a refusal, there was enshrined for all time the affirmation that the answer to prayer is sometimes to be found in the alignment of our wills and our purposes with God's. In the great ultimate situations of our lives, that is how the prayer is said; that is how it is answered; and that is how we receive the answer. The lesser situations have to take their tone and meaning from that source, and not from any quick deal we can effect with contemporary physics.

Fourthly, perhaps in the light of what has been said, we ought to look again carefully at what we do and what we expect in and from our intercessory prayers. Do we really expect God to feed starving babies now as Jesus fed the five thousand, or to match the needs of debt-ridden developing nations with sufficient national budgets? Do we expect wars suddenly to cease as a result of the prayers of the Church? If not, then what are we doing when we pray for such things? That God will have a care for them though we cannot? That their governors will see the light and change policy, or be inspired with magnificent economic acumen? Our prayer may be much more simply a hope that for them one day things will be right; it is an assurance that we are on their side and that somehow through our community with God this fact will be conveyed to them; it is a prayer for God's presence in their varied human situations and varied perils; and it is a constant stimulus to us to do what we can on their behalf.

Let us now, however, turn finally to tackle head-on the question whether the belief in the possibility of God's action in the world in response to prayer is to be marginalized in a culture which is totally convinced of the universality and inviolability of natural causality. These several theorems which we have just been considering are by way of being either caveats or negative assessments, and even the previous more positive accounts have not been conclusively encouraging. More serious is the fact that they fail to do justice, or if pressed do so grudgingly, to that element which has always been distinctive to petitionary or intercessory prayer, namely, its expectation, either explicitly expressed or implicitly understood, that God will act to effect the substance of the petition, and that he will do so in the world, and overtly, and not simply in the inward shaping of wills, feelings, and mental judgments. So it falls upon us now to blow the caveats, to be firmly positive and to attempt to redress the balance in favor of greater justice.

It has to be said right at the start that a belief in the efficacy of prayer in relation to events in the world, in history and within persons and their relations to one another is an inalienable part of the Christian understanding of prayer. Perhaps by concentrating upon problems that arise out of the physical sciences as they have developed in recent times, we have by our much foreshortened perspective allowed these recently raised problems to distort our presentation of God's part in the response to prayer, and to obscure the fact that in the many previous centuries of Christianity, even more serious objections to the validity of prayer have been encountered and accommodated. In fact, this conviction is so central to the whole concept and practice of prayer that to eliminate it is to destroy much of faith and hope.

Perhaps the time has come to be much less inclined to be thrown off-course in our commitment to the efficacy of prayer by arguments based on a conviction about the inviolability, universality and uniformity of physical natural laws. Granted that theology has always grown in the ambiance of a dominant culture and has been willing to take account especially of the points at which the culture and the theology seem to conflict, as was the case so often in the nineteenth and early twentieth centuries. Three reflections on this last subject put it into contemporary context. First, as we have just been finding, there have been several theologians in the present century who have taken the argument to those who accept unthinkingly scientific positivism as destructive of several aspects of theology, and notably of the efficacy of prayer as it relates to events in the world, personal lives and history. These apologists have done so on the basis of sound understanding of the relevant scientific theory. In *science versus religion* the situation really has changed. Secondly, widening the basis of the previous comment, we may add that the philosophy of science is never in what it itself would call a "steady state," and we have now reached the point at which, from the theological side, we take our stand on the central elements of the faith. Such firmness need not entail that we close our minds to what happens in contemporary culture, being willing to change when it is evident that a given belief is conditioned by demonstrably untenable fossils from an earlier culture. Such modification, however, is a long way from changing to suit the latest issue of *Nature.* We might put this last point in a converse mode, and say that we have to develop a disposition which is less prepared to assume that in a clash of culture and theology, the latter is by definition going to be wrong and will have to be modified. Probably faith is going to be a little more blind than it has come to be in the last hundred years, when it has tried to "see" everything — "a little more blind" in the sense of learning to shut out what is not important or relevant. A lesson we learned in first year physiological psychology was the capacity of the human eye to focus on the important in the visual field and to suppress the insignificant — a facility which the theological mind could well acquire. Thirdly, it could be argued that the doctrine of God the Creator, and of his lasting role in *creatio continua,* has never been properly related to the problems connected with petitionary prayer. It has always appeared to me to be strange that some theologians, in fact many, acknowledge the place of God's action at the initial creation of the universe, which has to be regarded as an "intervention" of major dimensions, and yet seem to experience immense difficulty in allowing that the process of *creatio continua* must entail "interventions," albeit of a less dramatic kind, all through the continued existence of the universe. To deny that is both to invalidate the doctrine of *creatio continua* and to subscribe to the noninterfering God of Deism.

CHAPTER 5

Prayer and Symbols

What Is a Symbol?

The nature and role of symbols as they appear in prayer cannot be readily separated from the part which they play in the rest of religious life, and I shall not here attempt to divorce the two situations. The general analysis of religious symbolism must obviously have considerable bearing upon anything we have to say about the place of symbols in prayer; what is of equal importance is that it is in the sphere of prayer that symbols play their most valuable role. There they must finally justify themselves, and there if they fail they will finally be rejected. Prayer is the world in which symbols live and have meaning. They become part of human existence, and for their part provide the shape which the religious life is to have, and the form which one's prayer life will take.

The word symbol as I shall use it is comprehensive. It will include more obviously objects such as crucifixes, icons, crosses on communion tables, crosses on walls behind communion tables, religious mosaics, stained glass windows; furniture in churches, such as altars, communion tables, pulpits, lecterns, baptismal fonts, reredoses and so on; and the buildings themselves, with their cruciform structure, or the utter plainness of four whitewashed walls, with their pointed steeples or their square towers. But religious symbolism must also include what goes on in these buildings and the use made of these furnishings and objects. It includes the whole liturgy, whether it is formalized or extemporaneous, with the prayers, the praise, the ritual acts of crossing oneself, closing one's eyes, kneeling, standing, bowing, the speaking as well as the remaining silent, and the processions, as well as the whole complicated actions of sacramental celebrations, whether we acknowledge two or seven. The comprehensive sense of the term "symbol" must extend finally to the concepts that are employed in all of these other spheres, concepts which unify what to an uninformed observer might well appear to be a sequence of happenings unrelated to one another or, as a whole, to their built-in environment. In fact it is the presence of a conceptual framework "in, with and under" the religious symbols which gives them their special status; the concepts are the commentary upon the symbols, the hermeneutic which provides them with their true meaning.

It may, therefore, be valuable, even at this early stage of our discussion, to offer a definition of symbol. In the light of what has just been said, it would read as follows: A religious symbol is a phenomenon existent in space-time, and identifiable materially or conceptually by both believers and unbelievers alike, but its differentia as a religious symbol is that for believers it carries a reference to a supernatural reality, this reference being specifiable in a complex variety of ways. The next major task to be taken up is the more precise specification of this variety, but before turning to it, I must first mention that herein lies the difference between a "sign" and a "symbol." A sign is unifunctional; it is an indicator to the presence of another reality, and its role is exhausted when we have reached or discovered or identified that reality. The symbol may be a marker to a reality beyond itself; in fact, minimally, it has to be. But in addition, it entails a wealth of relationship which we must now immediately explore, for the wealth of that relationship is the clue to the part which symbolism plays in prayer.

The Cognitive Role of Symbols

Symbols serve a wide variety of functions in religious life, most of which are relevant to their place in prayer. Bearing in mind the words of Mircea Eliade, "A fortunate conjunction in time has enabled Western Europe to rediscover the cognitive value of the symbol at the moment when Europeans are no longer the only peoples to 'make history,' and when European culture, unless it shuts itself off into a sterilizing provincialism, will be obliged to reckon with other ways of knowing and other scales of value than its own,"[1] we must first of all affirm the *cognitive* role which symbols play in religious life in general and in prayer in particular. The cognitive role is of this sort, namely, that in knowing the symbol in some way we are also given to know the reality. The symbol is not simply an occasion of knowing; it is a means of knowing. If I were to include the historical events of the incarnation in the category of symbol — an extension of the term which is not impermissible on the definition of symbol earlier given but which need not be pressed at this early point in the discussion — what I mean would be readily understood. We understand God's being, his purposes, his love, his mercy, in terms of the words and deeds of Jesus Christ. In a similar way, I am suggesting that the vast texture of symbolism which has been above quoted as constitutive of this concept may be regarded as the terms in which we apprehend God. It might be difficult to substantiate the claim on the basis of one event in the series of the incarnation separately from the others, even, for example, the death of Christ apart from his birth, or his sermons and sayings apart from his resurrection, but if we take the symbolism as a whole, then we can see as part of its function that it should be a way of knowing God.

This theorem may be clarified by means of three negative statements which all carry their contrary positives. The first is that the relation between the symbol and the reality it symbolizes, which enables the latter to be known through the former, is not of our creation. It is not a question of human searching after a variety of possible clues to an indeterminate reality, keys to open an otherwise firmly shut door, or for the most appropriate human figure or practice or concept to match the ineffability of the divine. Rather, is it that God himself gives the symbol, and in so doing constitutes the unique relation which it holds to himself. In Genesis 9:12f., it was a rainbow: "This is the sign of the covenant that I make between me and you and every living creature that is with you, for all future generations: I have set my bow in the cloud, and it shall be a sign of the covenant between me and the earth." The pillar of cloud by day and the pillar of fire by night in another circumstance were means chosen by God through which his people would be aware of his encompassing care for them. Once the principle is established, further examples rush to mind. For the Christian the most

1. Mircea Eliade, *Images and Symbols* (ET London, 1961), pp. 10f.

significant, of course, must be those chosen by our Lord: lilies in the field, as means of knowing the continuing providence of God; a child as the symbol of the greatest in God's kingdom — it is *that* kind of kingdom; and supremely bread and wine, through which in partaking we know the body and blood, the renewing forgiveness of Christ and of God. The principle can, I believe, be validly extended to those symbols which, while not part of the actual Word of God or of the total event of the incarnation, can be shown to bear immediate relationship to them, such as, the cross on the altar, the broken bread on the mosaic, the cruciform church, to mention but a few. These symbols, then, have been so closely related under God's will and purpose that they become the terms in which we know God.

The second negative theorem to be rejected is the view that the symbol is simply an associative mechanism which we adopt for purposes of recalling the sacred object to mind, a stimulus which we employ to activate the religious reality. The relation of association as the description of how a religious symbol stands to its reality is inadequate on three grounds: that it is purely external, that it is fortuitous and that it is expendable. The religious symbol carries a close connection with some specific situation in which it was created, and out of which it arose. The situation was the embodiment of some purpose of God, or of some aspect of his character or of his being; the symbol is the medium both of recall of that situation and of knowledge of it. Its relation to that situation cannot, therefore, be fortuitous since it derives from God's will. No more can it be expendable insofar as it points to some reality in God's nature.

The third negative theorem to be used to elicit a positive characterization of the religious symbol is that the symbol is not to be taken as a basis of inference to the religious reality, the premise in a proof of divine existence. If you were to combine H. H. Farmer's notion of "the world as symbol" with the cosmological proof of divine existence (a combination of which, may I hasten to say, Farmer was never guilty), you would have the kind of attempted inference which is here rejected. The religious symbol is in a more direct relation to the symbolized than the inferential process permits; the relation is more akin to that which obtains between the overt observable activities of a person and his or her inner intentions and purposes, where we know the inner reality *in terms of* its outward expression. Again we have an approximation only — hence the word "akin" — but the approximation is in the direction of that kind of immediate apprehension rather than in the direction of inference, analogical argument or deduction.

The link between this affirmation of the cognitive role of religious symbols and the subject of prayer lies in the fact that the symbolism which prayer shares with the whole of religion contains a cognitive component, and that prayer itself, in addition to all the other processes involved in it, rests upon knowledge, or acknowledgment of God. Some of this cognition may take place in other ways, but part of it is made possible by the symbolism which is employed in prayer. Interesting results may follow from a cross-check on the symbolism employed in prayer and in other kinds of religious activity, because the symbolism may vary and with it the conception of God entertained in the different contexts.

The Ontological Role of Symbols

There is a second function of symbolism which I can only describe as *ontological,* to distinguish it from the first which might be called *epistemological,* and to draw attention to the fact that it is the condition of the possibility of the first relation. The religious symbol is a way of knowing the religious reality because there is a real relation between the two, a relation existing in fact and not simply by human psychological association. Consequently, in knowing the symbol we are given the reality which it symbolizes. In a now classical formulation, Paul Tillich wrote that a symbol "participates in the reality it symbolizes,"[2] and in this way drew attention very clearly to the point under consideration, i.e., the ontological relation between symbol and symbolized. It is seen in its clearest form, perhaps, in the Roman Catholic doctrine of the sacraments, and particularly in the Mass, where the participation of bread and wine in the reality of the body and blood of our Lord warrant the claim of transubstantiation; however, it is no less clear in the Protestant Orthodox doctrine of Scripture, according to which the written Word of God becomes the Word of God *simpliciter,* or even in a non-sacramental service of dedication of a baby (which in some denominations is a substitute for baptism), where the liturgy followed shares in the holiness of the God to whom the child is dedicated. This ontological relation is

2. Tillich, *Systematic Theology,* I (Chicago, 1951), p. 177.

the basis of the veneration of relics no less than of the honor for God which requires us to take off our hats in Church or cross ourselves before the altar.

What I have never been quite able to accept is the quasi-Platonist account which Tillich tries to give of this relationship, which I agree is ontological. In Platonist metaphysics, the members of the sensory world, the world of opinion rather than of knowledge, participate to varying degrees in the Forms which constitute the world of ultimate reality. The degree of the participation of the finite world in the world of the Forms is the measure of its own relative reality, and carries with it an implication of unreality, illusoriness and falsity. No doubt Tillich would reject the overtones that attach to his notion of participation, but perhaps in any case it would be wiser to try some alternative account of how the ontological relation between sign and symbol is to be described. For my own part, I feel that we need scarcely go farther than the notion of religious symbol itself. The term "symbol" is, if the redundancy be pardoned, an incomplete symbol. It carries in itself a reference to the symbolized, and it is not constituted as a symbol until the referent and the connection between the two is established. Language, of course, allows us to speak of the symbol in isolation from the symbolized, and the symbol as a phenomenon in the ordinary world has an independent existence of its own. But if it is genuinely to be a symbol, then its relation to the symbolized is part of its existence; as symbol, it stands in an ontological relation to the symbolized, with which it forms the total symbol-situation.

This close relationship must carry, therefore, important implications for prayer. We use the religious symbols with which our faith supplies us as though they placed us in direct contact with the reality they symbolize. To enter into the symbol-situation in prayer is already to be drawn into the presence of the reality symbolized. This fact carries practical significance to the approach which we adopt to the symbols available to us for prayer. Quite wrongly, we all too often take the symbol as a thing-in-itself, an autonomous independent entity, for which we are required to cast a line to the other side, miraculously and improbably latching on to the reality out there, over there, or up there. In fact, there is no transition, miraculous, improbable, or fortuitous, from the symbol to the symbolized. To grasp the symbols as symbols is *already* to be gathered within the situation of which they are part, *already* to be carried to the reality which they symbolize. Such is the ontological affirmation which we make every time we pray.

The Mediative Role of Symbols

Because both of its epistemological and its ontological function in the religious situation, the symbol may summarily be described as having a *mediative* role. It mediates between the space-time phenomena and the realities or Reality of which the spiritual world is constituted. In doing so, symbols illustrate in a particularly clear way the "mediated immediacy" of our awareness of, and confrontation by God.[3] When speaking of the cognitive relationship effected through symbols, we noted how we know God *through* the symbols. The symbols are knowable in their own right, and *per se,* but when they become part of the religious-knowing situation while remaining the means by which we know God, they give way to, or are lost in the immediacy of, the reality that is known. The mediacy is the medium of the immediacy. This description of the position is virtually a paraphrasing of what was said under the heading of the ontological character of the symbol, where was observed the unitary character of symbol and symbolized within a situation which was comprised of both.

Once again the characterization of the role of the symbol, this time as mediative, is important for our understanding of prayer, and this for two reasons. First, if we accept, as we must, the saying of Jesus that "God is spirit, and those who worship him must worship in spirit and truth" (John 4:24), then we may be pardoned for regarding some form of mystical, nonsymbolized, even supraverbal, prayer as the true ideal at which we ought to be aiming. Such antipropositionism, or antisymbolism, as I would call it, tends in the direction of some immediate communion of spirit with Spirit, of a sort which would be inhibited by words, sentences and symbols. If what we are saying of symbols as mediative is correct, however, then we ought not to feel driven by any false desire for immediacy or perfectionism to dispense with symbols. Symbols are, on the contrary, the means which God has chosen both for his self-expression and for our communion and communication with

3. Cf. John Baillie, *Our Knowledge of God* (London, 1939), pp. 178ff.

him. Secondly, anyone who has any kind of Calvinism in the blood, even in the watered-down form of Barthianism, is bound to be obsessed with guilt feelings the moment he or she acknowledges the validity of symbols in prayer, in the knowledge of God, or indeed anywhere in worship. But the guilt feeling is a fantasy if created by the proper use of symbols — a point to which we shall have to return later. For the present, we allow that so far from apologizing for their presence in our prayers, we should rather embrace them as the normal means at our disposal for entering into the whole range of relationship with God. It is never a question of *whether* but *how* we may use them.

The Universalizing Role of Symbols

The *universalizing* function of religious symbols is not immediately grasped by its name and requires some explanation. There is a sense in which a person's awareness of God, or prayer to God, is a most personal and intimate experience and activity. In fact, the claim for the religious relationship is that, despite the infinity, the omnipotence and omnipresence of God, he relates himself with complete particularity to any individual believer and worshipper; one might say that if God loves all people with the love which he bears to each person, he also loves each as if there were none other to love. Emphasis is also laid on the *hic-et-nunc* character of the relationship, with God having something absolutely specific to say at this particular time, and the believer being required to relate to God, not in any vague or general way, but precisely, and uniquely. If this line were followed, then the whole experience would have to be presented as ineffable, in the sense of being totally private. The symbols are, in fact, the means by which this wholly private and personal experience, awareness, or prayer, is universalized and translated into a form which other people can understand and compare with their own experiences. It is thus that our religious experience can be checked, examined and criticized. The symbols, in a sense, externalize what is an intensely inner and inward experience and relationship, and make it so public that the world can see it, accept it themselves or reject it. Such universalizing and externalizing carries all the risk of exposure, and the risk is one which may bring on the disaster of adverse interpretation and even ridicule. Yet without such externalization, without the checking and cross-checking which it makes possible and in fact demands for its authentication, the religious awareness would be in danger of becoming subjective, in the worst sense of the term, and fanciful.

The public, universalizable character of religious symbolism has this consequence for prayer, that it provides both the control for private excesses or imbalances in one direction or another, and the opportunity for the individual to enter into the devotional heritage of centuries. The symbolism of Christian religion enshrines the fundamentals of the faith, and reliance upon it secures that the practitioner expresses himself or herself in the completest terms of that faith, and not in the slender creations of his or her own limited experience. As there is no guarantee that extemporaneous prayer will not prove to be every bit as repetitious as the most hidebound liturgy, with the additional disadvantage that you can be sure that the English will be a lot worse and the imagery a good deal more shoddy, so it is a mercy that from the symbols of the Christian religion we receive a constant enlargement in the expressions of our prayer and in our whole devotional existence.

The Communicational Role of Symbols

The *communicational* function of the religious symbol follows from the one previously mentioned. Because the symbol is universalizable and public, it is the medium of communication between believers, and the basis of their shared approach to God. Perhaps we have up to now been presenting both the religious life as a whole and prayer in particular in too private and individual a way, whereas something essential to both the general and the particular is to be found in the saying of Jesus that, ". . . if two of you agree on earth about anything you ask, it will be done for you by my Father in heaven. For where two or three are gathered in my name, I am there among them" (Matthew 18:19). The universalizable, public character of symbolism, then, enables the whole range of community activities which are the heart of the Christian fellowship. The language employed in the preaching of the Word; the concepts, ideas, or parables used in discussing the faith with one another; the symbolism of liturgy, sacrament and daily office; the shape of the Church and its several furnishings — all belong to the shared environment of Christian life and worship. The public character of the symbols makes possible the final unified self-offering of the people of God in dedicatory prayer; the symbolism of kneeling, shut eyes, folded hands, of language and concepts forms together the vehicle of the unity of that self-offering.

There are, however, advantages and disadvantages to this communicational role of the symbolism. It is, as we have seen, conditioned by its universalizability, and one moment in this quality is that the language so universalized is not some absolutely esoteric, in-language of a closed group. It is, in fact, very often the language of ordinary affairs that is used. On that ground, it is readily universalizable, and easily assimilable by those to whom its subject is communicated. When in Job we read of a God who speaks with a voice of thunder, who loads the clouds with moisture, to speak to whom we first require instruction (Job 37); or when the Psalmist says, "O God, why do you cast us off for ever? Why does your anger smoke against the sheep of your pasture?" (Psalm 74:1) we know what is meant by the writers. There lies, however, the disadvantage as well — for the language is open to refutation and alien interpretation as could not be some completely secret symbolism. It is in a sense because the symbolism communicates so clearly that it ensures the sort of radical criticism which it so often receives in the public forum. But no one would have it otherwise.

The Hermeneutic Role of Symbols

At an earlier stage in the discussion, I accepted Tillich's distinction between sign and symbol, while not necessarily endorsing the values which he gave to the two components of the distinction. One other feature of this distinction not so far mentioned is that while the sign offers no clue to what is signified, the symbol can claim to interpret that which it signifies — hence we have what I have called the symbol's *hermeneutic* function. The piece of wood on the sign post at Wagga Wagga which bears the emblem "Sydney" gives no clue to the metropolis which awaits the traveler at the end of 270 miles of Australian highway. But the religious symbol is expected to be an interpretative clue to the reality which it symbolizes. When Jesus says, "I am the light of the world," we accept the notion of light as a guide to at least one facet of Jesus' character, and we explore this facet to the very limit. The complex symbolism of the liturgy — the prayers of approach, adoration, confession, supplication, thanksgiving, intercession, not to mention the prayer of the veil or of the *ter sanctus* — is an irrefutable key to the interpretation of the character of the God who is worshipped in that context. For that reason, the God-concept of any theological system can be more accurately assessed from an investigation of the symbolism of the prayers and the religious practices of which the theology is an adjunct, than it can from the sophisticated descriptions of the theological system. It is no answer to this view to say that very often the prayer-concepts lag behind the radicalism of the theology, for that answer is simply an admission that the God-concept of the system has not sufficient intellectual and spiritual revolutionary power to transform the theology of prayer, or sufficient creative potential to devise a new liturgy and the proper language to go with it. As I have often said in the past, the test of any "new theology" will lie in its ability to set up a constructive religious life which matches its intellectual radicalism. So far in this area, we have to admit that many of the "new theologies" have proved either totally negative or singularly unimaginative.

The hermeneutic role of the religious symbol is of particular service to the neophyte, in that they supply markers to follow in that person's growth as a believer and in his or her devotional activities. Obviously they provide the terms in which to interpret a deepening communion and fellowship with God, but they also indicate how it is possible to enlarge that communion, and to articulate more precisely and more maturely the fellowship with God which lies at the heart of religious experience.

The Regulative and Prescriptive Roles of Symbols

There are two further characterizations of the functions of religious symbolism which now follow directly from the hermeneutic function, namely, their *regulative* and *prescriptive* functions. The first of these consists of the way in which the symbolism regulates or prescribes the behavior or speech of the practitioner who adopts the symbolism. In the behavioral field, to *bow down* in prayer is at once, if we are at least honest in what we do, to be embarked upon a prayer which acknowledges the majesty, greatness, goodness and mercy of God, and which from this acknowledgment leads on to other acts of confession and so on (the confession again being prescriptively determined or regulated by the act of devotional obeisance). In the linguistic field, to call Christ "Savior" is thereby to be committed to contrition for sins committed, to call afresh upon him for forgiveness, and to vow renewed obedience to him. As has already been noted, D. D. Evans, following J. L. Austin, has taught us that language is multidimensional, that it says and does many more things than those who see it as consisting of flat statements even begin to understand or appreciate. The symbolism for religion is of that category: It initiates a whole series of activities, statements, postures, attitudes, and is not in fact complete without them. It fulfills itself in them, as did once the Queen's statement, "I appoint you Governor of Kenya," which fulfilled itself in the political actions and statements which her appointee was thereby empowered to make. It is this integral relation, this regulative or prescriptive character of the symbol, which compels us to deny that it is simply a cue for what comes after the statement made by one actor on the stage which triggers off a speech by another, the relation being not much more than that of temporal sequence or the fortuitous occurrence of some associated word. The symbol *unfolds itself* in the behavior and expression which it prescribes, and exerts a regulative influence upon the form and character of that behavior and expression. Looked at in this way, symbolism can be seen to play a creative and foundational role in religion and in prayer, and not to have a repressive or restrictive character — which is unfortunately and mistakenly how it is frequently regarded.

The Normative Role of Symbols

It is a short step from speaking of the prescriptive and regulative role of symbols to a discussion of their *normative* role, that is, their capacity to provide standards for right and wrong attitudes, reactions, divisions, behavior and belief. It would be wrong to elicit this normative character of symbols from the meaning which the word has come to have in the history of doctrine, as a synonym for a creed. The normative role of the creed is well established: It provides the orthodoxy by which the false views of the heretical and the blasphemers are judged. It is the court of appeal when the Church itself seems to be in danger of departing from the faith once for all delivered to the saints. The symbols of the faith, as they have been defined in this chapter, have obviously not been ratified by Ecumenical Councils, or for that matter confirmed by acts of General Assemblies. Nevertheless, they have acquired, almost you might say by use and wont, or by habit and repute, a not dissimilar function of providing, in a less ultimate context than do the creeds, criteria for right thought and fitting behavior. When, for example, we try to modify a liturgy, taking it out of the sixteenth or seventeenth centuries and relating it to the late twentieth century, we are met on all sides by destructive criticisms as well as by helpful suggestions which have their origin in some conceptual symbol relating to what we are trying to do in the act of worship. If the discussion can be forced back to concentrate upon a comparison of the normative symbols which govern the different presentations of liturgy, then the real area of controversy will be exposed.

One of the major difficulties confronting those who plan contemporary Church architecture is the absence of some basic symbol to use in making their drawings and constructing their buildings. In the Middle Ages, the symbol of the cross provided the ground plan for most church architecture. In Calvinist Scotland, the symbol of the Word of God, read and preached, served a similar purpose. Church architecture in our day is doomed to failure so long as it consists simply of rearranging the furniture which these two basic symbols of cross and Bible distributed in such vastly different ways about the Church, or even of some kind of synthesis of the sorts of buildings which those symbols yielded. At the moment, we seem to be fumbling, and the fault, we must admit, does not lie with the architects. The Church, the living Church, must produce the symbolism. It is the absence of symbolism which is, I believe, responsible for the liturgical confusion from which today we are suffering. But without resorting further to jeremiads on the times or customs, we can notice certain positive and helpful ways in which the normative character of the symbol operates. It can, for example, act as a corrective of the less worthy items of our prayers of petition; it may be a catalyst to draw attention to the selfish streak in our so-called "prayers for others." It may provide us with a criterion to hack through the heavy, pompous, at times fatuous verbiage with which we clutter up even our private prayers, and which in our public prayers we feel to be necessary to induce a reverent somnolence in those who share them with us, or to secure the ear of God. Greater clarity in our symbols is the key to a clearer approach to God in thought and prayer, in word and action.

The Evocative Role of Symbols

A. C. Bridge places the concept of *evocation* at a very early point in his analysis of the role of images in art and of their place in religious belief, worship and behavior: "The method of art is to convey meaning by evocation rather than by exact description or direct statement; for the significance of a work of art is more than the sum of the connotation of its individual parts." He continues, "The subject of a work of art points beyond itself and evokes in the spectator an apprehension of the meaning which it is the artist's purpose to convey; it does not contain it."[4] We must discount at once the possible suggestion, implied by my making this quotation, that the symbols of religion are works of art, or that I have been thinking only of religious symbols which happen also to be works of art — though in fact many works of art are religiously inspired. But two of Bridge's points appeal to me and are relevant to our purpose. The first is that it is the role of symbols to point beyond themselves, and in the case of religious symbols, to point to a transcendent reality. The other point is that the symbol is calculated to evoke a response in the observer, as Bridge says, a response of apprehension of the meaning which it is the artist's purpose to convey, though in fact the response intended may be more total than one of apprehension alone. This evocative role of the symbol we must now further explore.

Obviously, Bridge is correct in drawing attention to the evocation of apprehension. We have already made the point that the symbol, if understood as a symbol, implies apprehension of a reality other than itself, and without that referential capacity the symbol as symbol cannot exist. But in a religious context, the symbol will be expected to evoke a considerable range of reaction in addition to that of comprehension. The intellectual reference may be perhaps predominant for someone in the initial stages of the religious process. Someone, however, who has already been related to the reality evoked by the symbol will very probably find that the emotional and volitional concomitants will im-

4. A. C. Bridges, *Images of God* (London, 1960), pp. 20f.

mediately present themselves. In the sacrament of the Lord's Supper, many young people partaking for the first time, with the catechetical preparation for first communion still fresh in their minds, will no doubt find their interest largely concentrating upon the intellectual aspects of the situation, when the bread and wine are brought in, the bread broken and the cup blessed. Those, however, who have partaken many times, will, on the appearance of the elements and through the celebration, find evoked in themselves a wide range of emotional and volitional reactions — emotional reactions stimulated by the memory of other celebrations in other contexts and with other people, volitional reactions created by recognition of failures in times past to fulfill promises made at the Table on previous occasions. This evocative function of religious symbolism explains the difference between what the Sacrament "means" to initiates and what it means to those who are more experienced, and the difference lies mainly in the range of evoked reaction. The point is sufficiently important to make to young communicants who feel that they are missing something which their elders seem to have found in the sacrament. Also, the evocative power of the symbol has to be allowed to operate on occasions on which we ourselves may feel unenthusiastic or unresponsive to the reality which the symbol presents. The symbol, because of its ontological relationship to the symbolized, can introduce us to the reality afresh, and by so doing evoke the responses which because of our indifference or coldness we were unable to produce in ourselves. The role of the symbol is to expose us to the reality which it symbolizes, and in so doing to evoke from us responses appropriate to it.

The Sustentative and Recreative Role of Symbols

Because of its evocative function, this capacity we have been noting to call up the reality it symbolizes, the symbol must also be credited with two further functions. The first of these I shall call *sustentative*, meaning thereby its power not only to initiate but to sustain the relationship between the believer or worshipper and the subject with whom he or she has to deal. If the symbol, as we have been arguing, constantly relates the individual to God, then it is putting him or her in touch with the power which renews, redeems, sanctifies and constantly sustains. Those who, treating religion phenomenologically, interpret symbols as talismans, are right in their recognition of the fact that symbols are thought to have the sustentative role of maintaining the believer's relationship to the deity, and they are closer to the truth in fact than those who try to dispense with symbolism, as if it were a substitute for the religious reality. The phenomenologist is, by the terms of definition of the discipline, restricted to the observation of the phenomena; the evidence of believers, however, is that *through the symbolism* of architecture, furnishings, posture, liturgy, or even in a sense through the absence of them all in the simplicity of an almost formless liturgy, they can maintain their relationship to God. The verse of the hymn "Abide With Me" which begins, "Hold Thou Thy cross before my closing eyes," is more than a request to see a certain physical object; it is more, too, than a metaphorical way of asking for divine assistance in the last hours of life. It is a request compounded of use, that through being given a vision of the cross of Christ, the person praying may, by that very vision, be not only reminded of Christ's saving power, but also actually be put in possession of it. The symbol, because of it immediate relationship to the reality of God's grace in Christ, is sustentative.

We have thought of the symbol initiating and sustaining faith, and trust in God, together with the vast complex tissue of the God-world relationship contained in such concepts as hope, love, forgiveness, and sanctification. The last of the functions which it may have in this same connection is that of *recreating* lost faith or shattered hope in the living and loving God. This role of the symbol has to be perhaps argued, because the first reaction might be to say that if the faith and the trust, the hope and the love have gone, then the symbol is indeed empty, meaningless and pointless. If, however, there is any truth in the case for the ontological function of the symbol, then the possibility opens up that the presentation of the symbol becomes also the point of self-offering of the reality symbolized by it. Because of its associations in so many of the contexts to which we referred in discussing the sustentative role of the symbol — and because of its immediately assimilable character as a space-time phenomenon, or as an ordinary mental concept — it may prove a ready recreative medium through which the ever available love, mercy or goodness of God may operate. The sight of an old keepsake, the discovery of a lost ring or an old letter, may do more than simply revive memories. It may recreate a lost affection, a forgotten concern, a forsaken tenderness. A *fortiori,* the sudden sight of a cross, the stillness of a wayside chapel, the sound of a familiar hymn, may be the turning point from lost belief to new determined resolution and obedience to Jesus Christ, and a recovered willingness to pray.

The Constructive, Structural and Integrative Role of Symbols

Religious symbol has a different, though not unrelated role, to which justice is not always fully done, that of providing a structural framework within which the religious life may be lived, a framework for Christian behavior in day-to-day affairs and for Christian action in the crisis, a framework too for prayer, for systematic reflection and for theology. When we think of symbols too much in terms of signs, we concentrate upon their referential character, their pointing beyond themselves to another reality. That function has obviously to be recognized. But at the same time, symbols relate to one another and can even be thought of as forming a structure, or a framework, as has already been said. The symbolism, for example, of the two natures and one person of Jesus Christ has been structurally integrated in theology with the human and divine aspects of the Church and the Bible as well as with the elements of the sacrament of the Lord's Supper. In fact, theological construction could be described as the attempt to systematize the symbol of the religious situation. For the devotional life, this structural role of symbolism is of value in that it preserves it from lapsing into a charge of free association, and sets up a system of support for growth and maturation. The trouble with much of our devotional activity is that it is conducted out of relation to that structural framework, and that it lacks also the integration which correlation with the framework would bring.

The Illuminative Role of Symbols

There is a famous patristic phrase used in relation to the incarnation which reads, "What Christ did not take he did not redeem," and which has often been taken to imply that logically, or in consequence, "What

Christ took he redeemed." The principle could be extended to the ordinary everyday situations where the things which Christ used in parable were given an other-worldly significance. Just because he could read off from everyday events and objects a whole range of messages and illustrations concerning the infinite care of God — from everyday things such as a lost coin, a lost sheep, a lost son, lilies in the field, a seed of corn sown in the ground, a pearl, a banquet, or a little child set in the midst — his lively sensitivity to the world as God's creation and as the object of his love was suffused with a new light, a new significance. It is this aspect of religious symbolism that I intend by using the word *illuminative.* The role of religious symbol, in addition to pointing us away from this world to a reality beyond it, is to enable us to view *this* world in a new light, to look at it in a different way. It was stated rather dramatically in the little poem about seeing things which "Christless eyes" had never seen, the sky above being brighter blue and earth beneath a brighter green. But it is not merely visual or closer intensity that was being suggested; rather, it was a perception of the *depth* of the world around, a world in which God cares for his people and provides evidence in that world for his caring. The situation is, of course, heightened when we move from the context of the doctrine of creation to those of incarnation and redemption, and the whole of human existence is illuminated by our religious symbolism.

The Liturgical Role of Symbols

The word "liturgical" may here appear to be repetition of what was included under the headings of "sustentative" and "recreative." Obviously, no attempt will be made to withdraw the ordinary sense of liturgical, and we have to say again that symbolism has a most important part to play in the changing of our liturgies and in the formulation and reformulation of our prayers. But a rather different emphasis has to be made in conclusion, in drawing together the many functions of symbolism in religion, namely, that it is *the* role of symbolism to *serve* the reality which it symbolizes, in whichever of the above-mentioned functions it happens to be operating. The symbol exists for the reality which is God. When it ceases so to serve, and seeks an existence in its own right, or when we give it that false independence, then it has to be condemned, and rejected. Of course, at that point it has ceased to be a symbol, which by definition points *beyond* itself and exists only *outside* of itself. But the self-existent symbol, the contradiction which it tries to be, is no longer a symbol: it has become an idol, a substitute-God, and is no longer part of the framework of the faith or of the service of the Church.

Symbols and the Future of Theology

As a result of this review of the varied functions of religious symbols, the question might well be asked: what then is the position of symbols in contemporary religion? Two immediate points must be made in reply. The first is that there appears to be a departure on a number of points from many of the symbols which have been effective for centuries, from cruciform architecture, from the traditional shape and progression of the liturgy and from long-familiar modes of address to God, to mention but a few. With this departure, no clearly discernible patterns, symbols, or concepts have emerged to take their place. The second point to make is that it is not likely that some totally alien, non-Christian concepts or symbols will suddenly materialize to take up the role which such symbols as we are familiar with have fulfilled in the past. What is more probable is that some concepts with which we are already familiar will come into predominance and will shape the symbols which are to be the vehicles of their expression. Remembering that earlier on we did include concepts among our roll call of symbols, we shall not too sharply separate the two.

The concepts which in my judgment could well come to play this master-symbol role in our theological and religious development are as follows. First, there is the concept of *reconciliation.* The religious symbols which are going to be effective for our time will be those which carry over into religion something of the secular concern of Christians living in the kind of world we know. In that world, there is brokenness of human relations over quite major areas of the world and of society, whether as a result of racial prejudice, economic inequality, territorial deprivation or political disenfranchisement. The Christian gospel has at its heart the message of reconciliation, and the symbol of reconciliation can draw together the gospel and the world, providing a vehicle both of understanding the faith and of effective action in that world.

Secondly, there is the concept of *the humanity of Christ.* What it means to be human, to be part of the stresses and strains of existence in this world, and how Christ should have genuinely entered this human situation — these are points at which Christian faith can most eloquently express itself, and where too the people of our time can most immediately begin to have their questions about themselves and about Christ answered. The part which the work or craft of carpentry has played in some popular presentations of the meaning of the incarnation is an indication of how the humanity of Christ is already beginning to act as a contemporary symbol.

Thirdly, I would speak also in this connection of the concept of *the aloneness and the involvement of God.* Here I have deliberately chosen to employ what appears to be a paradoxical concept, because both elements of the paradox are necessary. The "aloneness" of God I prefer to the notion of transcendence, otherness and so on, because it carries the social apartness, the attribute-difference which separates God from us, without committing us to spatial concepts, whether "outs," "ups," or "overs." But with that aloneness we have to hold on to his involvement, originally in Christ but continuingly through his Spirit, with human sin in its hatefulness, with human loneliness in its sorrow, with human despair in its hopelessness, and with all its aspirations and longings and desires for something better, more wonderful, more satisfying.

Fourthly, there is *the greenness of God's creation,* for perhaps the greatest and most important theological discovery of the years after World War II has been that of human responsibility for the conservation of God's creation, a heightened awareness of our role as the stewards of God's universe. "Universe" it has to be, for already we are turning the stratosphere into a scrapyard. It is a responsibility which has already captivated the imagination of even the youngest — especially the youngest — among us, as well as many whose connection with the theological basis of this responsibility is at best slender. This theme has also won a recognizable place in such new hymn books as *Songs of God's People,*[5] to supplement the very few hymns of a similar theme in the older sources. Because hymns are in many cases sung prayers, already the "green" cause is finding its way convincingly into our contemporary liturgies.

5. *Songs of God's People* (Oxford, 1988).

To embark on the elaboration of these symbols is, however, another subject, and one which cannot yet be developed at a theological level. It has to be born out of the faith and life, the worship and devotion of Christian people in the Church. It cannot be prospected or forecast — or worse, preprogrammed. But we do know that whatever the symbol, it can be expected to perform the several functions which have been outlined. Only as any new symbolism performs these will it be initiated successfully in Christian faith and sustained in Christian theology.

APPENDIX

Selected Prayers of John McIntyre

O God, it was a single goodness that created us, and not we ourselves.
It was a single wisdom that inspired us when our ideas failed and our thoughts were without purpose.
It was a single mercy that forgave us when we rebelled, breaking our human relationships and damaging our friendships.
It was a single hope that held us when we were all but overcome by frustration and uncertainty.
So may it be by a single light, a single purpose that leads us, that we face the life that begins anew for us today.
For Christ's sake. Amen.

O God, defend us,
not against the truth which reveals to us our true being and motives, character and purposes;
but against the lie which misrepresents and misjudges.
So give us patience to bear with those who will not understand when we speak in good will; and resolution not to be moved where — by weakness — integrity and goodness would be compromised.
For his sake we pray, who was the truth slain by the lie,
who, being reviled, reviled not again, remaining steadfast to the end. Amen.

O God, with Whom a day is as a thousand years and a thousand years as a day, and who dost make all things new continually in Christ;
give us renewal of heart and hope, of faith and trust, of love and understanding.
Of Thy mercy, restore to us the wasted years, the vain regrets, the unfulfilled intentions; and fill for us a world's emptiness with him that filleth all in all.
So grant us, in the silence, peace of soul, the comfort of Thy nearness.
For Christ's sake. Amen.

O God, the world in which we are called to live is not one of black and white but of different grays;
not of truth and falsehood but the compounding of both;
not of good and evil but the ambiguities that divide them;
not of light and darkness but the twilight between.
Give us, therefore, wisdom this day in our choices,
courage in our decisions,
and a continual discontent with anything less than the best that Thou hast revealed to us so wondrously in Jesus Christ. Amen.

O God, ours is the responsibility not only to seek the truth for ourselves, but having found it to impart it to others.
Give us both perseverance in our seeking, and in our communicating, patience.
May we at all times have sympathy to understand the needs of those with whom we have to do;
a care for their doubts and uncertainties;
and humility to admit our own.
Save us from a bondage to the past which can see no good in new thoughts, new approaches, new expressions;
from obsession with the present, which so easily becomes opportunism;
and from that anticipation of the future which evades present crises and demands.
For Christ's sake. Amen.

O Christ, our Savior,
who didst through the pain of the Cross and the joy of the Resurrection come to the glory of Thy exaltation to the right hand of the Father;
so make us sharers in Thy sorrow, that we may be joined to Thee in Thy glory for evermore.
As Thou hast bound Thyself to us by Thy humanity, with its nail prints and the wound of the spear,
so may we be bound to others by that same humanity,
to share their hunger, their suffering, their loneliness,
and thus in the end to share with them their exaltation in Thee.
For Thy dear sake. Amen.

O Christ, our Master,
who didst set Thy face to go to Jerusalem and to Calvary,
to bring love where there was hatred,
truth in the midst of error and misunderstanding,
and acceptance for all who were rejected;
may we in our turn show care to all who are neglected or despised,
a willingness not only to understand the truth for ourselves but to interpret it rightly for others,
and at all times, a spirit of devotion to our calling which has the courage to embrace self-sacrifice for Christ's sake. Amen.

Grant us, O God, Thy Spirit:
to lead us through the fallibility of our own searching to the certainty of Thy finding us;
to rid us of the error which we so readily mistake for Thy truth;
to inspire us with the love for Thee and for one another, which is the source of all forgiveness and the only possibility of reconciliation;
and to enable us in all things to honor Thee and to acknowledge Thy purposes for us.
Grant us, O God, Thy Spirit, for Christ's sake. Amen.

O God, who hast in the body of Christ knit Thy people together in one spirit of understanding, fellowship and peace;
grant that Thy people may ever fulfill in the world these same purposes of Christ.
So set upon the Church's ministry of healing and caring and teaching the seal of Christ's purposes, that we ever rightly support and inspire all committed to us.
For Christ's sake. Amen.

The Cliché as a Theological Medium

The Cliché as a Theological Medium

The trouble with a cliché is that you are rarely aware of using it yourself. Almost by definition, a cliché is something other people employ in speech or writing; but, like the beam in the eye of the beholder in Jesus' illustration (Luke 6:41ff.), it goes undetected. For my own part, having been taught in an institution in which the omnicompetence of the concept of *paradox* was accepted unthinkingly as the cliché-solution to the paralogisms endemic to systematic theology, I took at least a decade to realize that the utterance of the incantation, "It's a paradox," was not so much the end as the beginning of a discussion of the given subject. The point was brought home to me only when I recalled long afterwards a remark made by the late Professor Norman Kemp Smith, which I had at the time regarded only as a joke, that "Paradox is truth standing on her head, and it is the duty of a gentleman to assist the lady to her feet." Armed with this insight, I began to understand how effective the utterance about paradox was as a conversation- and argument-stopper, and equally how great a temptation to theological indolence it had been proving to be.

The experience was a sobering one, and from then on I have endeavored to be on the lookout for clichés similar to paradox, concepts and "OK sayings," which are part and parcel of theological thinking at any one time, and as unexamined presuppositions exert undue influence upon the course of arguments and even, if unexamined, impede adequate development of a given theme. Of course, there is a health warning on this process, namely, that of neglecting the thrust of Jesus' reminder to those who draw attention to what are but motes in our brother's eye.

Having observed the warning, however, we would be wrong to abandon the cliché, for it would not have passed into theological folklore had it not originally contained a fair degree of commonsense as well as theological truth. So, the task of assessing the cliché as a medium of theological expression takes on a more involved complexion. For an element of valuation has now entered, as it becomes necessary to judge, on the one hand, what credibility is to be assigned to the initial cliché, and, on the other, when a perfectly acceptable concept has begun to wear thin, or is discovered to contain elements which require closer consideration than was at first thought necessary. So, greatly daring, I propose to investigate a number of these widely accepted presuppositions, to tease out their possible meanings, and so to discover what truth they contain, what wrong implications they may carry, and how far their stereotyping precludes constructive and imaginative thought. So, to our task.

I

"We have no reliable historical knowledge about Jesus with regard to anything that matters."

This quotation comes from A. E. Harvey, *Jesus and the Constraints of History*,[1] but, in general terms, it reflects what theologians have been saying about the relationship of Christianity to history for close on a century and a half. The most influential, if not necessarily the earliest, expositor of such historical skepticism was Kierkegaard, who in 1848 wrote: "When Christianity is viewed from the standpoint of its historical documentation, it becomes necessary to secure an entirely trustworthy account of what the Christian doctrine really is. If the inquirer were infinitely interested on behalf of his relationship to the doctrine he would at once despair; for nothing is more readily evident than that the

1. A. E. Harvey, *Jesus and the Constraints of History* (London, 1982), p. 6.

greatest attainable certainty with respect to anything historical is an approximation."[2]

Few dicta in the whole history of theology have been taken up and repeated with so much dedication, and one might add, unthinking acceptance, as has the historical skepticism implicit in this quotation from Kierkegaard. In one form or another, it was adopted by Martin Kahler, Wilhelm Herrmann, Wilhelm Wrede, Ernst Troeltsch, and then by Karl Barth, who wrote, "Jesus Christ is also the rabbi of Nazareth, historically so difficult to get information about, and when it is obtained, one who is so apt to impress us as a little commonplace alongside more than one founder of religion, and even alongside many later representatives of his own religion."[3] Paul Tillich was even more explicit in his skepticism, "The Christological question is the question of Christ as the center of history. This question is however entirely independent of the problem of historical enquiry into the facts behind the rise of the Biblical picture of Jesus. The exposition of these facts can only lend probability — and with respect to the historical Jesus, a very faint probability. No religious certainty, no religious belief can be supported by such researches."[4] Emil Brunner encapsulates the skepticism of this whole tradition in the words, "Dependence upon history as a science leads to a state of hopeless uncertainty."[5]

But this trend did not exhaust itself in the first half of the twentieth century, as our thematic quotation indicates; as Peter Carnley agrees, it has remained very influential in the second half of the century.[6] In fact, the latter period has witnessed a shift in this kind of skepticism, from that found in Kierkegaard, and the theologians who followed him rather blindly, to an extremer form, illustrated by the quotation from A. E. Harvey above, and more correctly described as "historical agnosticism." For example, Kierkegaard, as it were, stopped short of the brink when he wrote, "The historical fact that God has existed in human form is the essence of the matter: the rest of the historical detail is not even as important as (it would be) if we had to do with a human being

2. Søren Kierkegaard, *Concluding Unscientific Postscript* (ET Princeton, 1941), p. 28.

3. Karl Barth, *Church Dogmatics*, I/1 (ET Edinburgh, 1936), p. 188.

4. Paul Tillich, *An Interpretation of History* (ET New York, 1936), pp. 246f.

5. Emil Brunner, *The Mediator* (ET London, 1934), p. 156.

6. Peter Carnley, *Christ, Faith and History* (London, 1972), pp. 165ff.

instead of God. . . . If the contemporary generation had left nothing beyond them but these words, 'We have believed that in such and such a year God appeared among us in the humble figure of a servant, that he lived and taught in our community and finally died,' it would be more than enough."[7] But Harvey's skepticism goes further, as does that of Dennis Nineham, who wrote, "Modern historical methods have rendered obsolete any talk of 'assured results' in relation to the figure of Jesus."[8] What we have now is full-blown agnosticism, which inevitably firms up, and consolidates the long-suspected antagonism of faith and history, with faith being always the diminutive contender and the probable loser.

So much for the cliché, as I have been calling it. Is there, after a century and a half, any way in which we can "assist the lady to her feet"? Two steps to that courteous end suggest themselves — the one immediate, and the other longer term.

The first suggestion comes from one of the clearest confrontations of historical skepticism to be presented in recent times. It appears in the article by Carnley referred to above, in which Carnley draws partly on a previous discussion by Norman Malcolm, in an article on "The Verification Argument" in the latter's *Knowledge and Certainty*,[9] Carnley seizes upon the logical inadequacies of historical skepticism, in the following way. He asks us to assume that a person at time t_1 has evidence which he believes justifies his assertion that event *E* occurred. The case for historical skepticism is that at some future time, t_n, evidence would come to hand which provided grounds for denying that *E* occurred, or that at time t_n, analysis of the existing evidence would yield grounds for a similar denial. Now, he continues, let us assume that at a given time, t_2, conclusive grounds emerge, which entail that *E* did not occur; therefore, at no previous time could anyone have known that *E* occurred. But "the argument for historical skepticism is a thoroughly *general* argument." So, even if it we have compelling evidence for saying that *E* did not occur, and that therefore no one could have known for certain that *E* did occur, that consideration in itself could not be proof of any

7. Søren Kierkegaard, *Philosophical Fragments* (ET Princeton, 1938), p. 87.

8. Dennis Nineham, "Epilogue" to John Hick, ed., *The Myth of God Incarnate* (London, 1977), p. 192.

9. Norman Malcolm, *Knowledge and Certainty* (London, 1965), pp. 1-57.

general conclusion that *no* statement about the past can ever be known for certain. Further, if we wish to demonstrate that at t_1 no one could have known with certainty that *E* did occur, then it is necessary that we be able at time t_2 to prove that at time t_1 the event *E* did not occur, and that the statement which says that it did is false. "But this is what the argument for historical skepticism denies."[10]

The author goes on to consider the implications for the part that historical material plays in faith and theological construction — and very interesting and relevant his comments are — but I should like to add a comment of my own. It is that, in addition to warding off successfully the demolition of the historical element in Christianity attempted by historical skeptics, whether of Christian or atheistic persuasion, Peter Carnley is indicating that the only way to deal with the historical element in Christian faith is the long way home, of examining each case on its merits. Agreed that such a proposal commits the enquirers to examination of the different varieties of criticism and their involvement in any given text or biblical situation. What is not permissible is the out-of-hand dismissal as irrelevant of such texts or situations, on grounds of historical skepticism. An excellent example of this process to which Carnley points is to be found in the same volume as that in which his own contribution appears (*Christ Faith and History*), an essay written by Professor John C. O'Neill, "On the Resurrection as an Historical Question."[11] The title indicates the readiness of the author to pursue painstaking historico-critical analysis, and in the event he does not hesitate to involve David Hume in the argument, or refuse to be stampeded by any form of universal historical skepticism.

My second and longer term suggestion as to how we are to handle constructively the treatment of the cliché which generated this whole discussion originates in a moment of truth disclosed by S. W. F. Holloway, in an essay entitled, "History and Sociology: What history is and what it ought to be": "The study of the past is at present in a very unsatisfactory state. Academic history is an 'intellectually invertebrate affair': it has no systematic theory, no accepted conceptual apparatus and no accepted canon of interpretation; its only rationale is the re-

10. Carnley, p. 185.
11. Carnley, pp. 204-19.

search methodology brought to perfection well over a hundred years ago by Leopold von Ranke, and handed on virtually unchanged from generation to generation."[12] These views may sound somewhat uninhibited and scandalous, offensive even to practicing historians. Any offense caused in the latter quarter is, however, unintended, inasmuch as the author's quarrel really is with the philosophers of history. In fact, by the time of Holloway's protest, a keen interest in the very subjects he mentioned, as well as several others closely related to them, had already been raised by the philosophers themselves, of which he appears to be ignorant. For example, F. H. Bradley had been writing about "The Presuppositions of Critical History" as far back as 1874, while early in the present century J. B. Bury, with such essays as "Darwinism and History" (1909), and "Cleopatra's Nose" (1916), was endeavoring to understand what it is that makes historiography an independent discipline. But it was not until the publication posthumously in 1946 of *The Idea of History* of R. G. Collingwood, himself both a philosopher and an historian, that the discipline which came to be known as "the analytic philosophy of history" seriously began. There followed in the next three decades a very steady stream of philosophers, such as Patrick Gardiner, Christopher Blake, John Dewey, W. H. Dray, Karl Popper, Carl G. Hempel, L. Pompa and W. H. Walsh, to mention a selection, who in an intensive way built upon Collingwood's foundations this discipline which had not existed previously — certainly not so comprehensively — in the history of philosophy. It is appropriate that the working manual for the discipline is the *Festschrift* in honor of the late Professor W. H. Walsh, edited by L. Pompa and W. H. Dray, *Substance and Form in History*,[13] in that it includes contributions by most of the philosophers who had been actively involved in the previous discussions.

What, then, of the historical skepticism which lay at the heart of the cliché from which we started, and for the treatment of which we are considering a longer term proposal than the "short way" which Peter Carnley so neatly set out? What has to be said now, and with all frankness, is that the reason for the popularity of historical skepticism,

12. In W. H. Burston and D. Thompson, eds., *Studies in the Nature and Teaching of History* (New York and London, 1967), pp. 12f.

13. L. Pompa and W. H. Dray, eds., *Substance and Form in History* (Edinburgh, 1981).

unduly prolonged it might be thought, for some hundred and fifty years, expressed in the terms quoted above, lay in the unthinking and unquestioning attitude of theologians to the grounds for its affirmation, and in their disregard for the very considerable investigations into the questions which Holloway had said were being ignored. What I fear has been missing, especially from the discipline of philosophy of religion, through its concentration upon problems of religious language in the 1960s and the 1970s, has been any serious attempt to come to grips with the analytic philosophy of history as set out by the writers abovementioned. Early and perceptive writers on the implications of history for one or other aspect of faith were R. R. Niebuhr, *Resurrection and Historical Reason,*[14] T. A. Roberts, *History and Christian Apologetics,*[15] A. Van Harvey, *The Historian and the Believer;*[16] but they were all writing before analytic philosophy of history had benefited from the philosophers listed above. What has become clear is that the terms of the old controversy over faith and history have changed, and the countenance once given to historical skepticism is subject to that change. In addition, it has to be said, there will be few areas of Christian doctrine that will escape reconsideration, for the reason that much of the script of modern theology has been written under the influence of historical skepticism.

II

> *"Metaphors are the means by which we speak of God."*

Reference has just been made to the concentration in philosophy of religion during the 1960s and 1970s upon the issues of the nature and validity of religious language, to the distortion to some extent of the treatment of quite a few central doctrines. By the 1980s, that concentration had been to some extent diluted, with at least one interesting result. This was that, out of the vast range of accounts of religious language previously on offer, the notion of *metaphor* emerged as apparently the most influential, as evidenced by the use that was made of it, for example, in

14. R. R. Niebuhr, *Resurrection and Historical Reason* (New York, 1957).
15. T. A. Roberts, *History and Christian Apologetics* (London, 1960).
16. A. Van Harvey, *The Historian and the Believer* (London, 1967).

the writings of Sallie McFague in *Metaphorical Theology*,[17] and Janet Martin Soskice in *Metaphor and Religious Language*.[18] Their writing had strong connections with the very adequate treatment of the subject of "metaphor" during the 1960s and 1970s, by Ian T. Ramsey in *Models and Mystery*,[19] Ian G. Barbour in *Myths, Models and Paradigms*,[20] and Richard Boyd in *Metaphor and Thought*.[21] There are differences of understanding and emphasis among these several writers, but without being guilty of unfair homogenization, we can grasp the main elements in a theory of metaphors — mainly as employed by theologians, although much that is similar can be said about their use in science, economics, political science and sociology — in the following ways.

(1) For example, though it may be the case, as Colin Gunton reports, that there are one hundred and twenty-five possible definitions of metaphor,[22] many of them bear a basic similarity to Aristotle's account in *Poetics*, 1457b 7-8, "that it is an alien name by transference." Gunton, who quotes Aristotle, offers his own interpretation of the term: A metaphor is "a term belonging somewhere else . . . used in unusual context," and, "a concrete image drawn from one part of human experience of the world and transferred to a new context."[23] Ramsey had said that metaphor is "a tangential meeting of two diverse contexts,"[24] and Ian Barbour, likewise, that "In a metaphor, a novel configuration has been produced by juxtaposition of *two frames of reference* of which the reader must be simultaneously aware."[25] Bearing in mind, therefore, Dalferth's warning about the multiplicity of definitions of metaphor, we shall not suggest that the above accounts are expected to be exhaustive or exclusive, but rather to represent a widely shared perception of what metaphor is about.

(2) Still pursuing a fairly broad line, we may add that, while some metaphors may lose that status and become literal in connotation,

17. Sallie McFague, *Metaphorical Theology* (London, 1983).
18. Janet Martin Soskice, *Metaphor and Religious Language* (Oxford, 1985).
19. Ian T. Ramsey, *Models and Mystery* (Oxford, 1964).
20. Ian G. Barbour, *Myths, Models and Paradigms* (London, 1974).
21. Richard Boyd, *Metaphor and Thought*, ed. A. Ortony (Cambridge, 1979).
22. Colin E. Gunton, *The Actuality of the Atonement* (Edinburgh, 1988), p. 27, from I. U. Dalferth, *Religiose Rede von Gott* (München, 1981), p. 218.
23. Gunton, pp. 28, 32.
24. Ramsey, p. 52.
25. Barbour, p. 13.

metaphors, as such, are not to be treated as literal, or regarded as literally true, or translated into equivalent literal terms. For example, as Gunton points out,[26] the word "muscle" derives from the Latin *musculus,* a small mouse, and so must have begun its life in a metaphorical mode, but eventually established itself in a literal sense. Despite the efforts of some of the literary critics to insist on its translation into literal expressions, its proper status as "metaphor" is to be secured, because of several potentialities which it bears, and functions which it fulfills, and could never achieve if it were literalized. To these we now turn.

(3) The metaphor creates the possibility of "epistemic access" to the outside world, the events that happen in it and the persons who live in it. These subjects are characterized in ways that would be impossible in flat, literal descriptions. This realist theory of knowledge is supported by a considerable line of writers on the subject, in opposition to those who would prefer to regard metaphors as intellectual fictions which have to be exorcised in the interest of truth. The difficulty inherent in the latter view is that it springs from a "mirror" theory of the nature of language and of knowledge, which then has to face two problems: First, how sure can we be that these mental fictions do indeed mirror reality? Without access to reality independently of the fictions, we are trapped on one side of the knowing situation, which was the problem also for the old doctrine of representative perception. Secondly, what we would have, on such a reading of epistemology, is not just subjectivism or idealism, but genuine agnosticism. The realist view which I have on occasion espoused takes the form of saying that metaphors are one of the ways in which we know reality, or, as shall be suggested later, one of the ways in which reality makes itself known to us. But the claim to knowledge must be made with modesty, as we recall that knowledge based on metaphor is tangential, the circumferences of two contexts intersecting, but not including one another.

(4) An attribute of metaphors which turns up frequently in accounts of them is their extensibility, their capacity to promote articulation, and "offer programs for exploring new situations."[27] The metaphor stimulates awareness of elements in the two situations or contexts which had not previously been connected. Max Black, in *Models and Metaphors: Studies in Language and Philosophy,* writes,

26. Gunton, p. 34.

27. Barbour, p. 43, reporting Donald Schon.

A memorable metaphor has the power to bring two separate domains into cognitive and emotional relation by using language directly appropriate to the one as a lens for seeing the other; the implications, suggestions and supporting values intertwined with the literal use of metaphorical expression enable us to see a new subject in a new way. The extended meanings that result, the relations between initially disparate realms created, can neither be antecedently predicted nor subsequently paraphrased in prose. We can comment *upon* the metaphor, but the metaphor itself neither needs nor invites explanation or paraphrase. Metaphorical thought is a distinctive mode of achieving insight, not to be construed as an ornamental substitute for plain thought.[28]

(5) Another theme which emerges in discussions of metaphor is that so far from our imposing our metaphors upon a neutral world, the world, on the contrary, when we open ourselves to it with the help of language — "if we have found the right metaphor — will enforce changes in meaning of the words we use."[29] Further, "this sort of epistemic success . . . is the very core of reference."[30] Ramsey had gone even farther with his view that "metaphorical expressions occur when two situations strike us in such a way as to reveal what includes them but is no mere combination of them both"; and "metaphor and model [are] ways of being articulate about what is disclosed to insight. But . . . it is not merely a matter of insight or imagination. I would stress what insight or imagination reveals, [namely], the ontological reference of metaphor and model alike."[31]

To gather together the various parts of this theme, for the quotations make slightly different emphases: not only are metaphors the means whereby we apprehend certain aspects of reality, they also are the means whereby a rich reality elects to reveal itself to us. When, in the metaphorical context, a profane term or concept is juxtaposed with some aspect of religious reality, the profane term thereby is transformed, and our world so much enriched.

28. Max Black, *Models and Metaphors: Studies in Language and Philosophy* (Cornell, 1961), p. 237.

29. Gunton, p. 45, paraphrasing Boyd.

30. Boyd, pp. 398f., quoted by Gunton, p. 45.

31. Ramsey, pp. 53, 54f.

The above cannot claim to be a comprehensive account of the state of play in the matter of metaphor at present, nor does it represent either the highest common factor or the lowest common denominator of recent and contemporary writing on the subject, which in fact is enormous. All that would be claimed for it is that such, or something very like it, has come to form the folklore in which metaphor is wrapped; or, using another figure, such in extended form is the cliché that we call metaphor and this is what it does. But it has now been so universally employed that the time has come to look at it more critically, and I do so as one who has employed it, together with its big brother, "models," and found it immensely serviceable and improving. In which direction, then, are we to move, if we turn upon ourselves and examine this idea and what has been said about it, or more honestly, what we ourselves have said about it?

1. To begin with, I must voice a suspicion, namely, that what has been happening in the immense popularization of the notion of metaphor in the study of religious language over the past fifteen years is that the term "metaphor" is itself being used metaphorically. I first came to this thought at a time when I was myself using the concept of "models" very extensively, and began to wonder whether a similar extensive use of that concept did not amount to using the notion of models as itself a model, a way of handling, for example, the different theories of the person of Jesus Christ, or of the atonement. In fact, I remember setting an examination question, which ran as follows: "State and discuss with illustrations the use of the concept 'model' as itself a model in contemporary theology." The primary use of the term "metaphor" is surely literary, and, given the element of assimilation, fundamentally descriptive. It is not for nothing that dictionaries, such as the *Oxford English Dictionary,* as well as grammar textbooks, such as J. C. Nesfield, *A Manual of English Grammar and Composition,* on which some of us were reared, classify metaphor under either grammar or rhetoric. It is, however, no disadvantage to admit that the theological use of metaphor, if I may so call it, is itself metaphorical, for by the admission, we are then free to run the range of activities with which scholarship in this area seems to have endowed metaphor in the recent studies which have been before us, and which might not be wholly appropriate if attributed to metaphor in general, or in its primary usage.

2. If we may now go on to unpack the cliché, we would have to draw attention to the fact that "metaphor" is in itself a fairly complex

structure. "Metaphor," as the textbooks will all tell us, is a figure of speech, or as the French would say, *une façon de parler,* a way of speaking, and so it is primarily an act of communication. As such, it involves the communicator, the two subjects from the different contexts, the relating of the two to one another (as noted above, creatively) and the final apprehension by the reader or the hearer of the situation communicated. So, while the metaphor often emerges as a kind of sound bite, an epigram or a *bon mot,* it is not to be regarded as a simple sentence, a proposition to be analyzed on its own; rather is it a construct out of the complex activity just described, which gives it its rationale. It is the elucidation of this structure, which enables us to put in place some of the things that were mentioned above in what I, perhaps lightly, referred to as the "folklore" surrounding metaphor in contemporary theology. For example, it is the communicator who has received the insight into reality in terms of the metaphor in the first place, or, alternatively, to whom reality so revealed itself, and who then imparted it in these terms to the person listening or reading. But the end of the process for the latter need not simply be an act of apprehension. Together with the understanding, there may be some emotional response, or some act of volition or a decision to embark upon some line of action. Metaphors have emotive powers denied to what we used to call "flat constatives," but these are not powers resident in them themselves; they are a function of the complex in which they emerge.

3. Mention has been made of the referential character of metaphors, which is part of a realist epistemology which considers that in using metaphors, we are making statements about the world as it is. Such a stance is taken in opposition to the view which regards metaphors as intellectual fictions imposed by the knower upon a neutral reality. I have already indicated my support for the realist epistemological stance, but I can also see that such an assertion can only be part of a much wider and more general realist epistemology. Writers such as Ramsey speak sometimes of reality "disclosing" itself, or God "revealing" himself, and metaphor is a major, if not *the* major, medium of describing these insights; in other words, metaphors are the media through which we describe a reality which thus presents itself to us. But the ontological reference thus assigned to the metaphors presupposes the existence of the subject revealing itself (reality) or himself (God), and they do not by their reference create the subject to which they refer.

4. Having so far, as it were, gone along with metaphors, I should now like to express an uneasiness that I have of late come to experience over their popularity, and my awareness of a "down side" to them which has long gone unacknowledged. Much has been made of the way in which the metaphor draws together two "diverse contexts,"[32] and the illumination that takes place as a result of the tangential meeting of two spheres. What is not so often acknowledged is that there is much that is not affected by the illumination, aspects of the two diverse contexts which are alien to one another. For example, for a very long time, the description of God as a loving Father was readily accepted; but in recent times, the metaphor has been rejected, not just by feminists, but also by people who have suffered at the hands of a human father. Interestingly enough, we were well aware of this down side of statements that involved some kind of assimilation, when we employed the notion of analogy, with its positive and its negative analogy. From the beginning, we were on the alert for the elements in the proposed comparison which fell within the one or the other, and we did our best not to confuse them. But somehow, the negative components in the metaphor have not been so closely scrutinized as has the negative analogy, partly because analogy, in addition to being a form of description, as in analogical predication, has also been a form of argument; partly also, therefore, because its roots lie in the precision of logic, while those of metaphor lie in the greater freedom of literature and speech. If we then pursue — perhaps a little perversely — what I am calling the down side of the metaphor, we soon begin to realize that the negative component is very substantial. For example, in the metaphors, "Their eldest son is the star of the family," "Hold fast to the anchor of faith," "he was fond of blowing his own trumpet," "Charles is a gem"; we are well aware that their eldest son is not a star, that whoever it was was not in fact given to marching about blowing some trumpet which he possessed, and that faith is not an iron anchor of heavy weight. In other words, the two ideas which in juxtaposition form the metaphor are in other respects totally different. This margin of difference is so great that in argument the metaphor is a dangerous counter to use, in that the opponent will waste no time in seizing upon the difference and turning it to his or her advantage. It is for this reason that I fear that the metaphor has retained a great deal of its literary provenance in its theological usage,

32. Ramsey, p. 52.

and lacks the degree of precision which the pressures of theologico-logic impose upon it. My suspicion is that when the pressures are on, metaphor has to fall back upon analogy, with its distinction between positive and negative analogy, to fight its battles for it in the logical arena.

Even while acknowledging the doubts which must inevitably arise from such strictures upon the place of metaphor in the analysis of religious language, I would not be prepared to remove it from consideration. I should like to offset such dangers as I have noted by insisting that the negative component in the metaphor be offset by a nucleation of other relevant metaphors, which among them reduce the danger of what would otherwise be misinterpretation. In the Scriptures, such a process unfolds when, for example, the metaphor of the loving Father is supported by the story of the prodigal son, by St. Paul in the hymn on love in 1 Corinthians 13, or by the accounts of the love of God in 1 John 4.

5. Having noted the corrective role played by the other metaphors which nucleate around a concept, as in the case mentioned, the metaphor of the loving Father, we have raised a very important further issue, so far unresolved in the study of the place of metaphor in religious language. It is the question of the criteria to be employed in the determination of the validity of a given metaphor. The question of the criterion of theological truth is serious enough when we are dealing with the run-of-the-mill statements that occur in doctrines and dogmas, the "flat constatives" mentioned earlier; but just because metaphors belong to what might be considered another order, and in addition seem to have certain internal difficulties of the kind we have just been considering, the problem is somewhat compounded. Certain criteria do come instantly to mind, the most important of which is the appearance of a given metaphor in Scripture. In the case of soteriology, a strong case can be made out for the view that almost all of the metaphors used to describe the death of Christ are scriptural in origin; similarly, not a few of those which appear in pneumatology are derivable from New Testament writers, such as St. Paul or St. Luke. On the other hand, when we turn to Christology, a different situation confronts us, for on the whole the metaphors which have found their way into canonical formulations can be easily traced to Greek philosophy, mostly of a strong Aristotelian flavor. In the event, these have been upheld by the Councils of the Church; have woven themselves into the texture of tradition and been found to sustain Christological convictions in cultures vastly for-

eign to those in which they originated; and so have themselves become part of the criterial structure of the Church's thought.

In addition to reaffirming the criterial role of Scripture and tradition in the assessing of metaphors, in the same way as other theological statements, we shall expect to encounter metaphors which are similarly not literal replicas of scriptural and traditional concepts, just because of the imaginative and creative element involved in the use of metaphors. The first stage check on such metaphors will obviously be their congruence with Scripture and tradition, and with that, the absence of sheer incongruity with the latter. When, however, the connection with Scripture and tradition in either of these two ways is not observable, as is the case with some of the metaphors to be found in, for example, Teilhard de Chardin or Charles Hartshorne, then two further criteria seem to have been accepted. The first is that the language embodying such novel metaphors (as well as other speech forms in evidence) must be acknowledged, by those who are aware of the scriptural and traditional originals, to be describing the same God, the same revelation, the same Christ, and so on, as the latter. The second supplementary criterion is that these new expressions should be effective communicators of the same ultimate truths as the originals, so that they too become the media of knowledge of God and of his grace to men and women who might otherwise fail to hear the Gospel. It is not for nothing that the creation of such new metaphors is likened to the use of another language to describe a situation to people who do not have the original tongue. In both cases the acid test is whether they understand and appropriate what has been said, as effectively as the others who received the message in their own tongue.

III

"*Persons are essentially relational in character.*"

or

"*The essence of persons is the relations in which they stand.*"

When the notion of persons as being always persons-in-relation was first mooted some fifty years ago, it very soon established itself as a dominant theological concept. The foundation for its popularity had originally been laid by Martin Buber's *I and Thou,*[33] but it was through John Macmurray, especially in his Gifford Lectures, bearing the collective title, *The Form of the Personal,*[34] that it became a philosophy of persons with emphasis upon the importance of the relationships into which they entered. The contribution of this insight into the nature of persons to philosophy and to theology in the second quarter of this century can not be overemphasized.

One immediate consequence was the opening up of an area of philosophical enquiry which had largely gone unnoticed in the whole history of philosophy up to that time, namely, the nature of our knowledge of other selves. In modern times, there have been centuries of discussion of the nature of our knowledge of the external physical world, and particularly of the ontological status of secondary qualities as they came to be called. Plato, followed by Aristotle, gave us an abiding interest in values and in universals, as well as into how we rightly conduct arguments. Philosophers and theologians of the Middle Ages gave themselves with religious devotion to understanding how we come to know God. But the question confronting us nowadays, namely, how do we know other persons, did not receive the rigorous analysis that these other major topics had received in centuries past. If the question ever arose, it was regarded as an amalgamation of perception, introspection and inference. It was only as we began to realize the specialness of our relationships to one another, together with the fact that, as persons, we live constantly in the I-Thou-God complex of relationships, that the understanding both of the nature of the self, and of how we know other persons, developed. The quality of such knowledge was soon discovered to depend on the character of these relationships, in commitment, affection, understanding, forgiveness, and so on.

Another valued consequence of this interest in the self and in persons was a fresh appreciation of the nature of our knowledge of God. Whereas in earlier centuries knowledge of God had been examined in the context of our knowledge of the external world, and at best in confirmation of accepted moral values, it now became clearer that our knowledge of other selves was a much better clue to the understanding

33. Martin Buber, *I and Thou* (ET Edinburgh, 1937).

34. John Macmurray, *The Form of the Personal,* 2 vols. (London, 1957, 1961).

of our knowledge of God than those earlier indications. This view of God as the Other, on the analogy of the other self, leading as it did to a reemphasis upon the transcendence of God as existing *totaliter aliter,* in his unutterable holiness and difference from ourselves, led some critics to reject its implications for theology. They drew attention to the confrontationalism which set God over against us, the seemingly excessively sinful account that it gave of humanity, as well as the secularization of society entailed by human fallenness. The end term of such strictures was the fear that the emphasis on the self or the person had produced the classic case of Luther's low view of humankind as *incurvatum in se,* "turned in upon itself."

But this conception of the self or the person as a closed entity ran counter to the mainline developments, for soon there were emerging the notions which formed our thematic clichés in this section. Persons are persons-in-relation. I encountered a much earlier form of this dictum, presented in a paper to the Heretics Club in Sydney just after World War II, but then in a sociological rather than a theological context. The author was arguing that the same "person" was in fact throughout the day, and by implication throughout his life, a whole series of different persons according to the relation in which he stood at the time: at breakfast with the family; in the car on the way to the office, sharing his inmost thoughts with some of the rather (as he judged) inadequate fellow commuters; dictating in the office to his secretary; a member of the board at its meeting; in the late afternoon on the squash court with his colleague; at the kirk-session meeting in the evening acting as session clerk; and finally arrived home, sharing a relaxed nightcap with his wife and half attending to the news. So varied were his attitudes and his behavior in these heterogeneous situations, that it would have been difficult to affirm which was the "true" person, or indeed, even, that there was any other than a series of what we would have to call *personae,* united solely by the fact that they are uniquely related to one body. That presentation is, of course, caricature, but in its simple form the saying is designed to draw attention to the facts that persons exist in communities, that they are enriched through the relations in which they thus find themselves, and that such relations form in many cases the fulfilling structure of their lives.

I should like to make three comments on this theme. The first comes from the late Professor John Anderson in Sydney University, which I have never forgotten, namely, that it is a logical mistake to try to define an entity by describing the relationships in which it stands. It is necessary, at some point in stating such relationships, to acknowledge its *own* being, by being able to speak about what it is in itself, and not to regard it as no more than a reference-point for the relationships. Anderson did cause a fair measure of consternation annually among first-year students, by adding that "God is love" cannot by itself be a definition of God, because love is a relationship, so that it is necessary to know in addition who God is.

Secondly, I am reminded at this point of a problem that first troubled me in Sydney, and has done since, when teaching the subject of Trinitarian theology, initially to students who had already been taught philosophy by Anderson — namely, the so-called personal properties of Father, Son and Holy Spirit within the Godhead. These are respectively, *paternitas, filiatio* and *processio* — paternity, sonship and procession. In each case, the personal property is an abstract noun, derived from the relation in which the particular person stands to one or both of the other two. If these personal properties are to be regarded as definitions of each of the persons, then the Andersonian principle has been violated, and we are back to our thematic cliché, that persons are persons in virtue of the relations in which they stand. We do, however, escape the Andersonian criticism, insofar as the members of the Trinity, who are distinguished from one another by these personal properties are, each of them, essentially God, and any full definition of them would be obliged to make that fact plain.

Having reached the matter of the relations obtaining among the persons within the Trinity, we must go further and note that we are now considering what is surely the archetype of the saying which triggered off this discussion. The revived interest in personhood which has been our subject in this section was always likely to impact upon any area of human thought where the notion of the person comes to be affirmed; and it did so in Trinitarian theology, causing embarrassment to those adhering to strict orthodoxy. The term "person" *(persona* or *hypostasis)* was now being construed in terms similar to the notion of a human person, raised, of course, to a higher dimension of wisdom, love, forgiveness and so on, with the result that the majority of writers in the past two decades have been affirming what they call a "social Trinity." In such a Godhead the Father, the Son and the Holy Spirit are thought of as forming a *societas* of equal persons united by mutual love and understanding, and in full communion with one another through the process of *emperichoresis* (interpenetration), much referred to in classical accounts of the intra-trinitarian relations of the persons. In fact, it is the firm emphasis upon the closeness of that *emperichoresis* which is claimed to save this notion of the Trinity from tritheism. On the other hand, it is fairly clear that this notion goes beyond orthodox accounts of the Trinity, which dissociate themselves from any suggestion that the persons resemble in any way individual personalities.

For my own part, I have felt now for some time that a social Trinity view of the Godhead is to a degree inescapable, so long as we refer to the *opera ad extra Trinitatis,* that is, God's activities in relation to reality — nature, humankind, and so on — external to himself. Dogma has always affirmed that the Son is incarnate in the world, as revealer and redeemer, and in carrying out this work he is an identifiable and integrated person. The work of creation has traditionally been associated with the Father, while the work of effecting the redemption and the sanctification of God's creatures has been appropriated to the Holy Spirit. These works of the persons of the Trinity *ad extra* are distinguishable and separable, in spite of the well-known saying that the *opera ad extra Trinitatis sunt indivisa,* the works of the Trinity in relation to reality external to God are indivisible. This latter saying I have usually interpreted to mean that when any one of the persons of the Godhead is working the work appropriate to himself, the other two persons are also involved, even though not primarily.

Having adopted the social Trinity interpretation to designate the presence of God in the world and history, I would like nevertheless to retain the canonical view of the nature of the persons within the Godhead and of their relations to one another, sharing in a single substance, and eternally related to one another by the relations referred to above, *paternitas, filiatio* and *processio.* I do not believe that a social Trinity can be accommodated within the intra-trinitarian picture, if for no other reason, then certainly because of the time-element in the former and the diversity of the inter-personal relationships which emerge in the *opera ad extra.* In other words, I accept the traditional distinction between the so-called immanent Trinity and the economic Trinity, but reject any suggestion that they are to be antithesized to one another. What I would prefer to argue is that the economic Trinity is the outward and perceptible form of the immanent Trinity, which is the eternal and inward being of the God who is Immanuel, with us from the beginning of time until its end. This social Trinity provides us with the paradigm for the way in which persons are related to one another — related, but each retaining self-identity within the relationship, even when benefiting richly from it.

IV

"For we are all one in Jesus Christ."

Of few points in the history of the twentieth century, with its record of uncontrolled destruction, inconceivable cruelty and spiritual darkness, could it be said, as it might have been of the year 1948, "Bliss was it in that dawn to be alive." It was the year of the first conference of the World Council of Churches, held at Amsterdam, and after the polarization and fragmentation of the War years, here was the affirmation of a bright new hope of unity with a profound religious foundation. Nor was it an affirmation calculated to inspire only the Church with a new assurance, after its many failures in wartime. With faithfulness to Scripture (John 17:21-23), the affirmation, on the strength of the promise of Jesus himself, was expected to serve the Gospel by creating in the world the knowledge that the Father had sent his Son, Jesus Christ. Almost fifty years on, it is a cause of disappointment and even disillusionment that somehow the words of Jesus, "that they may be one as we [Father and Son] are one" (John 17:22), have not brought the rich harvest of Church reunion and unity which the fresh appreciation in 1948 of the words of Jesus had anticipated. Yet throughout these years, it is no exaggeration to claim, few sayings of Jesus have been so often repeated. Sometimes they have been quoted as an incentive to proposed unions of one kind or another, with the implication that with one more heave the reality of unity will fall into our hands. Equally, they have been uttered at times when the evidence was running totally counter to any appearance of Church unity, this time with the implication that the unity is there, had we but the skill to lay it bare or the perception to intuit it in spite of the appearances. Why, then, is it that this Johannine saying of Jesus should have been repeated so faithfully all these years, without the galvanizing effect of Church unity which in that "dawn" we were led to expect from it?

I should like, in answer to my question, to argue that the Churches and their ecumenical theologians have been singularly at odds with one another in their interpretation of Jesus' saying. There are at least four ways in which the saying may be construed.

1. The first of these — and as far as I know, it is not an option at present entertained by the WCC — is the Roman Catholic view that the unity which Our Lord contemplated is that bodied forth by the Roman Catholic Church. It is a subject to which John Paul II addresses himself in answer to his interlocutor in *Crossing the Threshold of Hope,* who has been saying that "ecumenical dialogue . . . seems to have had its share of disappointments."[35] The Pope responds for a time, it would seem, encouragingly: noting, as we approach the end of the millennium, that Christians are more conscious than ever before of the fact that their divisions violate the words of Jesus in John 17:21 (p. 145); quoting the words of Pope John XXIII, "what separates us as believers in Christ is much less than what unites us"; allowing that, given the variety of cultures in which believers have lived across the centuries, their different approaches to "understanding and living out one's faith in Christ" (p. 147) need not be so much mutually exclusive as complementary; and finally, acknowledging that there may even be good in the history of the divisions between denominations in that thereby "the untold wealth contained in Christ's Gospel and in the redemption accomplished by Christ" has been revealed.

In the two chapters from which these thoughts are culled, however — namely, "In Search of Lost Unity" and "Why Divided?" (pp. 144-55) — there are judgments which are also less eirenical. For example, the Pope seems to draw back from his concession on the mutuality of differences, to affirm that some differences cannot be overlooked, insofar as they entail compromise of the faith (p. 147). The difference gap with the Orthodox is not wide, but the gap separating the Protestants from the Roman Church is greater, "since several fundamental elements established by Christ were not respected" (p. 148). The Buddhists in China and Sri Lanka took the gravest exception to the Pope's allegation in this same

35. Pope John Paul II, *Crossing the Threshold of Hope* (London, 1994), p. 144. Further references are given after quotations in parentheses.

book that "Buddhism is in large measure an "*atheistic*" system" (p. 86); and yet scarcely a voice has been raised in protest over his strictures on Protestantism. Of course, we are not informed what these "fundamental elements established by Christ" were which "were not respected" — perhaps the supremacy of the Papacy, or ministerial orders, or sacramental theology, or even women in the ministry — yet they were sufficient to earn the dismissal of the Pope. A not dissimilar dismissal appears when, after commenting upon the involvement of Christians of all denominations in missionary activity, the Pope observes that the people to whom the Gospel is thus preached must ask questions about the unity of such Christians, and about which of them is the true Church, since Christ "founded only one Church — the only one capable of speaking in His name" (p. 146) — an altogether thinly disguised affirmation of the Roman Catholic Church as that true Church. It is therefore difficult to see what precisely the Pope means by the "ecumenical movement" other than the reintegration of a Church that was once unfragmented.

So, when it is recognized that there is plurality among believers, it is argued that "it is necessary for humanity to achieve unity through plurality, to learn to come together into one Church" (p. 153). The plurality of denominations will turn out to be different ways of thinking and acting, of cultures and civilizations within the one true Church and not in parallel to it. Therefore, if in WCC circles we are still interpreting our unity in Christ in fully uniform and monolithic terms, then it is folly for us to think that this unity is one within which the Roman Catholic Church will be contained, as an equal among equals. The only fully uniform type of unity is the single unity of Rome, in which we would have to participate in the derivative sense of becoming part. In that unity plurality may still persist, but it does so, not as in the autonomous diversity of the Protestant Churches, but always within the parameters of those "fundamental elements established by Christ," of which we have already spoken.

2. A much less cerebral and more overt attempt to express the unity felt to be implicit in our Lord's saying in John 17:21 has been the plea for intercommunion (stated recently so persuasively in the document "Intercommunion: The Churches Agree and Disagree," published by the Unity Faith and Order Commission of ACTS[36] in February

36. Action of Churches Together in Scotland.

1994). This plea is born out of two circumstances. On the one hand, Christians of varying denominations meet in so many situations in which they are acutely aware of their shared experience of Christ — in Bible study, worship and prayer and ceremonies of mixed marriages — and a shared participation in the Eucharist would seem to be the spiritually appropriate fulfillment of such an experience. The exclusion which is the normal sequel in most cases serves at a single blow to unpick the good that has been emerging. It is indeed a frustration which we have all known.

On the other hand, just when so many joint studies of an ecumenical nature seem at last to be realizing the hopes of the heady days of Amsterdam 1948, the exclusion order above-mentioned has received rather draconian form from both the Roman Catholic Church and the Orthodox communion. The Catholic one runs as follows: "In general the Catholic Church permits access to its eucharistic communion and to the sacraments of penance and the anointing of the sick only to those who share its oneness in faith, worship and ecclesial life";[37] while the Orthodox ban reads: "For the Orthodox, 'communion' involves a mystical and sanctifying unity created by the Body and Blood of Christ, which makes them [the faithful] 'one body and one blood with Christ,' and therefore they can have no differences in faith. There can be 'communion' only between local churches which have a unity of faith, ministry, and sacraments. For this reason the concept of 'intercommunion' has no place in Orthodox ecclesiology."[38] The tone of both of these excerpts is so dismissive, and runs so counter to the spirit which has accompanied almost all of the ecumenical meetings and conferences of the past fifty years, that it has elicited a very sharp response from members in many Christian denominations. Their judgment appears to be that, setting aside the problems of faith and order, ministry and sacraments as apparently intractable, they feel that they should be able to meet around the table where for all Christians the body of Christ is broken and his blood shed, for the table is the Lord's and not the Churches'.

37. "Directory for the Application of Principles and Norms on Ecumenism," No. 129, dated 25 March, 1993; quoted from "Intercommunion," p. 2.

38. *The Dublin Agreed Statement* (London, 1984), p. 15; quoted from "Intercommunion," p. 2.

Given this motivation, a logic felt to be compulsive, and an objective considered modest and even minimal, namely, intercommunion, the supporting arguments are not unconvincing. For example, baptism, as the rite which introduces us into the Church universal and bonds us to Christ and to one another, has thereby already set us in unity with one another. To refuse someone who is already in that unity the Eucharist is a schismatic act. In any case, the Eucharist as the power which mediates the redeeming and reconciling grace of the crucified Christ is itself the means whereby the divisions which separate the Churches may be healed.

This approach is so simple and so persuasive at a first encounter that it is hard to understand why it does not carry more conviction, especially in the quarters to which it is directed. Yet the response to it has been so blunt and negative that there has to be some very sound rationale for it. That lies, I believe, in the two quotations, the one from the Roman Catholics, the other from the Orthodox, which are very close to one another. They both say that only those who agree with the denomination's faith, ministry and ecclesiology are to receive the Eucharist. In other words, the Eucharist is neither a neutral event upon which we may variously impose our own denominational interpretations, nor one from which, in receiving it, we may gratuitously occlude these theological components from which we dissent. It comes as a complex event, structured according to the ministry which celebrates the Church order within which it exists, the nature of the sacrament itself, and so on. It is impossible, or at least improper, to treat that event as less, or other, than it is. That argument is unanswerable in the terms thus stated.

So, if "intercommunion," despite its simplicity, turns out to be a non-starter — and it is a disappointment to have to say that, because for many people, weary with ecumenical attempts to share the Lord's table throughout his Church, it had become something of a last stand — what are we to do? My own opinion — and I am not considered a representative of my Church's ecumenical expression — is that there are no shortcuts in ecumenism, and so not in eucharistic theory either. It has to be the long way home, through discussions of the nature of unity, doctrine, ministry, ecclesiology and sacraments. It is also my conviction that, since this whole movement is a fire which the Spirit himself has kindled, it will not be quenched short of achieving what he had in mind for it. Perhaps that is a fact which we should all remember, both when we are obstructive, and when we are depressed about the Church's unity.

3. Our excursion into the subject of "intercommunion" was by way of exploring what could be said to be a minimalist interpretation of our oneness in Christ, in the hope that, if our oneness is established in the Eucharist, we can then go out to discover further unity in other places of our faith and ecclesiology. But that is not to be. So, we return to the text in John 17:21. The argument now is that the unity of the several denominations with one another in Christ is similar to the unity of the Father and the Son within the Trinity. The unity of the Churches thus affirmed is then taken to be a uniform unity, based, that is, upon the concept of the one essence in which the persons in the Trinity share, a unity, too, in which there is none prior or posterior but all are equal. When this argument is used, it is normally intended to reduce the differences that exist among the Churches in faith, order, ministry and sacraments, to a measure of agreement on these subjects, and where they persist to put on pressure for their reduction into an inclusive uniformity. Such an account of the unity of the Churches based on the doctrine of the Trinity, however, is flawed in its understanding of the relations of the persons of the Trinity to one another, and therefore of the implications for the subsequent account of the relations of the Churches to another within the unity of Christ. This criticism is valid whether we are thinking of the interpersonal relations *ad intra Trinitatis*, or in the *opera ad extra*. Thus, in regard to the former, it is a basic principle of trinitarian theology that the *opera ad intra sunt divisa*. Without the characteristic differences which "divide" the persons from one another, they would merge into undifferentiated unity. As we observed above, the so-called "personal properties" are little more than abstractions derived from the proper names of the persons; but the point that they were safeguarding was the distinctness within the Godhead of the persons, enshrined within the *opera ad intra Trinitatis*, the works of begetting, being begotten and proceeding, respectively. Without that distinctness, the fact of God's triunity would be in question. If we then follow out that argument into the derived analogy of the Churches, we say that the distinguishing characteristics of the Churches remain within the unity which is theirs in Christ, and that this unity is characterized by the plurality that obtains among them.

When we turn, however, to the *opera ad extra Trinitatis* and recall the assertion that they are undivided *(sunt indivisa)*, then we may be inclined to believe that the unity=uniformity understanding of the ideal relationship of the Churches to one another in Christ is the correct one. Three replies are to be made to this account of the matter.

First, an essential element in the description of the *opera ad extra Trinitatis* is the doctrine of appropriations, which affirms that each of these *opera* is associated with (appropriated to) one specific person within the Trinity, for example, creation with the Father, incarnation with the Son, and sanctification with the Holy Spirit. It is impossible to describe the *ordo salutis,* unless the distinctions implicit in that order are maintained. Without them, God's action in the world loses all definition and character. So, if the Trinity is the basis of our understanding of the relations of the Churches to one another, what we have is a recognition of the specific part which each of the Churches has to play in implementing God's presence and activity in the world, and certainly not a case for unity = uniformity.

Secondly, the point made in the scholastic dictum concerning the *opera ad extra* being *indivisa* is now usually interpreted as meaning that where any one of the persons is engaged in an *opus ad extra,* the other two persons are in attendance — the Son and the Holy Spirit at creation, the Father and the Spirit at the incarnation, and the Father and the Son in the process of sanctification. Once again, if the Trinity is the prime analogate for interpreting the kind of unity which obtains among the Churches in the world, then we see that unity to be one in which their identity is confirmed and sustained.

Thirdly, if we return to the social account of the Trinity, which as we argued above is acquiring considerable support, especially when it is held along with the traditional orthodox account of the relations to one another of the persons within the Godhead, the *opera ad intra Trinitatis,* we find that we arrive at a similar conclusion. The three persons form a *societas,* a group who participate in the Godhead, and yet remain distinguishable from one another, and consequently, the Churches, who similarly share a unity which is called "unity in Christ," within that unity retain their identity and fulfill special roles.

4. Another classic sentence quoted for the understanding of the unity of the Churches is 1 Corinthians 12:27 (to be taken, of course, with the whole passage, vv. 12-30), "Now you are the body of Christ and

individually members of it." I fail to understand why this passage has had so little effect upon the thinking in ecumenical circles about the relation of the plurality of the Churches to their unity in Christ. In the run-up to the passage which concerns us, St. Paul has spoken about one and the same Lord and Spirit and God, who endows believers with varieties of gifts (vv. 4-11). From v. 12 on, he advances the argument, showing that in fact the body *requires* the differences that exist between the different members in order to function properly. If the members were identical to one another, the entire body would be incapacitated. Further, while it might appear to the outsider that, though the members are all necessary to the body's well-being, some members are weaker or lowlier or less honorable than the rest, God on the contrary has invested them with special honor, and laid upon the others a responsibility of caring for them.

Now, I can appreciate that in the first instance St. Paul was directing himself to a pastoral situation in Corinth, where, it would appear, not only had there been an explosion of spiritual activity in the city, but the recipients of such gifts as he mentions had been trying to lord it over one another. So he had to specify the source of the gifts, their place in the life of the Church, and the obligations to one another that lay upon those who had the gifts. The analogy that may then be drawn by us, both as to how the Churches are related to one another within the body of Christ and to the Triune God, and as to their obligations of Christian caring towards one another, is so transparent and so primal that I find it inescapable as the basic analogate for understanding our plurality in unity in the Churches. It has, moreover, the support of the argument from the spelling out of the relations of the persons to one another within the Trinity.

V

> "*'Pluralism,' not 'exclusivism,' is the acceptable category for interpreting modern society, religion and theology.*"

Two sets of circumstances which have occurred, particularly in the United Kingdom in the past twenty-five years, have served to give the term "plurality" and its derivatives a frequency of use unprecedented in its previous history. The first has been the arrival in our midst of considerable numbers of people of other faiths, notably Muslims and Hindus. The arrival of immigrants in the United Kingdom is in itself nothing new. The difference is that whereas the old immigrants professed some form or other of Christianity, mostly Roman Catholicism, and on the whole blended into society, the newer immigrants often refuse resolutely to be indigenized, preferring to create sub-groups and subcultures within which they hope to perpetuate their own religion and morality.

The second noteworthy circumstance giving vogue to the term "plurality" is the rapidly growing interest in other religions, or other faiths, to use the more popular designation. This interest is, of course, partly due to the above-mentioned immigration influx, so that whereas previously "other faiths" formed the matter of textbooks, now they became part of the social fabric of daily life in some of our cities. The greater mobility provided by air travel, together with enhanced media communication, has also produced the closeness of a global village on the international scene. One result of this has been that in these twenty-five years, courses in religion and other faiths in universities have escalated to the point of pushing theology into a second place. I should like, then, to examine this much-thumbed notion of pluralism in the context first of society, and then of religion and theology.

In the former, pluralism appears also under the synonyms of multiculture and multi-faith, and the implication is that the proper relation with members of other cultures and faiths is "dialogue." No one is going to question the latter idea. Given that we live in close proximity with other groups, then a prime obligation is to understand our differences, and there can be no quicker or more satisfactory way of achieving that end than talking through our differences. Within such give-and-take, the notion of pluralism implies an egalitarianism of status with other faiths and responsibility to the culture and the faith which we ourselves support. The danger implicit in this process is that pluralism may seem to suggest that that is the end of the matter. On the contrary, certain issues remain to be addressed.

First, as was observed a moment ago, many of the immigrants of the second half of the twentieth century have differed both in faith and language from the native peoples of the United Kingdom, and have consequently and earnestly striven to maintain what is almost a closed community in ethos, religion and culture. This resolve is strengthened by their assessment of the culture into which they have come as being in many respects totally secular. Such intentions are laudable, and no question can be raised about it, unless eventually at the point where the ethos of the community may conflict with the legal structures and the sanctions which the host country adopts in relation to certain crimes. With the increasing and inevitable weakening of intercommunity barriers, such conflict is ever a risk, the consequences of which are simply postponed by the proposal which sometimes emerges from immigrant communities to have separated educational systems.

Secondly, while the principle of egalitarianism will be maintained as long as possible, it must not be allowed to obscure the responsibility which resides in the host nation to ensure that Christian values are safeguarded. I feel that this position has to be supported against the much vaunted claim that we are a post-Christian or even a non-Christian society. If that were the case, it would be necessary to rewrite much of the existing legal system and of the still widely accepted moral standards, which are acknowledged even when they are "more honored in the breach than in the observance." I fail to observe any rewriting of either of these codes by humanists, or New Age exponents. One of the Christian values is tolerance of those with whom we disagree, and that value guarantees the right of non-Christians to pursue their own lifestyle within the limits already indicated. But such insistence amounts to the denial of mutuality and egalitarianism of responsibility as among the different ethnic groups in the country; the non-Christian groups do not have an equal and mutual responsibility to maintain, say, Muslim or Hindu ethics, as an ambiance in which Christian ethics may be safeguarded. The reverse of this situation, or rather its mirror image, is experienced when British people live in countries in the Middle East, and have in public to honor the ethos and practice of the host nation. Such then are the limits of pluralism in a society of mixed religions, races and cultures.

Turning now to the applicability of the notion of pluralism to world religions and world faiths as distinct from the societies in which they express themselves, we can see at once that if it means no more than the multiplicity of religions and faiths, it is only a synonym, and does not require further investigation. If it means more, as I am sure it does, then pursuing the matter, we can see that it involves the following: the conception of the several world faiths or religions as coexisting in parallel; the acknowledgment of each by the other of its inherent truth, within its own system; the rejection of the old attitude of mutual criticism and attempted refutation of each other, such attitudes of live-and-let-live being dictated by the conviction that such systems are not so much intellectual stances as the ingredients of ways of life, which in themselves cannot be refuted intellectually. They are what they are by their own standards, and by these they shall be judged — not by the alien norms of another faith.

The flaws in this kind of argument — and they apply to the whole pluralist approach to the relations of faiths and religions to one another — are twofold. First, it fails to do justice to the intellectual element in the faiths, which it presents in social terms and lifestyle forms. But few, if any, of the faiths would be happy to be derationalized, or, alternatively, few of them could be adequately understood, if deprived of their intellectual structures. So, while it would be a mistake to reduce the faiths to the status of theological or philosophical systems, as was too often the case when they were studied without the benefit of anthropological and sociological research, they have to be credited with, in each case, a substantial intellectual content. The second shortcoming of the nonintellectual or anti-intellectual approach to the faiths so characteristic of pluralism is that, insofar as they have an intellectual component, they also make a truth-claim; and they make it as against the other truth-claimants. Put quite bluntly, there is no faith in which men and women believe which does not conceive of itself as other than true, and by implication, of others as false, at least in some respects. Having said so, I still believe that we have come a considerable way from the days of "conflict" as the way to regard world faiths. This advance is due to the influence of the pluralist conception, which, by holding the intellectual and the nonintellectual components together within the idea of a faith or a religion, reduces and cushions the sharpness of the encounter. That fact, however, ought not to conceal from us the ultimate clash concerning truth.

VI

"Peace" and "Justice" are the dominant categories in the Church's political action.

Throughout most of the years since the 1960s, whenever Christians have found themselves making public protest or taking part in a demonstration with a political or civil rights involvement, at some point in the procession a banner has appeared bearing the legend, "Peace and Justice." Gunnar

Stalsett, a Lutheran priest, sometime secretary of the World Lutheran Federation, and now rector of the Institute for Practical Theology at the University of Oslo, during a sermon at the celebration in July 1947 of the fortieth anniversary of the founding of the Federation, considered that "the call to participate in the struggle for peace and justice" went out at that celebration in 1947.[39] That call has echoed across the years, he adds, in the Federation's plea against nuclear war, its compassionate attempts to secure the cessation of the exploitation of the impoverished masses in Latin America, and its solidarity with the victims of apartheid in South Africa. That was 1947. But it was not until almost two decades later that the notion caught fire and became the inspiration of the public expressions mentioned earlier. Now it has come to be used, one fears, almost unthinkingly, and that in itself is an insult to a great idea, whose time as a result has come — and gone. But before investigating where this particular cliché is now going to lead us, let as pause a little to ask how it came to have such resounding and rallying popularity.

First, the objectives contained in the phrase "peace and justice" were such as could be easily identified with practical courses of action in a world of distressing injustice and threats of war. By contrast, the Christian ideal of love by its very nature seemed to be far removed from that kind of world, and to offer little indication of how it was to be implemented. Moreover, should it be necessary that violence would be required to ensure civil rights and realize the peace, then there would be no likelihood of clash with some commitment to nonviolence. In the interval since the 1960s, the threat of nuclear war may have somewhat diminished (even though the ingredients of such a war are still lurking in a few cupboards), but evidence of the grim reality of the violation of civil rights seems to be increasing daily. We still have a long way to go before we satisfy the ideals of "peace and justice."

Secondly, I am sure that the attraction of the formula "peace and justice" lay also in the common cause with communists and non-Christians in general that it gave to Christian activists. There was a certain sensible hard-headedness in this "common cause" argument, for by itself a purely Christian approach would be less well supported and more difficult of achievement. The other obvious point is that in many situations the "Christian" course of action is indistinguishable from the

39. Gunnar Stalsett, *Following Christ Together* (Geneva, 1994), p. 14.

non-Christian. Christians do not have a monopoly on moral rightness. Some Christian apologists once used such an argument for allying with the Soviets to defeat the Nazis.

Thirdly, anyone who had been brought up in the 1930s — or who had been taught by someone who had been brought up in the 1930s — on a strong diet of the ethics of Reinhold Niebuhr, might well have recalled what he had to say about the relation of justice to love. I shall later be claiming that the absence of Niebuhr's ethic from the present scene of Christian moral thinking is one source of its inadequacies. But someone in the 1960s or 1970s might well have recalled that the ethic of love is a moral "impossible possibility," and that there are certain socio-political situations in which justice is itself a form of expression of love; in addition, just because the distance separating the agents from the persons whom they are obliged to help often prevents them from direct expressions of love to them, the agents can take active steps to secure justice for the helpless.

But the mention of Reinhold Niebuhr, reviving as it does his prophetically penetrating book, *An Interpretation of Christian Ethics,*[40] takes us to the heart of the seriousness of allowing the theme of "Peace and Justice" to dominate our thinking about the standards we observe in analyzing and engaging in what we consider to be Christian activities. Two considerations compel us to rethink this domination, for such it has certainly been and continues to be. First, on the grand scale, the Soviets as such have gone from the scene, and the old urgency to find a highest common factor in the field of ethical motivation has disappeared. Admittedly, politics is still "a dirty business," but we would be less than responsible if we allowed that piece of worldly wisdom to be the last word or the only word to be offered in justification of our compromises in the situations that face us nationally and internationally. Secondly, I have always felt that, from the point of view of Christian ethics, the sole emphasis in the cry for peace and justice, as it has so often been, is pragmatic, temporary and penultimate. Surely the time has come for a characteristically and identifiably Christian input into the understanding and perception of the contemporary ethical scene in its socio-political, economic, international and personal dimensions.

40. Reinhold Niebuhr, *An Interpretation of Christian Ethics,* 2nd ed. (London, 1937).

Where, then, to begin? What has puzzled me most in the midst of the demonstrations and protests, which have all had an openly avowed moral tone, is the absence of the notion of *love* from the moral conviction which apparently inspired such activities. There may have been a number of reasons for this lacuna. For example, the 1960s were marked by a number of movements which used the term "love" very indiscriminately, and so brought it into disrepute. As such, in the kind of nirvana in which it flourished, and in the world of the flower people who gave it a home, it did not seem to have any place in the hard thinking which the moral crises of the day demanded. I recall how at that time I endeavored in *On the Love of God*[41] to offer a restructured understanding of the love of God, and its implications for our own response to that love in our daily moral endeavor for this very reason that the central element in the Christian ethic was in danger of losing its place either to more pragmatic and populist concepts, or to misunderstandings of itself. In those days professional theology did not offer any great assistance in this process of recovering a place for the concept of love in Christian thought and action.

It is, however, as I indicated earlier, to Niebuhr that we should be returning if we wish to correct the imbalance in ethical values created by an overemphasis upon peace and justice. In reference to Niebuhr, I mentioned the word "prophetic," and somewhat random openings of the work above-mentioned yield quotations which have a very contemporary ring about their context, and these passages offer shrewd ethical judgments:

> In a struggle between those who enjoy inordinate privileges and those who lack the basic essentials of the good life it is fairly clear that a religion which holds love to be the final law of life stultifies itself if it does not support equal justice as a political and economic approximation of the ideal of love.[42]

Again, we read:

> The problem of politics and economics is the problem of justice. The question of politics is how to coerce the anarchy of conflicting human

41. John McIntyre, *On the Love of God* (London, 1962).
42. McIntyre, p. 141.

> interests into some kind of order, offering human beings the greatest possible opportunity for mutual support. In the field of collective behavior the force of egoistic passion is so strong that the only harmonies possible are those which neutralize this force through balances of power. . . . All these possibilities represent something less than the ideal of love. Yet the law of love is involved in all approximations of justice, not only as the source of the norms of justice, but as an ultimate perspective by which their limitations are discovered.[43]

Let us now pursue some of the stages in the argument for an integral and organic relationship between love and justice. We have been so conditioned to regard love and justice as antithetic to one another that we have difficulty in setting them in any other relationship. We shall take up some mentioned by Niebuhr and extend ourselves into others inspired by him.

First, "love is involved in all approximations of justice." Justice, like any of the other major moral values, such as truth, honesty, and goodness, is regarded by all who pursue it as existing in an ideal form which is never realized. In the case of justice, which is our immediate concern, approximations may vary in the degree to which they fall below this ideal, when the ideal cannot be realized in the given circumstances, because egoistic interests, or unfair balances of power, or longstanding prejudices are heavily counteractive. Yet when approximations of justice are sought notwithstanding, it is because of the involvement of love in the situations. It promotes the highest level of justice which the situation will tolerate.

Secondly, as a result we can add that "love is the source of the norms of justice." Love enables us to judge which proposed course of justice is preferable to all of the others, taking account as it will of the varying claims and needs of the persons involved. This role of love in justice appears most recognizably within families, where the need of one of the children may have to be given priority over what are arguably the just claims of the others. Even on a larger scale, weaker and threatened groups within society may be given preferential consideration over others whose claims in terms of justice may even be higher. The norms

43. McIntyre, p. 150.

which enable such decisions to be taken in circumstances which might well prove controversial have their source in love.

Thirdly, love provides "an ultimate perspective by which limitations [of justice] are discovered." The trouble with "limitations of justice" is that they may in fact turn out to be just that — proposals less than justice requires. Just because love is the source of the norms of justice, it provides a standpoint from which to judge whether such shortfalls and limitations are not concessions to some pressures, biases or class interests within the situation. It does so in virtue of one of its essential characteristics, namely, its ability to identify with the parties within the situations, and so to view the obligations and tensions from the points where they apply. In brief, *justice cannot be justice solely in being justice.* The point of this epigram, in the wake of what we have been saying about love and the limitations of justice, is that love, and love only, can ensure that the varying claims of the different participants in the justice situations, with their idiosyncratic needs, can be fairly and justly met. Without the presence of that component of love, justice would entail a quasi-mathematical calculus for the measurement of such claims.

Fourthly, love supplies the inspiration for the pursuit of justice. The comment could quite rightly be made upon what has been said above about love and justice, that a desire for justice can itself provide motivation enough for most situations. Love, I would say, enters into the motivation in two ways. On the one hand, there is a kind of drive for justice which is, in the event, mixed with a strong element of vindictiveness and revenge, and which consequently results in a degree of overkill. The result is an unjust situation which soon evinces the unjust characteristics of that which it was designed to correct. The history of South America in the past twenty-five years yields ample evidence of this sort. It is the role of love to control such excesses and to provide the mean at which to aim. On the other hand, when the inspiration towards justice begins to wane, either through the discouragements of failures or the sheer intransigence of circumstances, it is loving concern for the victims of injustice that will reactivate that initial inspiration.

* * *

So, perhaps the time has come to revise the pejorative assessment which we have come to give to clichés when assigning them their place in the theological hall of fame. Those that we have looked at — and there are many more besides — certainly merit a place in the hall, for they have served the purposes of many theologians in their time. But, what has emerged from our study is that they seem now to have a second claim to be there, in that they have within them the seeds of further creativity if we have but the patience to nurture them. Thus encouraged, they may well have a new lease of life and eventually serve our purposes as profitably as they did our predecessors.

Bibliography of the Works of John McIntyre

1946

"Spiritual Reconstruction," in John McIntyre et al., *Spiritual Reconstruction: Addresses Delivered in the Conference of the Presbyterian Assembly, New South Wales, May, 1946*, pr. Paramatta, Australia, 1946[?], pp. 13-21.

1947

"History and Meaning," *Reformed Theological Review* 6 (1947): 7-23.

"In the Fullness of Life" [sic], *Australian Christian World,* July 18, 1847 [*sic*], pp. 5-6.

"In the Fullness of Time," *Australian Christian World,* July 25, 1947, pp. 3-4.

Review of *The New Modernism,* by Cornelius van Til (Philadelphia, 1946), in *Reformed Theological Review* 6 (1947): 38-42.

"Unity and Division," *Reformed Theological Review* 6 (1947): 7-29.

1948

Freethought and Christianity: Being Two Addresses Delivered by Prof. J. McIntyre to the Student Christian Movement in the University of Sydney on 27/9/48 and 6/10/48, pr. Sydney, Australia, 1948.

"God Was in Christ," *Reformed Theological Review* 7 (1948): 11-19.

Review of *Revelation and Reason,* by Emil Brunner (London, 1947), in *Reformed Theological Review* 7 (1948): 30-35.

"St. Andrew and 1948," *The New South Wales Presbyterian* 22 (1948): 1-13.

1949

Christ and History. Melbourne, 1949.

"Christ and History," *Reformed Theological Review* 8 (1949): 9-42.

"Christ as King in the Church, and in the World and History," in John McIntyre et al., *Christ the King,* Australian Student Christian Movement, 1949.

1950

Review of *The Inspiration and Authority of the Bible,* by Benjamin Breckinridge Warfield (Philadelphia, 1948), in *Reformed Theological Review* 9 (1950): 19-21.

"Reformed Dogmatics," *Reformed Theological Review* 9 (1950): 17-24.

"*Remoto Christo:* The Problem of the *Cur Deus Homo,*" *Reformed Theological Review* 9 (1950): 3-17.

1951

Review of *Early Christian Creeds,* 2nd ed., by J. N. D. Kelly (New York, 1950), in *Reformed Theological Review* 10 (1951): 97-98.

"The Incredibility of the Faith," *Reformed Theological Review* 10 (1951): 69-72.

1952

"The Proofs," *Reformed Theological Review* 11 (1952): 81-93.

Review of *St. Thomas Aquinas: Philosophical Texts,* trans. and ed. by Thomas Gilby (Oxford, 1951), in *Reformed Theological Review* 11 (1952): 72-73.

1953

"The Theology of Community," *The Coracle,* no. 24 (1953): 1-13.

1954

"The Holy Spirit in Greek Patristic Thought," *Scottish Journal of Theology* 7 (1954): 353-75.

St. Anselm and His Critics: A Re-Interpretation of the Cur Deus Homo. Edinburgh, 1954.

1956

"Christology and Revelation I," *Reformed Theological Review* 15 (1956): 81-89.

"Demythologization and Dogmatics," *Canadian Journal of Theology* 2 (1956): 85-91.

Review of *Nature and Grace: Selections from the* Summa Theologica *of Thomas Aquinas,* trans. and ed. by A. M. Fairweather (London, 1954), in *Reformed Theological Review* 15 (1956): 18-19.

1957

The Christian Doctrine of History. Edinburgh and Grand Rapids, 1957.

"Christology and Revelation II," *Reformed Theological Review* 16 (1957): 11-20.

"Christology and Revelation III," *Reformed Theological Review* 16 (1957): 44-53.

"Frontiers of Meaning," *University of Edinburgh Journal,* Autumn 1956, pp. 179-90; and *Scottish Journal of Theology* 10 (1957): 122-39.

1958

"L'analogie," *Revue de Théologie et de Philosophie* 8 (1958): 81-99.

Edited with Ian T. Ramsey et al., *The Library of Philosophy and Theology*. London, 1958-73.

"Science and Religion: Has the Situation Changed?" *Expository Times* 70 (1958-59): 15-18, 36-39.

"The Structure of Theological Education," *Expository Times* 70 (1958-59): 210-15.

1959

"Analogy," *Scottish Journal of Theology* 12 (1959): 1-20.

"Premises and Conclusions in the System of St. Anselm's Theology," *Spicilegium Beccense, I: Congrès international du IXe centenaire de l'arrivée d'Anselme au Bec,* Paris, 1959, pp. 95-101.

Review of *Spiritual Crisis of the Scientific Age,* by Greville Dennis Yarnold (London, 1959), in *Expository Times* 71 (1959): 45.

1962

The Availability of Christ. Edinburgh, 1962.

Review of *George Berkeley and the Proofs for the Existence of God,* by Edward Augustus Sillem (New York, 1957), in *Scottish Journal of Theology* 15 (1962): 420-23.

Review of *New Testament Apologetic: The Doctrinal Significance of the Old Testament Quotations,* by Barnabas Linders (Philadelphia, 1961), in *Expository Times* 73 (1962): 203-4.

On the Love of God. London and New York, 1962.

"The Place of Imagination in Faith and Theology: I & II," *Expository Times* 74 (1962-63): 16-21, 36-39.

1963

Review of *God is No More,* by Werner and Lotte Pelz (Philadelphia, 1962), in *Expository Times* 74 (1963): 230.

1964

Review of *Freedom and History,* by Hywel David Lewis (New York, 1962), in *Journal of Religious History* 3 (1964): 91-92.

1966

Review of *Science, Synthesis and Sanity: An Inquiry in the Nature of Living,* by George Scott Williamson and Innes Hope Pearse (London, 1965), in *Church Quarterly Review* 167 (1966): 391-92.

The Shape of Christology. London and Philadelphia, 1966.

Review of *Shapes of Philosophical History,* by Frank E. Manuel (Stanford, 1965), in *Journal of Theological Studies* 17 (1966): 522-24.

1967

The Christian Faith in Our Time. Edinburgh, n.d.

Review of *The Concept of Irony: With Constant Reference to Socrates,* by Søren Kierkegaard, trans. and ed. by L. M. Capel (New York, 1966), in *Expository Times* 78 (1967): 142-43.

Review of *Evil and the God of Love,* by John Hick (London, 1966), in *Interpretation* 21 (1967): 206-8.

1968

"Current Theology Around the World: Scotland," *Religion in Life* 37 (1968): 180-90.

Review of *The Evolution of Dialectical Materialism: A Philosophical and Sociological Analysis,* by Zbigniew A. Jordan (London, 1967), in *Expository Times* 79 (1968): 239-40.

Edited with Alec Cheyne et al., *New College Bulletin,* 1968-73.

"Obituary of Professor Karl Barth, Renowned Swiss Theologian," *The Scotsman,* December 11, 1968, p. 3.

"The Open-ness of Theology," *New College Bulletin* 4 (1968): 6-22.

1970

"*Cur deus-homo:* The Axis of the Argument," in Helmut Kohlenberger, ed., *Sola ratione: Anselm-Studien fr Pater Dr h c Franciscus Salesius Schmitt OSB zum 75sten Geburtstag,* Stuttgart, 1970, pp. 111-18.

1971

"Frontiers of Theological Existence," *New College Bulletin* 6 (1971): 10-15.

1972

Prophet of Penitence: John McLeod Campbell, Our Contemporary Ancestor. Edinburgh, 1972.

1973

"How Shall We Picture the Kingdom?" *Liturgical Review* 3 (1973): 14-18.

1974

Review of *The Concept of Meaning,* by Thomas E. Hill (London, 1974), in *Expository Times* 86 (1974): 27-28.

"Reflections on a Decade," *New College Bulletin* 8 (1974): 15-19.

"The Shape and Place of a University," *University of Edinburgh Journal* 26 (1974): 308-13.

1975

"College, Church and University," *New College Newsletter,* no. 4 (1975): 3-5.

1976

Review of *The Relevance of Natural Science to Theology,* by J. H. Austin (London, 1976), in *Expository Times* 87 (1976): 380.

"Theology and Method," in Richard McKinney, ed., *Creation, Christ and Culture: Studies in Honour of T F Torrance,* Edinburgh, 1976, pp. 204-30.

1977

Review of *Horace Bushnell's Theory of Language,* by Donald A. Crosby (The Hague, 1977), in *Scottish Journal of Theology* 30 (1977): 474-75.

Review of *The Leap of Reason,* by Don Cupitt (London, 1976), in *Scottish Journal of Theology* 30 (1977): 576-81.

Review of *Philosophers and Philosophies,* by Frederick Copleston (Turnbridge Wells, 1976), in *Expository Times* 89 (1977): 58.

Review of *Problems of Religious Knowledge,* by Terence Penelhum (London, 1971), in *Scottish Journal of Theology* 30 (1977): 279-80.

1979

Review of *The Holy Spirit in the Life of the Church,* by P. D. Opsahl, ed. (Minneapolis, 1978), in *Expository Times* 90 (1979): 281.

"Thomas Forsyth Torrance," *New College Bulletin* 10 (1979): 1-2.

Review of *Trinification of the World,* by Thomas A. Dunne and Jean M. Laporte, eds. (Toronto, 1978), in *Expository Times* 90 (1979): 187.

1980

"A Tribute to Miss Leslie," *New College Bulletin,* Autumn 1989, p. 3.

Review of *Falsification and Belief,* by Alastair McKinnon (The Hague, 1970), in *Expository Times* 91 (1980): 184.

Review of *Historical Theology: An Introduction,* ed. by Geoffrey Bromiley (Edinburgh, 1978), in *Scottish Journal of Religious Studies* 1 (1980): 74-76.

Review of *The Lure of Divine Love,* by Norman W. Pittenger (New York, 1979), in *Expository Times* 91 (1980): 283.

"The Place of Christian Studies in Religious Education Today," *Scottish Journal of Theology* 33 (1980): 257-72.

1981

Review of *Anselm and a New Generation,* by Gillian R. Evans (Oxford, 1980), in *Religious Studies* 17 (1981): 291-93.

Review of *Christian Faith: An Introduction to the Study of the Faith,* by Hendrikus Berkhof (Edinburgh, 1980), in *Expository Times* 92 (1981): 153-54.

Review of *Early Arianism: A View of Salvation,* by Robert C. Gregg and Dennis E. Groh (Philadelphia, 1981), in *Expository Times* 93 (1981): 88-89.

"The Theological Dimension of the Ecological Problem," *Scottish Journal of Religious Studies* 2 (1981): 83-96.

Review of *Whatever Happened to the Human Mind,* by E. L. Mascall (London, 1980), in *Expository Times* 92 (1981): 152-53.

1982

Review of *The Analogical Imagination: Christian Theology and the Culture of Pluralism,* by David W. Tracy (London, 1981), in *Expository Times* 93 (1982): 185.

Review of *Imagination and the Future: Essays on Christian Thought and Practice,* by John A. Henley, ed. (Melbourne, 1980), in *Scottish Journal of Theology* 35 (1982): 172-74.

1983

"Foreword" to *Four Centuries: Edinburgh University Life 1583-1983,* ed. Gordon Donaldson, Edinburgh, 1983.

"Imagination," *New Dictionary of Christian Theology,* ed. Alan Richardson and John Bowden, London, 1983, pp. 283-84.

"Theology and University: John Baillie," *New College Bulletin* 14 (1983): 18-22.

1984

Review of *Discerning the Mystery: An Essay on the Nature of Theology,* by Andrew Louth (Oxford, 1983), in *Religious Studies* 20 (1984): 305-8.

"Scripture, Authority and Tradition," *One in Christ* 20 (1984): 315-24.

1986

"New Help from Kant: Theology and Human Imagination," in J. P. Mackey, ed., *Religious Imagination,* Edinburgh, 1986, pp. 102-22.

1987

Faith Theology and Imagination. Edinburgh, 1987.

1990

"A Tale of Two Exchanges: The Christology of D M Baillie," in D. W. D. Shaw, ed., *In Divers Manners: A St. Mary's Miscellany*, St. Andrews, 1990.

"Imagination," *The Dictionary of Pastoral Care*, ed. Alistair V. Campbell, London, 1990, pp. 126-27.

1992

The Shape of Soteriology. Edinburgh, 1992.

1993

The Concept of Authority: Ecumenical Impediment or Ecumenical Opportunity? Irish School of Ecumenics, Occasional Paper No. 1, Dublin, 1993.

"Introduction" and "Epilogue" to *Hugh Douglas, One Man's Ministry*, ed. Colin Forrester-Paton, Edinburgh, 1993.

1994

"Historical Criticism in a History-Centred Value-System," in Samuel E. Balentine and John Barton, eds., *Language, Theology, and the Bible: Essays in Honour of James Barr*, Oxford, 1994, pp. 370-84.